Samson

Ellen Gunderson Traylor

Tyndale House Publishers, Inc.
Wheaton, Illinois

To Kenneth Petersen,
my editor, for carrying
the gates on his back.

The author has adhered to scriptural accounts in her writing of this novel. However, the chronology of events in the biblical account of Samson is difficult to pinpoint. Where the biblical record is unclear, the author has relied on the best scholarship and on a logical interpretation of events to establish chronology.

Library of Congress Cataloging-in-Publication Data

Traylor, Ellen Gunderson.
    Samson / Ellen Gunderson Traylor.
       p.   cm.
    ISBN 0-8423-5828-5
    1. Samson (Biblical judge)—Fiction. 2. Bible. O.T.—History
of Biblical events—Fiction. I. Title.
    PS3570.R357S26 1992
    813'.54—dc20   92-8670

Printed in the United States of America

99 98 97 96 95 94 93 92
 9   8   7   6   5   4   3   2   1

CONTENTS

*O*ut of the eater came something to eat.
*O*ut of the strong came something sweet.

JUDGES 14:14

PROLOGUE

*T*he sea was strangely vocal tonight, its distant roar rolling like soft thunder across the port of Gaza. Salt wind passed inland from the coast and whipped over the rooftops of the Philistine capital.

A dark-haired woman hugged the shadows of Gaza's central viaduct, clutching her mantle close against the chill. As she hastened toward the city square, where the temple of Dagon stood, she covered her face with her veil and hoped no passerby would identify her as a Jewess.

She had planned to be here before sunset, but the rickety cart and arthritic donkey provided for her journey from Zorah had made for slow going. Already twilight was far spent.

Old Rena, who had prevailed upon her to take this trip, had been quite persuasive. Her venerable husband, Manoah, was close to death and had a parting word for his long-lost son.

Surely Marissa could find the "lad," the old woman insisted. Surely Marissa could track down Samson's whereabouts and give him Manoah's exhortation. "My son, avenge yourself!" was the deathbed command. "Tell Samson to rise up against his enemies!"

It was with great trepidation that the younger woman undertook the task. Not only must she cross miles of unfamiliar terrain, but she would be traveling through the territory of Samson's foes.

Jews were not welcome in the land of the Philistines, especially not since Samson had been taken captive. If Marissa
were discovered, she could lose her life, and—short of this—
any manner of foul play could befall her.

After twelve hours of laborious travel through the hill country of the Danites, Marissa had reached the Maritime Plain.
Here the highway was wide and smooth, and the journey
quicker. But with the passing of daylight, Marissa's anxieties
had grown.

She had managed to enter Gaza's gate by mingling with the
traffic coming and going from the coast. But after dark there
were few carts in the streets, and fewer pedestrians. She had
tethered the donkey and wagon to a lamppost upon nearing
the central square and now hurried on foot toward the temple
compound.

Even if she traversed the pagan court without incident,
however, she could not be certain that Samson was incarcer-
ated there. But the last word received in Zorah was that he
had been captured in the vale of Sorek and hauled away to the
capital. Since the Philistine government, like that of the Jews,
was intimately connected with the national religion, Marissa
would begin her quest at the temple.

Though the old donkey and its cart had been feeble transportation, they were the best Rena and Manoah could offer.
Marissa, who had never married, and who lived on her wages
as a seamstress, had no conveyance of any kind, so the elderly
farmers had given her their hay cart.

But the humble appearance of her transportation was more
than offset by the fine garments she selected for the journey.
She would not enter Gaza in homespun clothing, she determined. Whatever became of her, she would confront the
Philistines in fine linen.

Marissa's garment had been years in the making. She had
begun it when only a girl, selecting the fabrics with her

mother's help and creating the intricate embroidered design on parchment before applying it to the cloth. Poppies of appliquéd velvet formed the border of her skirt. Scarlet, azure, emerald, and gold threads wound through the design, which was repeated on her bodice—and for this she had chosen the finest silk available in the village of Zorah.

As she ran through the moonlit square, it was not only fear that caused her heart to pound. It was the anticipation of seeing Samson. She had not selected her outfit to impress the Philistines alone. It was Samson she hoped to please.

After all, the gown had been made to be Marissa's wedding dress, lovingly designed when she had approached puberty, in keeping with tradition. And Samson was her betrothed. They would have been married two weeks ago, had his enemies not interfered.

As she passed through the shadows of the alien court, Marissa knew this might be her only chance to wear this dress for her beloved. And if she did not wear it for him, she would wear it for no one. For Marissa, no longer as fair of face and willowy as she had been as a young girl, knew she could never promise herself to another man.

Memories of Samson spurred her on. She had no idea how she would find him, or what condition he might be in if she did so.

Her thoughts were heavy with him when suddenly a rush of wings overhead startled her. Looking up she saw a hawk dive through the darkness, darting directly toward her between the gables of the columned buildings. Marissa stifled a cry and leaned into an alcove. She had heard that the guards of the Philistine temple kept hawks instead of watchdogs. Fearing she had been discovered, she stood still, listening to her drumming pulse.

When several minutes passed and the hawk did not return, Marissa breathed easier. But before setting out again, she bent over and removed her jeweled sandals. Perhaps they made too much clatter against the terra-cotta pavement and had given her away.

On tiptoe she continued through the cloisters, which now were lined with statues, tall and ominous, who stared after the trespasser with glazed eyes. Many of them represented gods of war, helmeted and bearing shields and spears. Each weapon, she noted, was made of iron, the special secret of the Philistines, the metal of military might that had made them kings of the coastland.

Marissa was no expert on Philistine gods or goddesses, but she did know that the temples of El, father of the gods, and Dagon, his son, would lie toward the center of the acropolis. And she knew the statue of Ashtaroth when suddenly it loomed before her.

She need not be told that the voluptuous thighs and hips, the pendulous breasts represented fertility. Any neighbor to the Philistines would have recognized this statue as the goddess of sensual love.

Marissa froze, her skin bristling, for this divinity not only symbolized the alien culture of Israel's enemies, but was the model for the females who had been Samson's downfall.

Casting her gaze to the pavement, Marissa slipped past the haughty Venus, tears scalding her cheeks.

Why now, of all times, must she be reminded of such things? Did it really matter that Samson had a weakness for such women?

Yes, it *did* matter! It mattered not only because he was Marissa's intended, but because Samson was a minister of the Lord, a judge in Israel, a Nazarite from birth, chosen to save his people from their enemies! It mattered because attraction to such females had always brought him short of God's glory and might even now have led him to defeat.

Of course, it also mattered because Marissa loved him.

A lump in her throat, she hastened on, at last coming within sight of Dagon's temple. Rising like a marble fortress across the acropolis, it was the most commanding building in Gaza. Gargantuan pillars, two of which supported the enormous gable and its many terraced roofs, stood sentry over vast courts.

The size and prominence of the structure showed that Dagon was Philistia's favorite god. Marissa knew Samson must be his prisoner, for the Nazarite had often put him to shame. She believed the mighty judge of Israel, son of old Rena and Manoah, must be captive in this very place.

Now that her destination stood directly before her, Marissa knew not which way to turn. The sheer challenge of reaching this site had so consumed her that she had thought little beyond it. Until this moment, she had been glad no one had spied her, and no one had challenged her presence in the Philistine headquarters. Now she wished someone could give her direction.

But she knew she must function more secretly now than ever. If she were to locate the prisoner and bring back any word of him whatsoever, only God could be her guide.

Upon her wrist was bound a phylactery, a tiny leather box attached by a delicate leather strap. Rena had given her this ornament at her bas mitzvah, the day of her emergence into Jewish womanhood. Because she had stolen Samson's young heart, she had long been dear to his parents. And upon that special day, years ago, Manoah and his wife had bestowed the gift.

Ever since, she had worn it, removing it only to bathe or to do cleaning. As she stood now before the pagan shrine, she clutched the amulet to her breast and breathed a prayer.

Ever so softly she walked up the broad stone steps of the sanctuary, whispering not the name of Dagon, but the name of the One True God.

Slipping between the mammoth columns, she entered the central court where a cascading fountain sang. Moonlight passed through the open roof, illumining the waters that rose resplendently about the likeness of a merman.

The huge bronze statue, Marissa knew, represented Dagon. Bearing a scepter shaped like a forked spear and wearing a tall conch-shaped crown, the god had the torso and arms of a man and the body of a fish. Reclining upon a rock, his tail resting in the water, he was graced all about by sensuous females, some entirely human and others shaped like mermaids, all in worshipful postures, adoring and fawning at his side.

Marissa shivered as she gazed upon the eerie being. And again she whispered Adonai's name, as if for protection.

Just as she did, the sound of quick footsteps interrupted the solitude. Her heart pounding, she wheeled about to find a small servant boy hurrying on some errand across the court.

Preoccupied, he focused on his destination, a low gate in the far corner beyond the fountain. He had not noticed the woman in the moonlit yard.

Though Marissa feared exposure, she knew this might be her only chance for help. Feeling safe with a young boy, she called out to him, hoping he understood her language.

"Sir," she addressed him, "I seem to be lost."

The lad stopped in his tracks and, searching the darkness, spied the source of the call. Cautiously he retraced his steps, until he could see her clearly. Then, to her surprise, he addressed her in her native tongue. "Yes, you are! No one should be lingering here after sunset. How did you get past the front gate?"

Marissa could not have told him how. She only knew she was on dangerous ground.

"Please, sir," she said again, "I do not know my way."

By now, the boy stood directly before her, studying her with awe.

"You are not Philistine!" he guessed. "Your speech is like mine . . . and his!"

Marissa knew it was not unusual for young Jewish boys to be taken captive by the Philistines. The fact that this poor lad was enslaved here made her heart ache. But she was on a mission and must not lose her focus. Drawing her shawl close, she inquired, "My speech is like *whose?*"

"You are an Israeli!" the boy exclaimed. "Why are you here?"

This last question was spoken more in wonder than in threat, but Marissa was not free to explain.

"*Whose* speech is like mine?" she pressed the youngster.

Drawing back, he surveyed her up and down, and his eyes stopped at the phylactery upon her wrist.

"I knew it!" he cried. "You are Jewish! Just like Samson!"

At this, Marissa was charged with courage and, bending down, grasped the boy by the arms.

"You know him!" she whispered fiercely. "Do you know where he is?"

Shakily the lad tried to pull away, fearing he had said too much. But Marissa would not let him go.

"You must take me to him!" she demanded. "I am his friend!"

The boy shook his head in earnest. "I cannot!" he pleaded. "Let me go!"

More firmly, Marissa clutched at him, her fingers like bands upon his slender arms.

"Do you have a papa?" she suddenly inquired. "If you do, you must know how it would pain him to lose you."

The boy said nothing, staring at her mutely. The question had stunned him, causing his body to tense.

"*Samson* has a papa," Marissa went on. "And his papa is close to death. I have been sent to bring Samson word from his father!"

At this, the boy grew limp, and his head fell forward. Marissa did not know how she had touched the boy's heart, but he seemed deeply shaken.

Slowly he heaved a sigh and at last looked her in the eye. Tears glistened on his face, and he nodded assent.

"Come," he simply said, slipping away from her. "I will take you to him, but you will not like what you see."

THE VERY DOOR toward which the boy had been hastening when Marissa had hailed him was the door through which he now led her. Beyond it, a flight of narrow stairs brought the two into a darker passage. Stairway after stairway led them down from the sacred compound into the warehouses of the Philistine priests.

Even if someone had drawn her a map, Marissa would never have found her way through the labyrinth where bags of dried fruits and cheeses, sacks of wheat, and casks of wine lined the walls.

Just as with the Hebrews, the Philistines were commanded to bring a tenth of all their produce to their temples. This tax went to support the priests, who, while dependent solely on this revenue, acquired great wealth from the system.

Doubtless other vaults stored sacks of gold and silver, but this wing of rooms was for food alone.

Marissa could not imagine why the boy took her this way. "Samson is a prisoner of your government," she said in exasperation, when they entered yet another maze of hallways. "This does not look like a prison!"

The boy turned to her with a sad face. "My lady," he said, "Samson would do well to be only a prisoner! He is not so lucky!"

"What do you mean?" the Jewess queried. "What could be worse than one of your dungeons?"

The boy made no reply, but only beckoned her on, and at last they came to a barred door along the farthest rim of the warehouses.

The door opened slowly as the child leaned against it with great effort, and as it swung back it grated ominously on rusty hinges.

The twisting corridor through which they had traveled was dimly lit with randomly spaced wall torches. But the chamber into which they now entered had only the meager glow of a solitary candle, which stood in a shallow saucer upon the floor. Its wick was close to drowning in the coin-sized pool of molten lye upon its tip, making it sputter and wane in the farthest corner of the cell, casting demonic shadows against the stone walls. In its distorted aura, a single item of furnishing was revealed, its shadow dancing against the floor like an awkward monster.

As Marissa's eyes adjusted to the dark, she made out the form of the piece, a great wheel-shaped rock resting on the pavement.

"A grinding stone!" she said marveling. "Then this must be a granary."

The boy nodded.

"They keep Samson in a granary?" she whispered.

Quietly the lad took her by the hand and led her to the far side of the wheel. In the wavering firelight, between the street wall and the huge grinding stone, a figure sat huddled, his face buried against his knees, his feet drawn close to his body.

"He is asleep," the boy said.

Marissa gripped the edge of the wheel, her knees weak.

"Samson?" she sighed, the word clinging to her lips like a feather. Even in this dejected place, he was beautiful, his physique a marvel of perfect manhood. His hair, which had always been his crowning glory, was shorter than usual, but still lay in dark waves against his muscular back and fell in ringlets across his broad shoulders.

"He sleeps very deeply, miss," the boy said. "He works very hard."

"He is a slave?" she replied, horror etching her face.

"Did I not say he would be better off a prisoner?"

Marissa gazed upon the bronze chains that shackled Samson's ankles to the wheel, and then her eyes moved to the circular path worn deep into the stone floor by oxen feet.

"Please," she beseeched the boy, "wake him for me. And bring the candle nearer, so he may see who I am!"

"I will wake him, miss," the boy said obligingly. "But the light will do no good. He is blind, don't you know?"

The woman sank back against the wheel, trembling. "Blind?" she rasped. "What have they done to you?" she wept, reaching for the one she loved.

At the sound of her cry, Samson roused. Apparently fearing that some guard had found him sleeping, he leaped to his feet. When he rushed to grab the wheel's handle, Marissa scurried aside and watched in horror as he threw his weight against it, turning it futilely round and round.

Candlelight glanced off of his determined face in grotesque angles. Stifling another cry, Marissa studied the matchless countenance, the noble features that had won a thousand hearts. But now, beneath his broad brow, two lifeless sockets gaped, and the once proud man seemed to cringe, as if in fear of a whip.

Stumbling backward, the visitor clutched her phylactery to her breast and staggered for the door.

Once she gained the hallway, she slumped against the corridor wall, her heart drumming fiercely.

Surely Adonai had brought her this far. Surely her mission was blessed of God. But how could she bear what she had witnessed? How could the great judge of Israel have come to this?

For a long while she waited, wanting to run, knowing she dare not.

From the room she could hear the boy calming Samson's fears and saying he had a caller. But Marissa could only quake in the shadows beyond the door.

Suddenly, flashes of old Manoah and Rena came to mind, and the story Rena had told of Samson's birth . . . how the angel had told her she would bear a mighty one, and how his name would mean "Little Sun."

Taking a deep breath, Marissa prayed for strength. She must complete her appointed task. She must encourage Samson to rise up against the Philistines.

For he was still the "Shining Star" of Israel. And he must avenge himself against his enemies.

The Nazarite

ONE

*E*ight boys, sweat-streaked and dusty, chased a leather ball through Zorah's village gate. Suspended overhead was the town's red and white banner, the same kind of banner that flew from the gate of every Danite stronghold.

Not that Zorah was a mighty fortress. It was barely more than a weekend market for a few dozen farm families scattered up the hills from Sorek Vale. But the people who dwelled here were proud of their village and showed it by displaying the conspicuous eagle-crested flag above the entry.

Today the banner-decked gateway served as a goal for a game of kickball, and the young athletes, four per team, traded the lead from hand to hand, first one side and then the other making a score.

Although the game was impromptu, it was not without spectators. From the sidelines, clusters of village children cheered and hissed, mostly radiant young girls clapping and screaming as some favorite showed his prowess.

Then there were a few adults looking on, stopping in their busy day to take a side in the matter. Among these was a couple, standing together in the door of the potter's cottage. Rena and Manoah, farmers from the hills, rested from their day of shopping long enough to watch their only child, Samson, score a goal.

"He is quick today," Manoah remarked. "Josef has been good for him."

Josef, the captain of Samson's team, was the lad's best friend. Though a couple of years older, Josef had always taken an interest in the boy who lived beyond the village walls, visiting him often at the farm and hiking with him in the rolling fields.

Together they had learned to love their mutual heritage as sons of Israel, to despise the oppression of the neighboring Philistines, and to dream of great feats against their country's enemies.

They had grown up together on games of war and military heroics. Together they plowed Manoah's fields, climbed the nearby hills, and traced the streams that ribboned them. They had dreamed of one day trekking to the mighty sea that spanned the coast of their tribal territory, and they had imagined the thrill of felling Philistine temples and pagan cities.

Their boyish hearts were intertwined by days and years spent in tandem. But their mutual admiration was based on their differences, as much as on their commonalities. For they complemented each other in many ways, as though they rounded one another out.

Though Josef was older, he was not as large as Samson. Wiry and lithe, he had a quick mind that made him a good strategist. Samson, while not so cunning, was stronger, and his physical powers were growing each day, lending action to Josef's well-thought plans.

Today, in fact, Samson's maturing strength was abundantly evident. Josef, having worked with him on maneuvers, had helped add speed to his power, and the muscular lad, dwarfing the other boys, moved down the playing field like a charging bull.

If he had been ignored by the girls in the past, they certainly noticed him this day. Not only was he playing better, but, having worked in the fields all summer, he was sun-burnished and rock hard.

His fine-chiseled face was framed by a shock of dark ringlets, which in themselves set him apart from the other lads, for his hair was not only unusually thick and heavy but reached nearly to his waist, having been allowed to grow all his life.

Fettered by a leather thong, Samson's raven waves clung to his glistening back, the sun glancing off them in a sheen of sweaty movement.

Observing him proudly, Rena and Manoah recalled without a word the long-ago day when a mysterious man, radiant as spring light, had appeared to them. Could they ever forget his words or his incredible promises? They would have a son, he had said, a son in their old age, when Rena was past the prime of life and Manoah was resigned to go to his grave childless. And not only would they rejoice in this miracle, but the promised one would be highly favored from birth, destined to deliver Israel from the hands of the Philistines!

When Manoah, always practical, had asked the stranger about the boy's upbringing, and how his parents might best serve God's purposes in his life, the messenger had laid certain strictures upon them. Rena was to abstain from wine and strong drink during her pregnancy, and she was to partake of nothing "unclean," but was to observe ceremonial tradition and priestly laws for purity.

As for the lad himself, the injunction seemed simple: he was to be a Nazarite "from the womb to the day of his death." Clear-cut as the commandment was, however, it lacked specifics.

Rena and Manoah had seen members of a nearby Nazarite order when they came down from the austere wilderness commune. Following rigid directives, these disciples appeared regularly before a local priest for prayer and cleansing, then returned at once to monastic life in the hills.

But while the Nazarites of the Zorah hills were cloistered and monkish, there were other orders that were less rigid, whose members circulated freely in society. These observed the rites and the strict dietary laws on a rotating schedule, living a normal life as husbands and consumers most of the year and devoting themselves to prayer and oblations periodically.

Therefore, when the messenger of God had appeared to Samson's parents, there had been good reason to ask for details.

But few had been given.

The lad's hair, they had been told, must never know the touch of a razor. It must be allowed to grow, uncut for his entire life, as a sign of sanctification. Beyond this hallmark, which was essentially common to all Nazarites, they were apparently free to select the degree of their son's discipline.

It might have been easier if they had had more guidelines. As it was, they had to depend on their own judgment and on persistent prayer throughout the boy's growing years.

It did not escape them, for instance, that in the near future they would confront the issue of celibacy. Did God mean for this Nazarite to lead a monastic life? Or would he be free to marry and have a family, observing the laws of a more liberal order?

Rena and Manoah had a preference. Long, barren years had filled their lives before they had known the joy of parenthood. Nothing would make them happier, in their advancing age, than a quiver full of grandchildren.

And though they would never have breathed a word of it beyond their own intimate conversations, they both admitted a fondness for one village girl in particular.

Tall and comely was she, graceful as a mountain lily and sweet as cedar air. Marissa, the seamstress's daughter, had always been a favorite, and in private confessions the old folks often dreamed what a marvelous wife she could be for their son.

Noting that she stood today with the other spectators, they hoped her keen interest in the game meant she noticed Samson's blossoming talents.

RENA AND Manoah were not the only ones who cared what Marissa thought.

Josef, something of a village star for his quick-footed antics on the playing field, could have had his pick of the cheering girls. But he played to impress only one: the tall damsel at the center of the klatch.

When he, on occasion, looked up from his sport to hail the little crowd, his eyes unfailingly sought out Marissa.

As for the girl herself, to her way of thinking Josef had no rival. Though he was shorter than she, and thin as a willow switch, he had always captivated her with his keen wit and clever charm. He had already made his bar mitzvah. Her mama said he would be a sharp businessman someday and would make some lucky girl a good husband.

Marissa, flattered by his attentions, blushed with adolescent ardor whenever he looked her way.

So far their common attraction had gone unspoken between them. Josef had not even told his best friend of his feelings. Samson was yet too young to understand, he reckoned.

But Josef meant to make Marissa his own someday. Of course, since he was only fourteen, "someday" was yet a few years off. But in this culture it was not too soon to plan for such things, and already he laid the groundwork, calling at her house from time to time and leaving wee bouquets in her door latch.

Samson would be his best man, he told himself when he thought that far ahead. And perhaps one day he and the farm boy would watch their own sons play together upon this very street!

Just now, however, he kept his mind to the game and his upcoming tactics. They were entering the fourth quarter. Calling his men aside, Josef passed a waterskin between them and clapped Samson on the back.

"Good job!" he praised him. "You are nimble today!"

The other boys echoed his sentiments, looking up to the powerhouse with growing admiration. "Well done!" they applauded. "Did you hear the girls cheer when you made that point?"

"Watch out!" one of them teased. "You might even turn *Marissa's* head!" To the village youngsters, there could be no higher compliment.

The team captain was not the only one who thought Marissa the most beautiful creature on earth. Though Josef laughed with the others, he was caught off guard by the comment. Suddenly, glancing up at the klatch of giggling girls—and at *his* girl in particular—the plaudit seemed less than humorous.

In one of those rare moments when one's whole view of oneself and one's destiny is laid bare to unexpected challenge, Josef wondered if such a thing could happen—and his mind was suddenly set in a spin.

Was it possible that he ought to keep an eye on Samson?

No, he told himself, *not Samson!* He was yet a child, a farm boy from the hills. He was surely no threat!

Yet it occurred to him that Samson's name had been shouted from the sidelines today nearly as often as his own.

Even now, as he looked up from the huddle, he heard the younger boy's name being rehearsed in admiring sighs.

All of this assaulted Josef in a span of seconds, throwing him off balance—but not so much that he failed to devise a quick defense.

While young Samson fumbled with the tribute, unused to such flattery, Josef made a rapid counter.

"Yes," he said with a gleaming smile, "you have done well today! In fact, I think we should save your strength for the time we will need it most."

Directing the big boy to the sidelines, he told him to sit for a while, until the end drew near. "Then I will call you in," he promised.

Bewildered by this sudden displacement, Samson objected, "I'm not tired, Josef. I don't need to rest!"

But Josef gave him a condescending pat. "Did I get to be captain by making bad decisions?" he argued. "Look at it this way: if the game is close you will pull us through! You can make the final score and be a bigger hero than ever!"

With a sigh, Samson moved to the shade of a nearby willow and plopped down compliantly. Trying to hide his disappointment, he sat with his knees to his chin as the game resumed.

Having no intention whatsoever to recall Samson, Josef sped onto the field, ready himself to be the hero of the hour. His plan might have succeeded, had it not been for a strange twist of fate.

The opposing team had the ball and began their offense by driving it straight toward the smallest member of Josef's team. Intervening, Josef greeted the serve with a square and powerful kick, sending it deep into the end zone.

Full of adrenaline, he shot forward, pursuing the ball toward the goal, darting around those who got in his way, certain of making a point. And so he would have, had an able opponent not tripped him, sending him to a skidding halt upon his stomach.

Breathless he lay on the street, watching in dismay as the ball rolled beneath a hay cart.

According to the rules, a ball out of bounds was still in play. Since the quarter was not over, it must be retrieved. Scrambling to his feet, Josef raced his adversary to the hay cart and, crawling underneath, reached for the leather prize.

But his eager attempt would go unrewarded. Just as he was backing out, the ball held tight in his hands, the tongue of the wagon jostled from its support, and the heavy load came crashing down, pinning Josef to the ground.

The next moments were a blur of cries and scuffling feet, as both teams forgot their differences and ran to help their playmate.

"Careful!" some adult warned. "Don't move him. If he's injured, it could make matters worse!"

A dozen men and boys pressed in about the wagon, and together they tried to lift it up. But it was stacked high with unbalanced hay and would not budge. Neither could they roll it off, for Josef was pinned between the wheels.

Samson, who had been sitting at the far end of the field, leapt to his feet the instant Josef was pinned. And when he arrived at the wagon, the others made room, anxious for him to add his strength to the obstinate task.

What followed would be recounted about the village dinner tables for nights to come. For in that moment, the boy who had captured attention in today's game elevated himself even further in everyone's estimation.

Josef was his best friend, and he was desperate to help. But as he placed his hands on the wagon's tongue, he did not try to move it immediately. Instead, he paused for a moment, raised his eyes to heaven, and with a husky voice, he cried, "O Lord God! Give me strength!"

Only then did he pull up on the bar—and with a mighty groan, he tilted the cart, hay and all, several feet in the air.

Gasping, the crowd fell back. And even Samson, surveying his outstretched arms and the load they supported, seemed astonished by the feat.

As though frozen, the gaping onlookers stood paralyzed, until someone remembered Josef. Quickly, the teammates pulled him from the trap, and as they worried over him, he sat up.

Josef's wounds were more ego-oriented than physical, however. As he looked about him, his face was marked more with shame than relief.

He knew who had saved him, and he was not pleased.

Jerking away from his consoling friends, he stood shakily to his feet, chagrined to think that an entire town had witnessed his humiliation.

Samson, only glad to see him unhurt, set the cart down and ran to his side.

But Josef had caught sight of Marissa, and he did not like what he read in her face. He did not like the pity she showed him, nor did he care for the wondering look in her eyes as she gazed upon his rescuer.

When Samson rushed to embrace his little friend, Josef was loath to be touched.

Turning on his heel, the ball still clutched in his fist, he suddenly threw it to the ground and kicked it viciously through the goal.

Then, spitting, he limped away, his face red with anger.

TWO

*T*hat evening, Samson paced back and forth before the low door of Josef's cottage, calling to him again and again.

"Friend," he pleaded, "come outside! It is Samson. I must talk with you!"

He knew Josef heard him, but the smaller boy made no reply. From within the house the sound of dinner preparations, the clatter of dishes, and the voices of the family spilled into the street. But Josef's face never appeared at the window, and no one stepped out to speak.

Long after the table had been cleared, Samson still lingered outside, kicking at pebbles and smacking his fist against his thigh. He knew that Josef must emerge soon. Since he had no sisters, it was always his duty to fetch water from the village well at sunset. When the door at last creaked open, sending a ray of yellow light across the dirt road, Samson called again.

"Josef!" he growled. "What's wrong with you?"

The wiry boy hurried past him with his bucket, shaking his head.

"Leave me alone!" he snarled. "You are no friend!"

Confounded, Samson caught up with him, grasping him by the shoulders.

"What have I done?" he asked. "Did I not show myself to be your friend today?"

He referred, of course, to the incident with the fallen wagon. When Josef only scowled, he was more bewildered.

Wrenching from Samson's ironlike grasp, the smaller boy rubbed his tender shoulder. "Keep your hands off me!" he fumed. "Must you always be so forceful?"

Surprised again by his own strength, Samson stood back. "I'm . . . I'm sorry . . . ," he stammered. "I didn't mean to—"

"You *never* mean to!" Josef whined. "You just *do!*"

"But I did not hurt you this afternoon," Samson argued, hanging his head. "I helped you."

"Ha!" Josef sneered. Then, mocking, he laughed, "Stand up straight. When you slump, you look like a barley bag!"

Hurrying for the well, he again left Samson behind. But, shaking off his dejection, the big boy straightened his shoulders and paced after him.

"Whatever I have done, I apologize," Samson said. "Can you forgive me?"

No matter how devoted he might be to his friend, however, Samson had a very low tolerance for ridicule. When Josef turned on him again, shouting, "Go away, barley bag!" anger swelled through him.

Visions of what he could do to his wiry tormentor filled his head. And before he knew it, he was racing toward the well, ready to show Josef what real pain was like.

But, just at that instant, voices from behind caught his attention, and he skidded to a halt. Coming toward him were girls of the village, carrying their own buckets for drawing the evening's water. Among them was Marissa, and as he watched her, Samson's heart went soft.

Side by side he stood with Josef, both of them forgetting their quarrel for the moment. Transfixed, they drank in the vision that was Marissa.

When she set her bucket on the edge of the well, they both eagerly grabbed for it.

"Let me help you," they offered in unison.

As though they squabbled over a kickball, they tugged the bucket back and forth between them, until the girl demurred, reaching for it herself.

"That's all right," she said. "I'll do it. It is hard to choose between you."

Choose between us? Josef thought. Since when was there a choice to be made? Hadn't he always been Marissa's only beau?

So, it is true! He grimaced at the thought. *Samson is a threat after all!*

The seething anger that had consumed him this afternoon welled up again, making him shake all over.

Thrusting the bucket into Samson's hands, he turned from the two who had always been his friends and fled back home, slamming the door behind him.

DEEP IN THE night, Marissa crept to her bedroom window and peered out across the village common. She had not been able to sleep since Mother had tucked her in, for thinking of the incident at the well.

She had not meant to hurt Josef. But neither had she wanted to discourage Samson's sudden show of interest.

Surprised at her own feelings, she lay awake, reviewing what had happened until she could lie still no more.

She had seen Samson many times in her life. But never had she seen him as she did today. In the past, he had simply been a farm boy from the hills, handsome to be sure, but too immature for her womanly interests. Today, however, he had captivated her, not only with his athletic prowess, but with the mysterious incident with the wagon.

Marissa had heard of cases where people were capable of unusual feats in moments of crisis. Without thinking, they could lift heavy objects or surprise themselves by risking great danger.

Such had not been the case today. Samson had not acted in haste or with thoughtless effort. He had called on a strength beyond himself, deliberately invoking the aid of God Almighty!

Even now, as she recalled his words of faith and the way his prayer was answered, a thrill went through her heart.

What kind of boy is this? she wondered.

And what kind of boy was Josef? In him, too, she had seen a different side this day—a jealous, caustic streak that surprised and disappointed her.

She could not deny the fact that when Josef departed from the well, she had been relieved. She had enjoyed being alone with Samson, and brief as that encounter was, it played over and over in her mind like a persistent melody.

Lowering the bucket into the well, Samson had brought it up brimful. Then, hoisting it easily to his shoulder, he had offered to walk her home.

When he set the heavy bucket on her doorstep, his hand had brushed hers. And hours later, she still relished that fleeting touch.

Across the village square, the well stood lonely now. But in adolescent reverie, she imagined Samson standing there.

With a sigh, she leaned her cheek upon her window ledge and relived his every glance and movement.

At last, falling into bed, she closed her eyes to savor dreams, the likes of which Josef had never inspired.

THREE

Samson and his father, Manoah, wended through the rolling hills above Zorah, wading through the swollen streams that crossed their path. This spring had seen unusually heavy rainfall, and while the streambeds were completely dry the rest of the year, the water was rapid and deep enough today to require careful fording.

Their destination was no more than five miles from town—an easy journey for an able-bodied man. But Manoah had not been well lately. He tired easily, and Samson had to slow his pace to stay beside him.

"Little Sun," the old man sighed, calling Samson by his nickname, "I fear we will never make it to Mahaneh-dan by your birthday, let alone by sunset."

Stopping along the trail, he sat down upon a rock and wiped his brow.

Samson's thirteenth birthday, the day of his entrance into Hebrew manhood, was three days hence. Long ago, Manoah had determined to take him to Mahaneh-dan, "the camp of the Danites," for his bar mitzvah.

The camp of the Danites was a wilderness retreat, frequented by members of various Nazarite sects. Year round, the strictest religious order lived there, but those of more liberal vows were welcome to make pilgrimage to the site for prayer and contemplation.

Since Samson had been a wee lad, his father had believed he would receive his full calling in that hallowed place, where men of deep spiritual understanding could guide him.

Just now, though, as his aged heart drummed miserably in his chest, he wondered if he would survive the journey.

Samson studied his father with concern. Sitting beside him, he placed an arm about his frail shoulders.

"Perhaps we should turn back," he offered, drawing the old man close.

"Absolutely not!" Manoah cried. "I have waited—*you* have waited a lifetime for this! We shall go on."

Struggling to his feet, he held tight to Samson's broad shoulder. With a glance toward the sun, he saw that it would meet the western ridge within the hour.

"We have traveled all afternoon, Father," Samson said. "We can camp here and move on tomorrow."

"Do you forget that sunset is the beginning of Sabbath?" the elder replied. "No Nazarite travels on the Sabbath."

With this, he was off again, pressing up the trail as though he moved against a great boulder.

Shaking his head, Samson followed. All his life he had been taught, rebuked, and admonished in the ways of the Nazarites. Though he feared to admit it, sometimes the lessons were tiresome.

He understood, because his parents had told him, that God had set him apart from birth for a special purpose. Just what that purpose was, he did not know. Manoah and Rena had agreed early on that the prophecy would be too great a burden for a young boy to bear. Therefore, the promise that he would free Israel from Philistine bondage was kept from him.

What he did understand of his calling was baffling enough. Never had he been allowed to taste grapes or anything fermented. Never had he touched any "unclean thing," such as a dead or diseased animal, and never had he eaten anything not yet blessed by a priest. Every few months he had been taken before the priest for ceremonial cleansing, and he had kept the laws of purity to a much finer extent than did his playmates.

It was not easy being peculiar. More and more he felt his unique status as he entered adolescence, that time of life when even the most devout child is loath to be "different" from his peers.

Samson's uniqueness, furthermore, was not confined to Nazarite observances or to the length of his unshorn hair.

It had been a year since the rescue of Josef from the fallen wagon. That had been the first public display of Samson's unusual abilities. But he and his family had known, long before, that he possessed amazing strength. Often he had come to his father's aid, lifting heavy objects or breaking up fights between barnyard animals, usually with a force that astonished both son and parents.

Sometimes, however, his strength was dreadful, an attribute that required extreme discipline to manage. And while he was increasingly admired by adults and children, no one but himself knew the burden such a "blessing" could be.

Since his public revelation, he had often been challenged by boys of lesser ability. Like small, yipping dogs snapping at the heels of a bear, they could be tormentors, sorely trying Samson's patience. When, upon occasion, he had yielded to their taunts, repaying them with his terrifying fist, they had run crying to their mothers. One fling of Samson's arm could send a boy sprawling; one light grasp could bruise him black. It had been no easy thing for Samson to know his own strength, harder yet to keep it in check, especially when it developed faster than he could comprehend.

He ardently loved the Lord and his native land. But he was still a youngster, and while he had been afforded fine spiritual training, his God-given body—the very body with which he was intended to perform some special service—could be a dire distraction.

Plodding up behind Manoah, he gave a sigh of frustration. "At this pace, it will be impossible to reach the ridge by sundown," he complained, "let alone the camp! We have no choice but to rest here tonight and travel tomorrow, unless you want to lose a full day!"

Taking Manoah's elbow, the youngster helped him up a steep incline. But when his father made no reply, he forced the issue again. "Besides, we didn't bring enough provisions for such a wait! We have no choice!"

Dusk was descending. As the sound of crickets rose to meet the graying light, Manoah sat down again, a look of resignation on his face.

Gritting his teeth, Samson looked down upon the old man. "We are almost there," he muttered. "We will see the camp from that ridge!"

But Manoah was adamant. Gesturing to the burnished sky, he argued, "See now! Sabbath is upon us! Even if we should starve to death, we will not take another step!"

With a toss of his dark head, Samson paced back and forth, until, utterly exasperated, he gave a rebellious chuckle. "Oh, Papa!" he cried, reaching down and scooping the elder off the rocks. Carrying him like a baby, he began to run up the hill. "What better time to walk with God than on the Sabbath?" he challenged.

Aghast, Manoah pounded his feeble fists against the lad's rock-hard chest. "Put me down!" he railed. "You defy the Lord!"

"How do I defy him?" Samson quipped, still racing up the hill. "Is it wrong to use the Sabbath to seek after him?"

Wide-eyed, the elder held on tight as Samson bounded over rocks and brush.

"You twist the Law!" he wept.

"I twist nothing!" Samson laughed. "What do I twist?"

Suddenly, he stopped his chase. Already they had come to the crest of the ridge, and setting his father down, he turned him to gaze upon the vale below.

Sprinkled along a distant brow were the lights of Mahaneh-dan.

With a quivering heart, Manoah looked up at his son, finding, as he often had, an expression on the boy's face of teasing innocence that defied suspicion.

"A strange lad you are," he said, gimlet-eyed. "Prophet or scoundrel, I cannot tell."

For an uneasy moment the two locked eyes. But then, with a shrug, Samson turned to go on, and Manoah followed.

They would reach Mahaneh-dan before midnight, and by way of the Sabbath.

FOUR

*T*he camp of the Danites nestled on the shoulder of one round hill, unhidden, as though it dared the forces of evil to approach it.

From the distance of the ridge where Samson and Manoah had first sighted it, it was no more than a cluster of yellow lights resembling the unwalled encampment of some wandering tribe.

As the two travelers drew nearer, however, the lights were distinguishable, each burning low within a permanent shelter, shining in a topaz patch through a single window. These shelters were the cells of the Nazarites: austere, made of whitewashed mud smoothed into hollow, hivelike cones. Each housed only one man, and they were arranged in a ring about a fire that was central to the commune.

Since it was very dark when the Zorahites came upon the settlement, the caves that formed the backdrop for the camp were less visible. As the father and son descended into the valley, however, the glimmer of other solitary fires could be seen, peeking out from the rock rooms burrowed into the far hill.

The caves were the original shelters of the camp, and the eldest leaders still resided in those mountain vaults. As the sect had grown, requiring additional living space, the commune could have moved elsewhere. But considering the ancient plot to be sacred ground, they opted instead to construct mud houses on its slope.

No guard stood watch at the rim of the camp. In fact, there was no gate or barrier of any kind. When Manoah and Samson reached the circle, they were greeted by intimidating silence.

Except for the huts' firelit interiors, there was little hint of life about the place. The huts themselves might have been tombs, save for the sound of low snoring which issued from some of them.

Of course, the newcomers had arrived after dark. Even so, they had anticipated a greeting of some kind. As Samson and his father stood doubtfully at the edge of the cluster, wondering how to proceed, the long-dreamed-of arrival seemed anticlimactic.

"Let's rest here," Manoah suggested, sitting down beneath a tall broom tree. "At dawn we will introduce ourselves."

Though not the least bit weary, Samson agreed. Reclining upon the ground, he gazed up into the slate black sky. The desert hills were much quieter than even the country setting of Manoah's little farm. At least there, the sound of lowing cows or bleating goats sometimes disturbed the night, or the rumble of some other farmer's cart could be heard upon the nearby highway. Here the night was oppressively quiet, broken only by the rustle of leaves in the branches overhead.

Scanning the midnight sky, Samson let his thoughts wander among the million stars that graced the heavens. As though scattered from some gigantic broken necklace, they seemed to have taken their places at random, rather than according to divine scheme. Pulling his mantle close to his chin, Samson wondered if he was like some fallen star, full of fire, but cast across time without purpose.

Such questions often filled his mind in moments of solitude.

Why had he been so strangely endowed? The hallmark of his nameless calling, his remarkable strength, coursed through him on command, a servant of his own will. Yet he knew it was not his own, but came from beyond himself and must be disciplined with reverence.

Remembering the day he rescued Josef, he sighed and shook his head. He had called on God's help, yet the very act of rescue had alienated his best friend.

Then he thought of the good that had come from that same brief episode. Marissa had opened her eyes to him that day, and it seemed her heart was his, an unexpected prize.

Folding his arms beneath his head, he stretched out upon the ground and closed his eyes. Remembering her smile, he imagined what it would be like to kiss her. Never had he been so bold as to act out that fantasy—but it was a pleasant one, all the same.

Indeed, the girl haunted him, her lithe beauty and gentle manner wooing him in powerful ways.

Ashamed, Samson sat up. Beside him, Manoah dozed, leaning against the tree with his face lifted toward heaven. *Likely he dwells on holy things,* the lad thought. What would he think if he knew of Samson's ruminations?

Sometimes the youngster resented the way Marissa so easily invaded his mind. Too often her face and her smile disturbed his meditations. He wondered at the odd stirrings she provoked—the quickened pulse, the tightening of the groin.

Never had he shared his adolescent yearnings with anyone. Certainly no one would understand. And surely such feelings were evil. Especially for a Nazarite, a "called one," like himself.

Suddenly, the awkward interlude was split by the shuddering wail of a ram's horn trumpet. Lurching upright, Manoah and Samson braced for a challenge, thinking themselves the cause of the alert.

As they waited, exposed to whatever should follow, apparitional figures emerged from the huts, almost ethereal in their long, white habits and hooded cloaks.

The visitors had seen such figures before, when they made their annual appearance in Zorah for the blessing of the priest. But they had never before seen them in the moonlight, nor in the eerie quiet of these hills.

Holy awe fell upon the intruders. Would there be some divine retribution on their trespass?

To their surprise, however, the specterlike figures seemed oblivious to their presence. Walking straight for the center of the circle, they passed by without heeding the Zorahites and seated themselves about the main fire.

As Samson and Manoah looked on, half-a-dozen men came out from the caves above, distinguished from the others by their advanced age and venerable white beards. These were the elders, the remnant of original leaders who had established the commune years before.

Breathing more easily, the Zorahites watched the spectacle with curiosity. Apparently the blast of the ram's horn had signaled a midnight meeting. As the elders joined the circle, the congregation began to chant softly a familiar hymn of Israel:

> "I will sing unto the Lord, for he has triumphed
>   gloriously:
> The horse and his rider he has thrown into the sea.
> The Lord is my strength and song,
> And he has become my salvation:
> He is my God, and I will prepare him a habitation;
> My father's God, and I will exalt him.
> The Lord is a man of war:
> The Lord is his name."

As the chorus rose and swelled, filling the night air with holy urgency, Samson felt his spirit soar with it. Though the two visitors sat outside the bright circle, enveloped in black night, they blended their voices with the others' and sensed a kinship with the Nazarites that transcended sect and dogma.

For they were brothers with them, all men of Israel. And the song, which had been sung by Moses and all the children of Israel upon their deliverance from Egypt, was one of racial solidarity.

If anything distinguished the Hebrews from pagan cultures, it was their sense of divine calling. Nazarite and commoner alike believed that they were set apart for the glory of God.

Indeed, Israel was a concept more than a political entity; a concept sorely tested by oppressing neighbors. As the Gentiles saw it, Israel had no land of its own. While the Jews maintained that the ground upon which they toiled was vouchsafed to them by Adonai, the Lord, Israel had no king like other lands and was considered a vassal, a tributary of the Philistines.

Israel's only identity lay in the hearts of her people, even as her unity lay in the leadership of various "judges" whom, they said, God raised up to bring them to righteousness.

As Samson joined in the refrain, he forgot the distracting thoughts that had invaded his mind earlier. Nothing, not even Marissa, could be so important as the cause of Israel.

At last the music tapered to a hush. All about the fiery circle, faces were upturned and eyes were closed.

The eldest of the elders rose before the worshipers, and in a somber tone he began to speak.

"The Lord is a man of war," he said, repeating the last lines of the hymn. "The Lord is his name."

The audience nodded agreement, and he went on.

"Though we do not see it, the Lord leads Israel today as surely as he did in the days of Moses."

Again the audience concurred, murmuring enthusiastically.

"He led us through Abraham," he declared. "He led us through Isaac and Jacob. He saved us through Joseph and delivered us through Moses and Joshua!"

Applause followed, and the men laughed for joy.

Then silence descended, and the Nazarites stirred uneasily, wondering at their master's contemplative pause.

"But, my brothers, the mighty men of old are no more," the elder groaned. "There has been no patriarch in Israel for three hundred years. And the sacred land promised to us through Abraham, and won for us by Joshua, is overrun with enemies. We no longer possess it in honor, but share it with heathens!"

The men did not like to be reminded of this. Aliens within their own promised land, they and all their countrymen had relied for centuries on the sporadic guidance of a string of "deliverers," the loosely-inaugurated judges through whom God chose to speak.

Continuing his rehearsal of Israel's history, the elder told of the many such governors who had led the nation for the generations since they had entered Canaan. Valiant warriors like Deborah, Gideon, Abimelech, and Jephthah stood out among a host of lesser greats for their victories over Israel's enemies. Nearly a dozen of these leaders had held the nation intact, but each had been called upon to fight the easy apostasy into which the people repeatedly wandered.

As the preacher reminded them of the judges' heroic feats and bold discipline of the wayward Israelites, the listeners had mixed feelings. Hope stirred at the mention of God's providence, but the tendency of the people to turn from the truth was discouraging.

Israel's most recent history was even less hopeful.

"We have been blessed with countless deliverers," the elder declared. "But where are the judges today? It has been forty years since anyone led us. Forty years since our last judge, Abdon, passed on to his reward. Nor has anyone risen to take his place! An entire generation has flirted with the Philistines, losing its integrity to pagan ways, and no one has called us back!"

None of these ideas were new to Samson. He had heard similar woeful reminders all his life, in town gatherings and during homilies delivered on Sabbath mornings. Why should they impress him now?

Whatever the reason, they struck a chord deep within him. Sitting in the dark beyond the circle, he was unknown and unnoted by any of the Nazarite monks, yet the elder's message reached directly into his heart, as though intended especially for him.

Shaking himself, he pulled his mantle tight to his cold shoulders. Perhaps it was the setting that troubled him: the crystal black night and the starlit eeriness of the hill; the spectral images about the fire, bent and hooded and droning in sad Israeli chant.

But he knew he was only rationalizing. There was no avoiding the haunting sense of God's voice.

What it meant for him, or how he should apply it, was too deep a question for one so young. All he knew just now was that something strange transpired within his spirit, something he would not begin to understand for a very long time.

As the elder concluded his talk, Samson was lost in introspection. It was not until the audience was again on its feet, singing a benediction, that the youngster returned to the moment.

When he focused again on the proceedings, the words of the closing hymn struck him with fresh impact. Though it was the same refrain which had earlier been sung, it targeted his heart like a spiritual arrow.

"The Lord is a man of war," the hymn insisted. "The Lord is his name."

FIVE

*I*t would be dawn before Samson and Manoah were recognized in camp.

When the meeting broke up, the two Zorahites huddled together on the bleak hillside, trying to sleep. For Manoah rest came easily, his old body exhausted by the journey and the late vigil. But for Samson, there would be no peace. All night his spirit was restless as he reviewed the evening's message.

When the crickets quieted before twilight, Samson was still awake, eager for the first stirring of the camp. As he surveyed the circle of huts and the dying embers at its center, his gaze was caught by a movement in the mouth of one cave.

Remembering that this cave had been the one from which last night's speaker emerged, Samson brightened.

Yes, the elder stood there, his white habit silhouetted against the dark opening.

Had Samson known his name, he would have called to him. But to his surprise, the elder scanned the slope where he and his father rested, as though he knew someone was there. When the old fellow spied the two Zorahites, he walked straight toward them.

"Father!" Samson whispered, nudging Manoah. "Wake up! Someone is coming!"

Manoah sat up, his bones aching from the night on the cold ground. Groaning, he rubbed his eyes and glanced in the direction of camp.

"Peniel!" he gasped, astonished. "It is Peniel who approaches!"

"You know him?" Samson marveled. "Why didn't you tell me?"

"I did not recognize him last evening. It is only now, as he walks toward us, that I know him."

It was true that the old man had a distinctive gait, as though one foot was twisted.

"He was a boyhood friend," Manoah explained, standing up in greeting. "Because he could not run and play with the rest of us, he was always given to contemplation. When he was about your age, he became a Nazarite, but I did not know he dwelled at Mahaneh-dan."

By now the elder was upon them. And he was equally surprised to see Manoah.

"Friend!" he hailed him. "Do my eyes deceive me?"

"No more than mine do me," Manoah laughed.

Happily they embraced, seeing past their creases and wrinkles to a time when they had been boys together.

"Something told me we had visitors," Peniel said. "When did you arrive?"

"Last evening," Manoah replied. "We heard your talk at midnight."

Samson's father evinced no shame as he said this, and Samson wondered if he realized he confessed to traveling on the Sabbath.

There would be no reprimand from Peniel, however, who was only glad to see his old companion after all these years. As Samson was introduced, the elder studied him with care.

"This is my son," Manoah said. "Samson will be thirteen years old in two days. We have come here in the hopes that you would celebrate his bar mitzvah with us."

Peniel looked the lad up and down, walking around him and surveying him from every angle. Tenderly he reached forth a wizened hand and stroked Samson's long curls.

"Your hair has never known the cut of a razor," he noted.

Samson did not reply, but his heart surged with the same urgency he had felt the night before.

"He has been raised as a Nazarite from birth," Manoah explained. "His mother and I were told to sanctify him."

For a long time Peniel was quiet, receiving the statement as though it needed no explanation.

"He has never eaten anything unclean, nor approached the dead, nor . . ."

Peniel raised a hand, hushing Manoah and nodding.

"You were here last night?" he asked Samson.

"Yes, sir," the lad replied.

"And you heard me speak?"

"Yes, sir."

For some reason, the admission was fearsome.

The elder stepped back, looking at the ground. In silent wonder he closed his eyes, his gnarled fingers twining and untwining through his long beard.

"I knew someone was here," Peniel whispered. "I knew my message was for someone beyond the circle."

SAMSON WALKED with Peniel deep into the hills above Mahaneh-dan. Far below lay the camp, where they had left Manoah to rest in the elder's cave.

This trek was not as slow as the journey from Zorah. Though Peniel was an old man, and though he was crippled, a lifetime in the wilderness had hardened him, and he managed the hike with relative ease.

"So, in only two days you will be leaving your childhood behind," Peniel observed. "How does it feel to meet your manhood?"

Samson considered the question carefully. There were many ways he could have replied. He could have said the prospect was exciting. He could have declared it a challenge. Instead, he spoke his heart.

"Sometimes I am afraid," he said.

Peniel paused in the path, detecting the sadness in Samson's voice.

"You see," the lad continued, "for me . . . it is different."

"Different?"

"In two days I will be a man. But I have never really been a child."

The elder took a seat beside the path and placed his walking stick across his bony knees. Leaning forward, he encouraged Samson's openness.

"I am not like the others," Samson sighed, "not like my friends. I have always been bigger . . . stronger . . . "

Peniel smiled broadly. "Such a curse!" he teased. "I was always different, too." Rubbing his twisted foot, he shook his head. "Are you not grateful for your endowments?"

Samson's face colored and he tried not to stare at the atrophied ankle.

"This strength of yours, has it been difficult to manage?" the elder asked.

Samson took courage. "Sir, it has," he replied.

"It lures you from the spiritual," Peniel guessed.

Never had the youngster shared his struggle. Never had he been able to put it in words.

"It pulls me in many directions," he confessed, tears welling in his eyes. "And yet, I am told it is a gift from God."

Peniel studied the lad with compassion. In the sunlight that glinted off the morning hills, he saw the pubescent shadow of a beard along Samson's noble jaw. Though by tradition he would enter manhood at thirteen, he was maturing earlier than usual.

"The tug of the world and the call of the senses can be powerful," Peniel agreed. "Sometimes the most spiritually gifted are the most sorely tempted."

Samson shuddered. It seemed the elder plumbed his very soul. But how could one so set apart, one who had lived in the wilderness most of his life, possibly relate to such a fleshly battle?

The lad would have asked, but Peniel was now deep in contemplation, hands outstretched, eyes closed.

After a long while, the elder stood up, tilting his head back so that his hood slipped off, revealing a snowy mass of unshorn hair. "Samson would have me tell him his way will grow more easy," he said, as though speaking to the sky. "He would have me tell him that temptation will fall away."

Yes, yes, this was what the lad wished to hear. He wished to hear that he would outgrow his childish temper, that weak and foolish folks would not enrage him. He wished to hear that he would lead a normal life, being a village craftsman or a farmer like Manoah. He wished to hear that he would have Marissa, and that she would satisfy him, and that no great or awful thing would be required of him.

He wished to hear that the tumult of his spirit and the boiling in his veins would one day die away.

But Peniel would speak no such thing. Instead, his eyes now open, he approached the lad and placed his hands upon his head.

"You are a called one, and your path will be hard," he said. "You are a Nazarite, and the Nazarite way is for those who find it difficult to renounce the world."

Deftly his hands moved over Samson's head as he pulled up first one strand and then another of the long, dark curls.

Within moments, he had arranged the hair into seven locks, each held apart by a fine braid, the adornment of a Nazarite initiate.

Then, reaching down, he pulled Samson close, looking him full in the face.

Suddenly, as they stood thus, Samson could see himself in the elder. He saw them both as equally crippled, equally weak and strong.

And it seemed, for one brief moment, that life's mysteries might bear the seed of resolution.

A village bar mitzvah, while free of much ceremony, was a glorious occasion. Everyone turned out to greet a boy on his thirteenth birthday, to receive him into the manly society of the community.

Although Samson's birthday had actually been yesterday and had been observed in Mahaneh-dan, his hometown would not miss the opportunity to celebrate the occasion as well.

Even as Samson and his father were still some distance from the village, descending the last hill on their way home from camp, the sound of music and revelry rose to meet them. When they arrived at the edge of town, they were greeted by banners strewn across the modest gate and by a chorus of twirling girls clapping tambourines above their heads.

"Samson, Samson!" the girls sang. "Man of Israel you are! Childhood is behind you, the world is at your feet! Samson, Samson, serve Adonai! Man of Israel you are!"

Samson scanned the group of singers, hoping that Marissa might be among them. To his disappointment, she was not. Perhaps she was in the marketplace, waiting for him. Lifting his chin, he thought confidently on the words he would speak to her, if he could only get her alone.

His three days in the Danite camp had infused him with zeal, assuring him of God's special calling. Though he could not foresee what that calling would demand, the visit with the Nazarites had accomplished what his father had hoped for: the inward confirmation that the Lord had singled him out for great things.

The confidence instilled during those three days not only encouraged a sense of spiritual destiny, but also bolstered Samson's self-worth. In the past, he had hung back from declaring his heart to Marissa, but he would do so no longer. Tonight, if he could only be with her in private, he would share the secret of his love.

The splashing fountain at the center of town was muted by music and festivity. As Samson and Manoah entered the marketplace, folks shouted and waved to them from nearby rooftops, and young people surrounded the handsome celebrity, marveling at the arrangement of his hair.

Not only would they be celebrating a bar mitzvah this evening; they would be acknowledging the ordination of a Nazarite. Three days before, Samson had gone into the hills, a favored son of Zorah; tonight he returned, a man marked for holiness.

As he had hoped, Marissa was waiting near the fountain, standing on tiptoe, stretching her tall body even taller to catch a glimpse of him. As their eyes met across the square, her face declared an adoring heart.

But as she noted the mark of his calling, the seven locks of his hair, her hand moved lightly to her throat, and he wondered what she thought.

Had it been proper, he would have flown to her side. He would have taken her in his arms and assured her that his sacred office would never take him from her.

But it was not proper. There were too many people here, and there was tradition to observe.

Chanting and singing, the crowd pressed in about Samson, ushering him toward a small, striped tent at the end of the square. There he would receive the blessing of the town priest, and he would partake of one swig of wine. Since he was now a Nazarite and was to avoid strong drink, this would be his only permissible taste of the fruit of the vine. It would be given only for the sake of custom, a mark symbolic of manhood.

As the crowd led him toward the tent, his gaze continued to fasten upon Marissa. Manoah, who walked beside him, nudged him in the ribs. "Son . . . ," he whispered, directing him to the priest.

At the door of the tent, the holy man waited, Samson's mother standing beside him. Over her arm was a handmade shawl, which she had woven for Samson years before. It would be placed upon the lad's head this day, denoting entrance into the Danite fraternity.

As Samson drew near, Rena kissed him upon the cheek. She would not be allowed to accompany him into the tent, for no woman was allowed within the male sanctum of a bar mitzvah shelter. But she handed the shawl to Manoah, who would, in turn, pass it to the priest for the official covering.

Following the priest into the tent, Samson obediently knelt before him, bowing his head as the holy man prayed over him. In simple ceremony, he was draped with the Danite mantle and then received the cup of wine.

This was a sacred moment, almost as sacred as the moment when Peniel had prayed over him, arranging his hair in the seven locks and separating him to the Nazarite life.

Although his heart raced with religious emotion, it also lingered behind him, where Marissa stood watching.

He hoped it was not wrong to think of her as he sipped the priestly wine. But he breathed a prayer for forgiveness, just in case.

ALL EVENING long, the town celebrated. Zorah was not a wealthy place, and its people were hardworking folk. But when they had an excuse to party, they did so with gusto.

Well past midnight the lanterns strung across the square illumined a merry scene. Though the occasion of a bar mitzvah was of religious significance, the revelry was anything but somber. When enough wine had been drunk, enough songs sung, and enough dances danced, everyone was in a carefree mood, and the village rang with frivolity.

Samson, who had a keen eye for the girls, had never enjoyed so much female attention as he did tonight. One after the other of the village maidens locked her arm in his, laughing gaily as she danced him around the court until he thought his head would burst. When Marissa was his partner, he hoped the night would last forever, that he might feel her touch upon his hand and smell her perfumed hair against his cheek for hours to come.

There was one youngster attending the party, however, whose heart was not so merry. Watching from the sidelines, Josef did not mingle with the others, but observed his old friend with seething jealousy.

Josef had always been small, but he had compensated for his size with agility and cleverness. Tonight, though, as he compared himself to Samson, he felt more frail and insignificant than ever.

Sitting alone behind the fountain, he cupped his pointed chin in his hands, his elbows resting sharply on his updrawn knees. Shoulders stooped, he looked on as Marissa danced with the bar mitzvah boy. As his keen black eyes darted from Samson's fawning expression to the face of the love-struck girl, he heaved a sigh.

Bitterly he followed the town legend, who spun and wheeled about the square rewarding every girlish gaze with a confident smile. Even the adults in the crowd were enamored with Samson, and Josef knew that some of the locals believed the boy to be supernaturally endowed.

Smirking to himself, Josef shook his head. He knew Samson too well! He knew his volatile temper and lack of self-control. Josef had never believed Samson's talents anything but human.

"You are the brawn, and I am the brains," he used to tell his burly playmate.

Suddenly, as he recalled this, a spark of challenge flashed across his envious soul.

Yes! Samson was only human! He was big and strong, but never had he been as smart as Josef!

"Brains versus brawn!" he whispered to himself. "You have been a fool, Josef! If you are to beat Samson, you must use your head!"

He knew all too well that he would achieve nothing if he tried to woo Marissa. Considering her addlepated infatuation, such a course was hopeless just now. He must first undo his opponent, and the rest would take care of itself.

Absorbed in such ruminations, Josef plotted how he might gain a foothold.

If I am to beat him, I must join him, he concluded.

And what better time than now, when the entire town could witness his charitable spirit.

When the musicians took a break, and the young people joined the older folks about the banquet table, snacking on yet another round of food, Josef slipped forth from the shadows and walked up behind Samson.

Tapping him on the shoulder, he stretched out his hand, and when Samson wheeled about, he thrust it toward him with a smile.

"I have not congratulated you," he said, loudly enough that everyone could hear.

Astonished, Samson studied Josef's proffered hand and at last returned the gesture, shaking it energetically.

"Congratulations!" Josef declared. "We have been boys together, and now we are both men!"

Wide-eyed, Samson drew him close, clapping him on the back.

"Friend!" the celebrity laughed. "This is indeed a happy night!"

Then, pulling Marissa into the embrace, Samson hugged them both together.

"Could any man want more than this?" he shouted to the crowd.

Applauding, the town echoed his sentiments, and as the music began again, the people danced around them—Josef, Marissa, and the grateful bar mitzvah boy.

SEVEN

*M*oonlight spilled across the common as the music at last died away. Giving Samson a final round of congratulations, the revelers said their good-nights, and departed for their homes.

Rena and Manoah, their hearts overflowing with joy, had headed home some hours ago. And even Josef had bid farewell, smiling as he shut the door to his cottage.

As a few villagers helped the priest lower the bar mitzvah shelter, storing it away until the next boy came of age, Marissa gazed fondly up into Samson's radiant face.

"I must be going," she said. "Mother will be waiting for me."

His heart drumming, Samson took hold of her hand. He had promised himself that he would not let the night pass without declaring his heart.

"Walk with me," he managed to say, his voice cracking with adolescent tension.

When Marissa did not withdraw her hand, but wove her warm fingers between his, he felt a familiar surge rush through his veins.

The brook, he told himself. *Take her to the brook.*

Though the pristine ribbon of water that ran along the edge of town was only a few feet from the square, it seemed miles away. Trying to ignore the priest and the whispering villagers,

Samson hoped no one would follow him as he led the girl to the sheltered bank.

Willows and sycamores graced the narrow stream, and when Samson had found a quiet bower, he turned Marissa to him, studying her lovely face.

He was not good with words. He had practiced what he should say, but just now he could not recall a syllable.

He should have been embarrassed. Surely she wondered at his strange hesitance. But for now he could think of nothing but her beauty, and lost in her eyes, he lifted her hand to his cheek.

When he felt her tremble, he knew he must speak.

"Do not be afraid," he whispered. "I brought you here to tell you . . ."

To tell her what? he wondered. Did he really want to say those words?

Straightening his shoulders, he pulled back a little and lowered her hand from his face.

"I am a man this night," he said. "I have much I want to say."

"Yes?" Marissa spurred him on.

"I . . . much happened to me at Mahaneh-dan."

"Yes," she said again, scanning his Nazarite hair. "You are a man of God."

"So I am," he replied, then quickly added, "but it will make no difference."

Bewildered, Marissa shook her head. "No difference?" she said, marveling.

"No difference . . . for us," he stammered.

He was handling this badly.

"What I mean is . . ."

"What *do* you mean?" she whispered.

Overhead a light breeze filled the treetops, and the melodic sound of the brook coursed through Samson's soul.

Drawing the girl close, he tilted his head back and looked far away into the stars. He remembered the insistent call of God, the first night when the monks had gathered. He remembered wondering what it meant for him and his future.

"I am a man this night," he sighed. "I am free to speak my heart."

Marissa may have questioned whether he addressed her or the sky. When he drew her even closer, breathing into her ear, she felt his pulse envelop her.

"I am a man of God," he declared. "But I am also a man. I love you, Marissa."

Yes. Yes, he loved her. She had longed to hear it!

But as he lifted her chin and pressed his lips to hers, she trembled at his eager insistence.

Sinking into his embrace, she let the glory of young love enfold her.

But it was a tortured love. She could sense anxiety in his too-strong grip.

And the mystery of his torment clouded her heart.

The Lion and the Riddle

ONE

*J*osef reined his horse over the last hill west of Zorah, speeding ahead of a small wagon train, as if to hurry it toward town.

The fact that the wagons were empty of the goods he had taken to the coast proved that his venture to Ashkelon had been successful. When he had headed out from Zorah, the wagons had been piled high with copper pots, bolts of fabric, and boxes of honeycomb—special wares of the hometown merchants. All these he had sold within a few days in the coastal market.

Due to his clever salesmanship, he had become merchant general of the village, though he was only twenty-two years of age. In fact, all of the craftsmen, potters, dyers, jewelers, and farmers of the area had come to rely on Josef to peddle their products in distant cities, even awarding him ten percent of his receipts.

Josef was therefore, at an early age, a wealthy man. And though he would always be slight of build, as lithe as a paring knife, his reputation for sharp dealing had gained him great stature in his community.

Just now, however, business was the last thing on Josef's mind. As he raced his horse through the town gate, he looked eagerly for Samson.

In a few weeks, it would be seven years since Samson had been ordained a Nazarite, seven years since his bar mitzvah. He would soon be twenty, and he had received permission from his mentor at camp Mahaneh-dan to marry. Everyone in Zorah knew that old Peniel had released their Shining Star to take a wife, and everyone knew Samson's choice would be Marissa.

Though there had been no formal announcement to that effect, people saw the handsome young man go courting at the girl's house. They saw the flowers he left on her doorstep, and they often saw him walk with her along the brook and fields that bordered Zorah. They knew that the night lamp burning in her parlor meant she sat up late, likely finishing the dress she hoped to wear at her wedding. As the time of Samson's birthday drew closer, everyone in the village anticipated news of a betrothal.

That such news had not yet come, they attributed to the fact that the Nazarite spent so much time away from home, abiding more at Mahaneh-dan than with his parents.

Indeed, Samson had become a holy man. For the last seven years he had taken his calling very seriously. Though he would never be a Nazarite of the strictest order, he abided by the rules laid out for him since youth, avoiding strong drink and contamination by anything unclean. He carefully observed all of the laws of Moses, adding to them the special rituals of his sect. He spent large amounts of time in seclusion and allowed his hair to continue uncut.

As a result of his dedicated life, he was greatly respected and was often called upon to offer his opinion at village councils. Of late, he had even been asked to mediate in legal disputes. In many people's minds, he was a judge among them. And he would gain even greater status when, as the citizens expected, he took a wife.

All of this filled Josef's mind tonight as he looked for his old friend. But he had a special reason to be concerned about Samson's future—a special reason to try to intervene.

That reason was Marissa, whose light burned bright in her cottage down the way.

Josef knew that Marissa would be able to tell him Samson's whereabouts. The realization angered him, but he would use it to his advantage. If he had his way, the girl would soon have no involvement in Samson's life.

Dismounting from his horse, Josef stood before Marissa's low door, nervously wiping his hands down his cloak, then rapping lightly with the knocker. By the eager response, he supposed the young lady expected to open the door to her lover. When she threw it back and saw Josef instead, her crestfallen face confirmed his suspicion.

"Oh, Josef," she said, nodding as congenially as possible. "Have you returned already from your trip? I was expecting—"

"Samson," he filled in. "Where is he?"

"He is due back from Mahaneh-dan this evening. Are you looking for him?"

"Yes," he replied. "I have a gift for him." Peering past her into the parlor, Josef saw Marissa's nuptial gown draped across her footstool, a spool of thread and a needle lying beside it. "A wedding gift," he added, with a biting tone.

Marissa's face colored as she followed his gaze to the lovely garment. "I was just . . . mending," she stammered.

"I see," Josef said, his lips pulling back from his teeth. "I will go to meet Samson. If he arrives here before I find him, tell him I am looking for him."

MENDING, INDEED! Josef thought, as he spurred his horse up toward the hills.

Behind him in town, his servants unhitched his caravan and bedded the mules down for the night. Tomorrow he would settle his accounts with the merchants, but for now no one would miss him as he went to meet his Nazarite friend.

As he traveled the twisty road, which was little more than a path, he considered his good fortune. Not only had his trip to the coast been financially successful, but he may have found a treasure on the journey that would solve the problem of his heart.

While his horse picked her way up the heathered hill, he savored the memory of his short stay in Timnah, a Philistine burg just seven miles west of Zorah. How many times since he had begun to caravan had he stopped in that little village? Yet never before had he laid eyes on its loveliest inhabitants, Jezel and Zerah, the daughters of Mardok.

Had Josef not been determined to make Marissa his own, he would have coveted the girls for himself. Especially Jezel, whose elegant glamour outshone her winsome younger sister. But the girls could be put to better use. Josef believed that if he could only pass them before the gaze of Samson, just once see to it that he glimpsed their beauty, he might have a chance of turning the Nazarite's heart from Marissa.

Josef knew what it was to be a sheltered Hebrew boy. He remembered how it had felt to set foot in a Philistine town for the first time, to see a scarlet-clad harlot upon a street corner, her tinkling hip-bells and bangled bosom advertising her wares. Though he was now an experienced traveler, he still found painted Gentile women to be of heart-stopping wonder. And he figured that Samson, sheltered from birth and accustomed to monastic purity, would be even more vulnerable than he to the wiles of such females.

Intellectually, Josef hated all things Philistine. Yet he had not been immune to the temptations that the Gentile world presented. Sometimes he felt guilty for his indiscretions. He wistfully remembered days of innocence, and youthful dreams of squashing Israel's enemies. Never, when he was a child, could he have dreamed he would eat at pagan tables, drink heathen wine, or enjoy their fleshly liberties.

But, he reasoned, business was business. One could not forever be idealistic and maintain good business relations. Didn't his fellow Jews suspect that his much-lauded success and the profit *they* made from it were largely due to his liberal attitude?

Nonetheless, he remembered what it had been like to see a Philistine woman for the first time. And if Samson was still the same lad who had danced a dozen girls to exhaustion the night of his bar mitzvah—the lad whose impulsive character Josef knew only too well—he was certain he would be easy prey to Gentile advances.

Getting Samson out of Zorah would be the tricky part. Josef was still pondering that challenge when his horse snorted, stopping in the path and lifting her nose to the evening breeze.

"What is it, girl?" Josef whispered. "Is someone coming?"

Through the gloaming, he made out an advancing figure, tall and broad shouldered.

"Samson!" he called.

"Josef?" the Nazarite cried. "Is that you?"

Soon they were face-to-face upon the path, Josef climbing down from his mount and embracing his friend with gusto.

"Samson!" he laughed. "I was told I might find you here. I have just returned from the coast, and I have a gift for you!"

"A gift? But why?"

"A wedding gift! You *will* be marrying Marissa, won't you? That is all the talk."

Samson shrugged, kicking at a pebble and smiling bashfully.

"Of course you will. And I will be your best man! But first you must take my gift."

"Very well," Samson agreed. "But see that you tell no one. We have made no announcement."

"You have my word!" Josef promised, clapping him on the back.

"So," Samson sighed, "where is the gift?"

"You must come with me to Timnah to pick it up," Josef said enthusiastically. "I reserved it for you during my trip."

"You left it in Philistia?"

"It was necessary," Josef said with a smile. "Besides, it is only a few miles down the road, hardly far enough from Zorah to qualify as Gentile! Don't let that trouble you."

TWO

*T*he sunlight that kissed the hills leading down toward Timnah seemed especially bright this morning. It was hard to be somber on such a day.

Still, it was no easy thing for a Nazarite to set foot in Philistine territory.

As Josef had said, Timnah was very close to Zorah, in the same vineyard country as Samson's hometown. But it was by no means Jewish. And though it was tiny, its licentious reputation was typically Gentile.

The Jews had a name for the pagan peoples around them. *Goyim*, they called them. It meant simply "the people," or "the people outside," and was always spoken with an edge of disgust. If one was a proper Jew, even condescension was too kind an attitude to express when speaking of goyim. One must display revulsion when using the word.

Of course, it was necessary to have contact with goyim. The Israelis were surrounded by them, and so they were obliged to trade with them and engage them in various business dealings. People like Josef were especially useful in Jewish communities, for they dared to work more closely with the goyim than most Jews did. Josef carried the burden gracefully, and his fellow Israelis were grateful for it. He would never admit he might actually enjoy his traffic with the "unclean."

As the two young men made their way down the westward highway, the morning sun was warm against their backs. Josef journeyed on foot, leading his horse by the reins, walking with Samson, who had never owned a mount.

Such a good friend he is! Samson thought. Memories of their childhood, of the times they had played in the fields and hills around Zorah, pricked his heart. Sometimes, in recent years, he had felt that Josef shunned him. Surely today showed that he had been mistaken. Josef's affection had not cooled, though their lives had taken them down very different paths.

When Samson laughed out loud, Josef looked at him in curiosity. "What is it?" he asked.

"I was just remembering all those wars we fought when we were boys. We were always the victors because the enemy was invisible. But we must have killed thousands of imaginary Philistines!"

Josef laughed with him, so Samson did not notice the twinkle fade from his friend's smiling eyes.

"Yes, I remember," he said.

"And the war horses!" Samson exclaimed. "Those glorious Philistine horses! We must have captured ten thousand!"

Josef quietly nodded, and Samson did not see that a cloud crossed his companion's face.

What did impress Samson was what seemed a sudden insight. Yes, the Philistines raised marvelous horses, strong as the iron which was the Philistine secret, and swift as spears made from that iron. Josef's horse was just such an animal, purchased on one of his journeys into Philistia.

"You little weasel!" Samson cried, throwing a heavy arm around Josef's narrow shoulders. "Now I know what you are up to!"

"You do?" Josef queried, trusting he had not, indeed, guessed the truth.

"You are giving me a horse, a Philistine horse! And you wish for me to have the joy of selecting her!"

Josef cleared his throat and pulled away from Samson's embrace.

"Well," he said with a laugh, his face crinkling, "you *shall* have the pleasure of choosing her, but . . . if she is a horse, she is a sweet little filly, indeed!"

TIMNAH, sitting in the rolling, emerald green country above the Maritime Plain, seemed heedless of its small size. Announcing itself gaily to all travelers, it sported colorful banners along its low wall and gave a warm invitation to all who passed its way by means of a tall, beckoning statue of its patron goddess, Ashtaroth, which was stationed just outside the iron gate.

If Samson had thought to avoid direct contact with Philistine stimulus, he was quickly shocked into reality. The goddess of sensual love smote his eyes, targeting his heart with erotic arrows.

Whether or not Josef was affected by the sight, Samson did not notice, so stunned was he by the statue's prurient appeal.

Like racing fire, his blood rushed to his cheeks, and he feared to set foot in the city. Turning to his friend, he stammered, "I'll wait here, Josef. You go in and bring them out to me."

Knowing that his ruse was up, Josef chuckled nervously. "Oh, come on, Samson. I can't do that. It wouldn't be fair to the owner. Besides . . . it's not horses I have brought you to see."

Samson stood in the statue's shadow, glowering at the gate and then at Josef.

"What kind of game are you playing?" he demanded. "Why *have* you brought me here?"

"If I am your friend," Josef said smoothly, "I should do what I can to make you happy. And if I am to be best man at your wedding, I want to be sure you have thoroughly thought through your options."

Bewildered by this gibberish, Samson barely resisted as Josef wound an arm through his and led him through the gate.

"Trust me," Josef continued, directing him down the main street. "After all, who knows you better than I? And who knows the *world* better than I?" Gesturing toward the boisterous marketplace, he chuckled, "You *have* led a sheltered life, you know."

THREE

*H*ow Samson came to be sitting, only hours later, in the house of Timnah's leading merchant, laughing and languishing in the arms of a Gentile woman, drinking wine from her cup, he would never completely recall.

The brief stretch of time between his entrance into the forbidden town and his indulgence in such activities was a blur and would always remain so.

"Come, Samson," Josef had prodded, leading him to the door of Mardok's house. "Don't be afraid. We will stay only a few moments. At least *meet* the women. If they are not for you, you will return to Zorah more convinced than ever that you have made the right choice."

"But I have never had any doubt about my choice," Samson argued, hanging back.

Pulsating music spilled into the street from the courtyard. Josef winked at the younger man and gave him a nudge. "All right," he said. "Forget the women. But we are here now. Where is it written, 'Thou shalt not have fun'?"

With this, Josef led Samson through the portal.

Perhaps it was the sunlight outside that made it seem so, but to Samson, the patio was oddly dark, despite the fact that it was open to the sky. Josef took his guest by the arm, leading him from stranger to stranger, introducing him. When Samson avoided their gazes, Josef quipped, "At least be polite! This is a party, not a funeral."

But, for the Nazarite, it was a sore trial. Standing in the midst of the pagan court, he felt very much the alien. A quick survey of the gaudy interior and the lounging revelers convinced him he was out of place.

When he turned for the exit, Josef caught up with him, rebuking him beneath his breath. "Are you afraid? None of this can touch you. After all, you are a Nazarite, a holy man. You are strong enough to sift the grain from the chaff!"

"Why should I put myself to the trouble?" Samson snapped. "Let them have their grain and chaff together!"

But just as he would have escaped, a glimpse of Mardok's elder daughter stopped him in his tracks.

When the girl, who was unlike any Jewess he had ever seen, smiled at him across the room, his knees grew weak.

Sidling up to him, she breathed deeply. "Why, Josef," she gasped, "where have you been hiding this treasure?" Before Samson knew it, she was running her hands over his muscular arms, embracing him as though he were a long-lost cousin.

Her name was Jezel, and so strange was her beauty that Samson was her instant captive.

Of course, had Samson spent more time around Philistines, he would not have thought her beauty so unusual. But she was the first Aryan woman he had ever seen: tall, Hellenic, with hair the color of summer wheat and eyes the color of spring cornflowers. Blue eyes! He had never before seen blue eyes!

Marissa was dark, typical of the Semitic people, and while she was unusually tall, her body was more willowy than Jezel's. Samson had always loved Marissa's graceful slenderness, but Jezel was more fully endowed, blessed with curves and roundness, as well as the stature which had helped to make the Philistines a mighty people.

And, in keeping with her imposing physical presence, Jezel was anything but shy. While Marissa had always been quiet and circumspect, Jezel was daringly flirtatious and full of laughter.

"Here, darling," she said, slipping a wine goblet into Samson's hand. "Join the party."

In that brief interlude, twenty years of abstinence fell away. Taking his first sip of wine since his bar mitzvah, Samson let Jezel lead him to a seat across the room, where another light-haired beauty waited.

Between Jezel and Zerah, the host's younger daughter, Samson had not a minute to consider his boundaries.

"Come, come," the younger sister cooed, pulling him to a cushion upon the floor. "You have arrived just in time for the magician!"

Eager for a show, the revelers in Mardok's courtyard took seats all about the pavement, clapping and swilling drinks and calling out to a curtain set up beside the fountain.

Soon the curtain parted, and a man dressed in a flowing robe and a resplendent, pointed hat stepped forth. Beside him was a female assistant, poured into a clinging white gown and painted like a peacock, her hair full of purple feathers and her suggestive bodice studded with rhinestones. Samson, who had never seen sleight of hand, was instantly taken in by a volley of the trickster's art, thanks to the distracting assistant who drew his focus off of the magician's hands at just the right times.

Water seemingly flowed from an empty glass, coins disappeared from the sorcerer's open palm, empty boxes bloomed with flowers when a velvet veil was lifted off of them. Amazed, Samson tried to imagine how such things were done, and he began to wonder if they were the work of an evil spirit. But his fears were assuaged as the two young women cuddled against him, lisping admiration, stroking his bare arms and twining their fingers through his Nazarite braids.

Mardok, meanwhile, stood with Josef not far from the threesome. If the two men nodded together, whispering a mystery, Samson did not notice. He was lost in the wonders of Philistine magic, the wonders of foreign women.

For now, he had forgotten Marissa.

FOUR

*W*hen Samson returned to Zorah, he did not go to Marissa's house. Nor did he go to see Peniel at the Danite camp. What he did, in fact, was avoid those contacts at all costs.

Had his relationship with his orthodox parents been different, he would have avoided them, too. But Rena and Manoah would be no problem. While Samson had never abused the power he had over them, both he and they knew it was real enough. They all knew that it was the son, not the parents, who was in control.

Of course, he was prepared for their disapproval when he told them where he had been and what he had been doing. Though he was a powerful person, he had never openly defied them.

"You went *where?*" Manoah shouted when Samson explained his delay. "We expected you to come straight here from Mahaneh-dan! What purpose could you possibly have in going to Timnah?"

Samson had braced himself for this inquisition, but no amount of preparation made it easy for him to see the look on his mother's face. Avoiding eye contact, he still sensed the horror in her expression as she quietly stood behind her husband, her hand raised to her throat.

He knew her unspoken thoughts: *Gentiles . . . goyim! My son has mingled with goyim!*

"Let me explain," Samson said, his own throat dry and his mouth smiling only from one corner. "I think you will be happy for me."

"Happy!" Manoah cried. "Do you hear that, Mother?" Turning to Rena, he drew her protectively to his chest. "Samson says we should be happy he has broken his vows! Happy he has walked on unclean soil!"

Samson could see that this would call for most delicate handling. When Rena began to weep, very quietly, her feeble shoulders shaking, the young Nazarite wondered if he could, indeed, persuade them.

But he had given much thought to what he should say.

"Hear me out," he resumed coolly. "You trust Josef, don't you? Everyone respects Josef! Do you think he would mislead me?"

When the old folks made no reply, looking at one another in bewilderment, Samson knew he had scored a point. Josef had done well by the family, making a fair profit for Manoah and Rena on the food and handmade goods they had consigned to him. They were no less appreciative of his business sense than anyone else in Zorah.

"Well," Manoah sighed, "what does that have to do with anything? Josef has been a good friend, but he had no right to entice you against your vows!"

"I am not one of the zadokim," Samson objected, referring to the strictest order of the Nazarites. "It is permissible for me to deviate from my regimen . . . if the cause warrants."

At this, Rena pulled away from Manoah's embrace, brightening a bit.

"So, you had good cause?" she sighed. "What cause, Samson?"

The Nazarite paused a moment, as if in sober reflection. With a face of intense sincerity, he replied, "You know that Peniel has given me permission to marry."

Of course, they knew. It was all they thought about and the delight of their future hopes. For months they had awaited the announcement that Marissa and their son would be wed.

But how a trip into Philistia could facilitate their dream, they could not imagine.

"Yes," Manoah said. Then, the fire of joy leaping to his eyes, he laughed. "Of course! You went there to purchase gifts for the bride!"

Such a purpose would be straining Samson's vows, but it might be forgivable.

When the young man's gaze went to the floor, and he did not offer immediate reply, the parents grew anxious again.

"Josef took me to Timnah to purchase a wedding gift," he said. Before he could explain further, Manoah rushed forward, throwing his arms about his sturdy neck.

"Praise Adonai!" he cried. "So, you have set a date for your marriage!"

At last, knowing he should not toy with his parents, Samson admitted the truth.

"Josef presented me with a gift, but the gift was not a bride-price. It was the bride herself. I do not wish to marry Marissa. Instead, I have seen a woman in Timnah, one of the daughters of the Philistines. Father, I want you to get her for me . . . as my wife."

Manoah gripped at his old heart, clutching his tunic to his chest. A stammer pushed through his white lips, barely recognizable. "But, Son . . . how . . . why? Marissa . . . Lord God!"

Trembling terribly, Rena leaned against her husband, tears quivering down her face.

"Is there no woman worthy among all your people," she wept, "that you go to take a wife from the uncircumcised Philistines?"

So horrified was her expression, one would have thought a parade of demons had passed through the room. Manoah clung to her weakly, scarcely believing this was his son standing before him.

Trying to be strong, Samson swallowed hard. "I . . . I never knew I would be drawn to anyone but Marissa," he confessed. "But it has happened. If I am to be a spiritual man," he reasoned, "I must have the Philistine girl. I will be distracted until I make her my own."

Then taking a deep breath, he made it clear that he expected his parents' cooperation.

"Get her for me," he demanded, "for she looks good to me."

FIVE

*I*t was not proper for Jewish elders to move quickly. Always circumspect, they walked with hands folded and heads raised in austere dignity. But today, Manoah was almost running, straining his old muscles all the way to Mahaneh-dan.

Seven years ago, when he had gone with Samson to request a blessing on the lad, he had barely been able to walk through these hills without stopping every few feet. Today, however, he was spurred by anger, as well as zeal. He must speak with Peniel. He must fill his friend's ears with the fury of his Israelite heart.

Already, only a half-day out of Zorah, he descended toward the evening lights of the Danite camp. Heedless of the deepening dusk and of the vesper songs arising from the vale, he rushed into the compound, calling for the elder.

"Peniel, Peniel!" he cried, hailing the white-habited monks who retired to their hivelike huts. "I must speak with Peniel!"

Raising their hooded heads, the holy men scrutinized the hobbling intruder. "Peniel must not be disturbed," one replied, stopping on the path. "Our brother is at prayer!"

"Prayer time will wait!" Manoah insisted. "There is an emergency!"

Pushing past the man who had objected, Manoah headed directly for Peniel's cave. Barging in, he stood between the elder's small fire and the dark entryway.

At the sound of the invader, Peniel, who sat cross-legged upon the stone floor, was jolted from his private devotions.

"Manoah?" He marveled, peering past the fire. "Is that you?"

As Peniel blinked to clear his vision, Manoah drew near and sat across from him.

"It is I," he announced. "But just *who* are you?"

With a befuddled laugh, Peniel shook his hoary head. "What do you mean?" he asked, pushing back the mantle of uncut hair that cloaked his shoulders.

"You claim to be a holy man!" Manoah raved. "A teacher of the Nazarites. Years ago I put my son's spirit into your keeping, and you have failed me!" In an accusatory torrent, he cried, "Was Samson not the Lord's from birth? Even from *before* birth? When he was living under my roof, subject to my inadequate teaching, he was a holy lad, clean as snow!"

"Yes . . . ?" Peniel questioned slowly, stunned by his friend's outburst.

"But, you have ruined him! You . . . his mentor . . . his spiritual guide . . . whom his mother and I entrusted with his soul!"

Thoroughly shaken, Peniel rubbed his knees and leaned toward the fire, prodding it with a stick. Trying to be patient, he asked, "What has happened, friend?"

"You gave Samson permission to marry," Manoah replied. "And so he shall!"

Shrugging, the elder reminded him, "Only with your approval. You know this."

"But I never approved a marriage outside of the law!" Manoah spat.

His brow furrowing, Peniel studied his old friend. "Nor did I," he answered. "You know I would not."

"Well, that is his intention!" Manoah declared. "He wishes to marry a Timnahite woman!"

When Peniel only stared at him blankly, the old father rushed through the story, punctuating each syllable with resentment. "And so he returned to us, having been to the Philistine town," he blurted out. "Now he tells me I must get the infidel for him! Can you imagine? I should pay bride-price for a *heathen?*"

As Manaoh chased the tale with more blistering accusations, laying all responsibility on Peniel, the monk listened quietly, fingering the tendriled beard that wound down his chest.

The law of Moses gave specific injunctions regarding marriage "outside the covenant." Intermarriage with certain foreign groups was strictly forbidden. Since the Israelites had had little contact with Philistines at the time of Moses, there was no specific law forbidding marriage with them. But most proper Jews looked askance at such unions. Since a Nazarite was supposed to be "holy unto the Lord," more was expected of him than of even the most orthodox commoner. Marriage to a Philistine was unthinkable.

"So, what have you taught him all these years?" Manoah demanded. "Have you cared nothing for his vows?"

Peniel realized such a charge was ridiculous, that it was spoken in the heat of unreason. The old hermit, who knew better than anyone the struggles of Samson's nature, could have responded with his own smarting anger. But instead, his gaze drifted past Manoah to the cloaking dark beyond the door.

With a patience borne of years in spiritual questing, the monk listened to another voice as it whispered through the chambers of his sanctified heart.

While Manoah continued to vent his pain, Peniel heard him, but did not hear him. He attended, but did not attend. For the fragrance of a quieter spirit moved past the doorway, spilling quietly into his hallowed soul.

"Peace, Manoah," he finally whispered. "Listen to me."

So gentle was Peniel's command, it missed Manoah's ears. But when it was repeated, Manoah ceased his fuming.

Staring out the door, the monk presented a peculiar challenge. "Is the Lord the master of the law, or its servant?" he asked.

Unable to decipher the Nazarite's meaning, Manoah made no reply. In confounded silence, he followed his friend's gaze toward the night sky.

"Let the boy go," Peniel said. "He has been the Lord's since birth, and whatever befalls him is within the providence of God. Let Samson go, and leave him to the providence of God."

*W*inter would soon be coming on. It had been several months since Samson had seen the woman of Timnah. Anxiously he had passed the summer working beside his father in the fields. Eagerly he had awaited the passage of harvest, when the bulk of the family living was made. As the only son in the family, he could not leave for Philistia until the seasonal work was finished.

Not that the old man had reconciled himself to the idea of a mixed marriage. He had, in fact, been most difficult to live with ever since he had come back from visiting Peniel. Begrudgingly he had accepted the monk's advice, but he still harbored grave doubts as to the "providence of God" in the matter. And he made no secret of his frustration.

At last, however, the growing and reaping seasons were past. If the fateful trip was to be made, if Manoah was to see the Philistine woman and offer bride-price, the thing must be done before the chill of winter.

Now, when a Jew traveled from Israel into Philistia, he was not, in truth, traveling from one country into another. Palestine, the land of the Philistines, surrounded and encompassed all things Jewish, so that Israel was a state of mind rather than a political reality. The Jews did not admit this. To the orthodox, the land promised to Father Abraham *was* Israel, and the profaning dominance of "foreigners" was only a sad commentary on the spiritual state of the chosen people. The Jew did not see himself as an alien here, since Israel had arrived in Canaan at about the same time as the invading sea peoples, the Philistines. But ever since the time of Joshua, the region had been contended territory.

Since the Philistines presently controlled the area, the best the Jews could do was keep to themselves, their little villages and pockets of settlement representing the "true" Israel. Therefore, to journey into a Philistine town was to journey "out of Israel" and "into the land of the heathen."

A few brave souls, like Josef, had learned to travel easily between the cultures. But this was done at risk of becoming "polluted." To maintain one's clean status under such conditions took a convincing cleverness, which Josef had well mastered.

When Manoah finally agreed to make the trip, he insisted on bringing Rena. Samson, concerned that the journey might be too much for his aged mother, had objected. But so great was Manoah's unhappiness over the coming venture, and so dependent was the old couple upon one another, that in this matter, the son had no influence.

Though it was only seven miles from Zorah to their destination, the three still had not reached Timnah by nightfall. The cold of late fall was quickly descending, and they huddled beneath their mantles until they reached the vineyards that marked the entrance to Timnah vale.

Samson, relieved to see the lights of the village along a westerly slope, suggested that they camp among the vines and enter town at morning. "It will be safe here," he said, gesturing to the terraced hillside that bordered the road. "No one stays here after harvest, and we can sleep behind the boxthorn."

Moonlight glanced off of a series of low retaining walls that led up the hill, between which were the remains of harvested vines, hanging from their support poles like skeletons. During the growing season, especially during harvest, workers literally lived in the vineyards, the landholders residing in stark stone buildings erected on the high places as watchtowers.

Completely enclosing the vineyard was a living hedge of cactuslike plants, and where the plants did not grow, another wall, topped with dead spiny burnet, deterred animals and thieves from entering the precious plot.

Trying the gate, a low door set in the hedge and the only legitimate entrance to the vineyard, Samson found it was unlocked. Leading his weary parents through a maze of terraces and lifeless branches, he reached the door to the watchtower itself. When he found that this, too, was unlocked—there was little reason for the owners to secure it this time of year—he laughed quietly. "See, God is with us," he said.

Manoah did not appreciate this comment. Snorting, the old man led his wife to a dark corner and spread his mantle upon the floor. Together the two lay down, and Samson gently placed the woman's cloak over them as a blanket.

"Rest now," he said. "I will sleep outside."

Like a shepherd who sleeps across the entrance to the sheepfold, Samson positioned himself across the path from the watchtower, ready to defend his family against danger.

Not that he anticipated trouble. The vineyard gate was shut tight, and the boxthorn hedge seemed forbidding enough. Even so, it would be a night of restless sleep for the Nazarite. It was true that he moved toward his objective, the woman of Timnah. Still, he was not without a conscience. Tonight, in this private hour, he was haunted by uncertainty.

In truth, the uncertainty had been there all along. Samson had known, in the depth of his spirit, that he had taken a willful turn. But he had not allowed introspection, so full was he of desire for Jezel.

When thoughts of Marissa or of his holy calling had pricked him, he had managed to put them aside. But tonight, in this strange and eerie place, he was compelled to dwell on the very thoughts he had worked so hard to avoid.

As he tossed restlessly, it seemed he had been here before. At least he had been stirred with the same uneasiness before. When had that been?

Samson stared upward, and the flint black sky drew his eyes into its fathoms as though it were a vacuum, sucking his thoughts past the stars until they seemed to streak past him. All about, dry vines rustled in a silent breeze, waving to him like scrawny, voiceless hermits.

He remembered the night he had first entered Mahaneh-dan, how alien the place had been, how peculiar the hooded monks had seemed as they made their dark pilgrimage to the nighttime circle. Chanting and droning, they had been his first glimpse of holy solitude, and he had not liked the initial impression.

Later that evening, when Peniel had spoken, his ancient, cracking voice had risen above the hivelike huts, lingering over the hills, dying away into a night as deep as this one. Samson recalled the old man's sermon, its theme so out of keeping with his present pursuit. The monk had spoken of holiness, of the need for Israel to return to her God. He had said they must have a leader, that Israel had been without guidance for too many years.

As though he were once more hearing Peniel's voice, Samson felt again the sting of his words, as though the prick of the message was meant for him alone.

Suddenly, unbidden thoughts of Jezel interrupted his sad remembrance. Cringing with guilt, Samson buried his head on his updrawn knees and tried to sleep.

Whether he actually slept or not, he was not certain. But as the lonely moments passed, the eeriness of the dead vineyard pressed in upon him, the night breeze filling his ears with the chant of the Nazarites, heard so long ago:

I will sing unto the Lord, for he has triumphed
  gloriously:
The horse and his rider he has thrown into the sea . . . .
The Lord is a man of war . . . a man of war . . . .

Surely he slept, for it seemed he was a boy again, reliving pretend wars he had fought against the Philistines. In a dream, he roamed the hills above Zorah, laughing and carefree, chasing phantoms with sticks and stones, side by side with his little friend, Josef.

Over the crest of a hill, a thousand warriors appeared, arrayed in Philistine armor. The sun glinted off of their iron shields and spears, but they were no match for the two boys, who had the God of Israel on their side.

As always, the young soldiers led a fearsome army of devout Jews, who, despite their primitive weaponry, quickly embarrassed the foe, sending their stamping, snorting horses to retreat, and laughing in derision at the enemies' cries.

At this point, the dream should have ended. For now the two boys would have turned to other sport, frolicking in the streams or rolling down the grassy slopes until they were dizzy.

But it did not end. Instead, the Philistines reappeared, this time not in the form of men and horses, but as lions—hundreds and hundreds of them. Terrified, Samson raised his arms over his head, defending himself against the charge of an especially vicious beast.

Suddenly, the space between reality and fantasy disintegrated as the Nazarite awoke to the roar of a true-life, pouncing lion. Flying over the hedge, crashing through the dry burnet, the snarling cat made straight for Samson's throat.

It was near winter, and the cold hills were devoid of easy prey. The scent of the man must have drawn the beast to this daring attempt. With no time to think, Samson leaped to his feet, barely avoiding the first attack.

Skidding through a rubble of gleanings left on the harvest path, the cat wheeled about and charged again.

But he did not anticipate the man's strength.

Like a bolt of lightning, unearthly power whipped through Samson's veins. Lifting his broad hands, he caught the cat in midflight.

With dazzling speed, Samson gripped the lion's throat, holding the beast in the air with one hand, and clutching its underbelly with the other.

In one mighty flash, he pulled his arms wide, tearing the cat asunder. With a groan, he threw the beast aside, watching as life spilled from it.

Shaken, still struggling to realize that this was real life and not a dream, he scanned the hills above the vineyard, as if on alert. Then, throwing his head back, he shouted aloud, a cry of triumph, a cry of warning, a cry of praise to the Lord of hosts.

SEVEN

*O*nce again, a party was in full swing in Mardok's courtyard. But this time, it was no casual social gathering. This time it was a wedding reception that attracted the entire town of Timnah.

It was spring in Palestine. Samson's visit to this place before winter had brought the hoped-for results, as Manoah and Rena had begrudgingly consented to his wishes and paid the bride-price for the fair-haired Jezel.

Of course, the humble Jewish farmers were not wealthy. It had strained their hard-earned income to pay even the minimum for the girl—two she-asses and a dozen bags of barley grain. Mardok could have been insulted by the paltry offer. But his daughter was so enraptured with the handsome, young Israeli, and so dear to her father's heart, that he accepted it.

"On one condition," Mardok had stipulated. "Samson will not take Jezel from Timnah. If he wishes to be her husband, he will reside with her here, in her hometown."

Hearing this, Manoah had gasped, clutching his chest as though he would faint. And Rena fought back tears of shame.

If anything would have dissuaded Samson from his chosen course, it would have been this ultimate disgrace. But, much to his surprise, Manoah bowed his head, as if in prayer, then raised sad eyes to the Philistine and nodded.

"So be it," the old man agreed. "If this is our son's desire, we will not stand in his way. We gave him to the God of Abraham before he was born. We have no hold on him."

Thus it was that faithful Manoah and his wife sat in the rollicking court of a pagan businessman, sinking like shadows into the wall, observing heathen excesses in silent despair.

There would be seven days of this foolishness. They, as the groom's parents, would only need to endure one night of the misery. But that one night was the worst, for it was the night of the wedding, which would be performed by a pagan priest. And the hated ceremony would conclude with Samson's disappearance upstairs with his bride, for the consummation.

Shame washed over the two parents as they saw their beloved son submit to a priest of Baal! How could his holy upbringing have produced such results?

As the son of Dagon, Baal was the most popular deity of the Philistine farmlands. God of grain and crops, god of storm and fertility, he received his power directly from his father, the god of the sea. Cringing, Rena and Manoah watched as the priest, followed by a string of dancing girls, anointed Samson and his bride with oil and honey, symbols of life and abundance.

Manoah struggled to control the revulsion that filled him at the sight. Had Samson not been anointed already, when he was but a lad? Had he not received the blessing of Zorah's Hebrew priest when he entered manhood? Had he not received the mark of a Nazarite when he was in Mahaneh-dan?

Why this holy man should submit to a counterfeit anointing, Manoah could not imagine. And he grumbled the name of Peniel beneath his breath, until Rena nudged him to be quiet.

Reaching into a small pouch that hung from her belt, the old woman handed her husband a waxy piece of honeycomb. "Here, eat this," she said, trying to comfort him. "It will all be over soon."

Placing it in his feeble hand, she wrapped his fingers about it and raised it tenderly to his lips. Tears welled in Manoah's eyes. Why would Rena wish to remind him of this precious gift, bestowed upon them by their son?

Never would they forget how, during this latest trip to Timnah, they had come to the vineyard again and Samson had left them on the road, racing through the gate and leaping up the terraces toward the watchtower. He needed to see something, he had announced, and they must wait where they were.

They did not know that he went to see the carcass of the torn lion. He had never told them of his strange night upon the vineyard path and the attack of the mountain cat. He wished to spare them such a story and did not want them to know he went to look upon something dead, a taboo that had bound him all his life. Furthermore, he did not care to hear their interpretation of his vision—that the Philistines were evil, or that his intended bride was unclean.

Returning from his little side trip, he had been full of smiles, and thrusting a heap of honeycomb into their hands, he had bid them eat, that they might not be so glum.

"Where did you get this?" Rena had asked in astonishment.

But Samson did not say, treating the secret as though it were sacred.

Now, as the pagan priest and his dancing girls surrounded the wedding couple, tossing grain upon them and passing wine through the crowd, and as Samson took his bride by the hand to lead her up the stairs to the nuptial chamber, Manoah groaned and shook his head. But Rena pressed the honeycomb to his withered lips, ignoring the loud music and laughter that flooded the court.

"Eat, Papa," she whispered, leaning close to his ear. "Samson is a good boy. We must believe."

JOSEF STOOD at the closed door of Jezel's chamber, listening from the hallway to the secret sounds of love that pressed through the portal.

As Samson's best man, it was his duty to do this and to report the consummation to the guests downstairs.

The assignment brought delight to his heart. Not that he cared for the groom's ecstasy, but the wedding of Jezel and Samson was a major step in his plan to wrest Marissa's heart from the strongman's clutches.

Stepping away from the door, he went to the balcony rail and nodded to the crowd, signaling that the deed had been done.

With a loud cheer, the wedding guests turned to merry-making, and Josef hurried downstairs to embrace Rena and Manoah. Under different circumstances, this would have been the happiest day of the old couple's lives, but Josef knew they were miserable, and he tried to console them.

"There, there," he said, patting the weeping mother on the arm. "I know you had high hopes for him. But he has always been a headstrong fellow. We must leave this matter to God."

Manoah put a protective arm about his wife's shoulders and glared at Josef's beaming face.

"Headstrong?" he snarled. "Perhaps. But it was you who set temptation in his path. You brought him to Timnah, knowing he would meet this girl! He says you called her a 'wedding gift'!"

Feigning surprise, Josef seemed offended. "He said that?" he gasped, flashing an angry glance toward the bridal chamber. "Why, I am shocked! I brought him here to choose a gift, it is true. I never dreamed he would meet Jezel!"

Studying Josef's persuasive face, Manoah gave a sigh. With a shrug, he led Rena to the door. "We must be going," he muttered.

"Let me walk you to the street," Josef offered, taking them by the arms. "When you reach Zorah, give my regards to Marissa."

EIGHT

The wine-swilling crowd lolled about the wedding couple until the wee morning hours, laughing and dancing and joking. So light was Samson's head with drink and with love that he barely realized his parents had departed. If it did dawn on him, it gave him only momentary pause.

Jezel was by his side, in his lap, entwined about his neck. For now, that was all that mattered.

And, of course, his party guests. They mattered, too.

In Philistine tradition, a group of "companions" had been assigned to him. So wealthy was Mardok that he had hired thirty in all, young men of wit and charm, who would make the groom's heart merry and keep the festivities lively. After all, seven days was a long time to keep enthusiasm at a peak, and their duty, while pleasurable, was necessary to the party's success.

Besides, Samson was an Israeli. If Jezel's marriage was to last, her new husband must be won to the Philistine way. Mardok knew there was no better method to accomplish this than to surround him with fun-filled company.

Josef, while himself an Israeli, mixed easily with the young men whom he knew through his trade contacts. Encouraging the evening's playful spirit, he sat close to the newlyweds and often whispered in Samson's ear some clever quip or flirted freely with the bride.

As morning approached, and the party was still rowdy, the best man proposed a toast. Hoisting a goblet of wine, Josef called for quiet.

"To the groom!" he cried.

Everyone echoed him, quaffing their drinks and laughing heartily.

"It is a custom among our friends," he addressed Samson, "that the groom should ask his companions a riddle. Whoever answers it correctly receives a prize from the groom."

"Hear! Hear!" the crowd cheered.

"Tell us, Samson, do you have a riddle?" Mardok inquired. "Make it a good one, for these fellows are clever."

Loosening Jezel's arms from about his neck, Samson leaned back upon his pillows and thought a while.

"I can guess it, Samson!" someone called.

"No, I!" cried another. "Make it as hard as you can!"

As Samson pondered the matter, he surveyed the revelers' jolly faces. These were delightful folks. Why had he been trained to believe the Philistines were unclean? Yes, he knew their ways were ungodly, but could they help it that they had been born into a culture alien to the Lord?

At last, breaking into a smile, Samson leaned forward and winked at his companions.

"Very well," he nodded. "Let me put a riddle to you. But it will be so difficult that it will take you all week to solve it!"

"Ha!" the crowd roared. "Try us!"

"In fact," he boasted, "if you can tell it to me within these seven days, I shall not only reward the one who solves it, but I will give you thirty linen cloaks and thirty tunics, one for *each* of you!"

Astonished, the crowd could scarcely believe his generosity.

Josef flinched at Samson's impulsiveness, but said nothing. If the Philistines doubted the groom's ability to make good on the offer, they did not question him, and his friend dared not cast distrust on his character. Samson was obliged to hold up the bargain or lose the goodwill of his new family.

Conferring together, the Philistines took the offer, another great cheer ascending from the court. And Jezel, flattered by her husband's risk on her behalf, planted a kiss upon his lips.

But the happy guests were not prepared for the balance of the deal. While they were still overwhelmed by Samson's giving spirit, he added the clincher. "If you are unable to tell me the answer, then *you* shall give *me* thirty linen cloaks and thirty tunics!"

What any man, Jew or Philistine, could want with such a wardrobe, they could not imagine. Only kings were so well outfitted. But in their exaggerated mood, they let him alter the traditional rules and played along.

"Give us your riddle," they laughed. "We are ready!"

Unfortunately, Samson had no riddle in mind. He was not used to such games and was unaccustomed to the levity of jokes and puzzles. Nevertheless, he had committed himself. He knew he must put forth a mystery for them to contemplate.

Mutely, he studied the waiting crowd who pressed close about him, ready to pounce on any challenge.

Ready to pounce, like mountain cats . . . like lions . . . Philistine lions!

Jolted by the memory of his vineyard vision, Samson recoiled. Yes, these *were* Philistines . . . the goyim of his youth . . . the enemy!

Looking up at them, the Israeli suddenly saw each face as alien, overlaid with deception, underlaid with hatred for all that was godly. This he wished to deny; this he could not escape.

When he began to speak, it was in words he barely understood himself, words unrelated to a wedding, words holy and profound:

"Out of the eater came something to eat,
And out of the strong came something sweet.
Now tell me the answer if you can.
Prove to me, who is the better man!"

NINE

Samson lay asleep on the wedding bed where he had made Jezel his own. This was her room, and the aroma of her perfume was heavy upon the sheets. But he did not dream of her, nor had he thought tenderly of her for the past three days.

He had been in hiding ever since he had presented his riddle. He had not shown his face to the crowd since that moment, refusing to drink with them, refusing to converse. And while the party went on and would fill out the week, an ugly mood had settled over the court.

In all the traditions of Jew and Gentile, there could be no greater insult than for a groom to desert his companions. He might more easily abandon his bride than his partying friends. But this Samson had done, retreating behind a cloak of fear and depression which no one downstairs could comprehend.

No one, that is, save Josef. He knew that Samson struggled in his spirit—that Samson had no place marrying a Philistine, no place in company with the heathen.

But Josef's goal was closer to fulfillment. Leaving Samson to fight his inner battles, he partied with the others, savoring his secret victory.

As for Samson, as he slept upon his wife's bed, dreadful scenes filled his head, scenes of war and blood and conquest.

He loved Jezel, but he hated her people. And part of him hated Jezel.

Even more did he hate himself and the demon that drove him. Or was it a demon? Were not his energy and his strength the gifts of God, though they sometimes made him vulnerable to temptation?

His head drummed with pain as he tossed and turned upon the bed, fighting the Philistines of his soul. When glimpses of Marissa passed between the battles, his heart ached as it had never ached before. And he clutched his chest in shame.

Just then, a knock at the chamber door woke him. Lurching upright, he called through the haze of a departing dream, "Marissa! Is it you?"

The door creaked open into the darkened room. It was Jezel who entered, not Marissa. But the bride had not caught Samson's words, and she did not know he had been dreaming of a Jewess.

"Husband," she pleaded. Though her tone was hushed, he knew she had been crying again. Hour after hour she had come seeking him, pleading with him to return to the party, to lift the shame he had laid upon her family.

Until now he had been able to disregard her. But this time she wanted more than simple courtesy.

Tiptoeing to the bed, she knelt beside it and took his broad hand in hers. Kissing it, she let a tear splash upon it and lifted sad eyes to his stony face.

"I will not come down," Samson insisted. "I will stay here until the feast is ended."

"I know. I know," Jezel sighed. "I will not ask you again. Though I do not understand you, I will not ask you to join us again."

"Then what do you want?" he barked. "I shall be a husband to you in time. Only let me alone until the others are gone."

Pulling back, Jezel flashed angry eyes. "You think I have come for love?" she snapped. "Do not flatter yourself!"

Grimacing, Samson withdrew his hand and instantly she became kittenish.

"Oh, husband. I am sorry. Forgive me. You know I love you."

Climbing onto the bed, she pulled his arm beneath her head and nestled against his chest.

"It is only that I fear you do not love *me,*" she cooed. "How can you stay up here with your secret and not tell it to me?"

"My secret?" he said.

"You only hate me, and you do not love me!" she cried. "You have propounded a riddle to the sons of my people and have not told the answer to me!"

Bemused by her playful ways, Samson laughed and rested his head upon his pillow, drawing her close. "So this is what troubles you?" he sighed. "I have not even told the answer to my father or mother. Why should I tell you?"

Jezel was wounded. "Your father and mother? What have they to do with this?" she inquired.

"Never mind," he replied. "I shall not reveal the riddle until the seven days are over."

With this, Jezel became all the more insistent. Her chest heaving, she pulled back and sat curled beside him, heavy tears coursing down her cheeks.

"Oh, Samson!" she wept. "How can you be so cruel? Do you not see what shame you have heaped upon my family, disappearing from the party, and . . . and keeping your love from me?"

Moved by her girlish sobs, Samson's heart grew warm and pliable. As he enfolded her in his powerful arms, he caressed her neck and passed his fingers down the soft skin of her bosom.

She put him in mind of love, and he was ready to forget his isolation. But as he kissed her, she pleaded once again, "Tell me your riddle. If you love me, tell me."

Almost he did so. Almost she made him set aside hatred for the Philistines. For she was herself a Philistine, and he *did* love her.

But he was a strong man. She did not move him against his will.

What he willed just now was to take her, body and soul. And so he did.

TEN

*I*t was the eighth day, the day after the feast had ended. Samson was in a rage, and the strength of his anger compounded the strength of his great body.

He had fled Timnah by night, not out of fear, but in pursuit of revenge, and he had not stopped running though it was now morning.

He headed toward the coast and the Philistine Pentapolis, the five major cities of this alien land. He knew he would enter at Ashkelon, one of the maritime capitals.

Not that he had given much thought to his destination. His only intention was to find Philistines in large number, to level retribution upon them in one of their most publicized places, and to return to Timnah with spoils of war.

His "companions" had guessed his riddle. Just before sundown on the seventh day, they had come to his room. Pounding upon the door, laughing and jeering, they had cried, "You owe us thirty cloaks and thirty tunics, Samson! We have solved your puzzle. What is sweeter than honey or stronger than a lion?"

Leaping from bed, Samson had thrown back the door on a sea of mocking faces. Below, in the courtyard, stood Jezel, huddling close to her pagan father and fearing for her life.

From deep within Samson issued a growl, low and animal-like, as he realized his bride had betrayed his secret. After seven days of pleading and manipulation she had managed to wheedle it from him, only to give it away!

"If you had not plowed with my heifer, you would not have discovered my riddle!" the strongman bellowed, pushing through the crowd until he stood at the gallery rail. "Jezel, how *could* you? You know I am not a wealthy man!"

Weeping, the woman crept toward the stairs and beseeched him. "Forgive me, husband," she whimpered. "These men threatened evil against my family if I did not reveal the secret! They said they would set me and my father's house afire! How could I refuse?"

At these words, Samson's heart burned like a coal within his breast. Gripping the rail in vicelike hands, he nearly ripped it from its pins. But, summoning self-control, he flew down the stairs and out the courtyard door.

That had been last evening. With a taste for blood upon his tongue, he now approached Ashkelon.

A wet breeze whipped salt air through his long hair as he descended the last crest of the highway. Below, the walls of the city stretched like a seductive snake along the shore. How penetrable they looked, laid bare for the breaching!

So this is the Pentapolis! he thought. *This is the iron land.*

Laughing like a wildman, he chased his echoing derision down the hill and headed directly for Ashkelon's immense gates. He might have been the dreaming boy again, the sporting friend of Josef. There were guards upon the walls, but their hands were palsied upon their bows, as the mighty Israeli tore colossal chains from the barred doors and pushed through the fortress as though it were so many apple crates.

Claiming the city with daring as much as brute strength, Samson swept through the streets, picking men up by the throat and shaking the life from their lungs. One by one he took them, before they had time to think, before they could defend themselves or decipher what had transpired.

Like a titanic whirlwind, the Israeli bashed through homes and brothels. He threw men into the gutters and laughed at the cracking of their backs.

Thirty in all he took, and not one more. When he had snuffed the life from thirty souls, stripping the bodies bare, he turned again for the gate.

Tomorrow the coast would be afire with vigilante spirit. The overnight legend of the powerhouse Jew would be the talk of Philistia, and the reward upon his head would be a king's ransom.

But, despite his seeming revenge upon the goyim, Samson would return to Timnah unrequited. Though he would bestow upon the riddle-guessers their tunics and their cloaks, he would never forget their duplicity.

He had only now begun to know true hatred. And it was a righteous hatred, indeed.

PART THREE

Jackals
and
the Jawbone

ONE

*T*he night Samson swept through Ashkelon, Josef was breaching another wall. The door was more humble than the gates of a Philistine city, but it presented as great a challenge.

It was the door of Marissa's cottage, and it took as much courage for Josef to knock upon it as if a queen lived behind it.

But then, Marissa had been queen of Josef's heart since he was a boy. He had schemed to reclaim her since the day the wagon fell upon him and Samson shamed him in her presence.

Straightening his robe and smoothing his short-cropped beard, the young caravanner tried to assure himself he was worthy of her interest. Then, taking a deep breath, he reached out and rapped lightly with the knocker.

A shadow crossed the parlor's yellow light, and soon the girl of his dreams stood before him.

To Josef she had always been the most beautiful woman on earth. If her face was a little drawn, he knew it was from sorrow. She pined over the loss of Samson, but he would turn her heart to happier things.

"Good evening," he said, bowing low.

Bewildered, Marissa peered around the door. She had not seen Josef since the day he came with a "gift" for Samson.

"Good evening," she replied.

"I have just returned . . ."

"From Timnah," she guessed.

"Yes. I . . ." The embarrassed suitor shuffled awkwardly. "Would you care to walk with me? The evening is cool and the willows are full of breezes."

"Not really," she said, pulling back into the shadows. "Thank you, anyway."

"Come, come, my lady," Josef insisted, holding out a hand. "It will do you good."

Marissa looked at him, considering. Perhaps he was right. She had kept close to home for too many days, every day since Samson had left for his . . . wedding.

The very thought of Samson's betrayal still pierced her heart like a white-hot prod. She had not been comfortable with Josef since she chose Samson over him. But she had no reason to be unkind. Perhaps it would be good to walk again beside the brook.

Lifting a shawl from a hook inside the door, she stepped into the evening air. Gently, Josef took the little mantle and wrapped it about her shoulders. If his hand touched her too familiarly, she pretended not to notice.

As they walked, a thousand questions raced through Marissa's head. She longed to ask Josef about her beloved. She wanted to know about the bride, what she looked like, and how she had so easily wrenched Samson's heart from its secure place with herself.

But not one question would be voiced. Marissa had not yet accepted her loss, and to speak of it would make it much too real.

Therefore, it was Josef who broached the topic.

"That was quite a party in Timnah," he said.

Marissa blanched. "I'm sure it was," she sighed.

Her lips quivered with unspoken pain, and Josef drew closer.

"You would do well to forget him, my dear," he crooned. "I would not criticize my friend. But he *is* an unpredictable sort."

Downcast, Marissa sniffed back tears. "If you knew this about him, why, oh, why, did you ever take him into that God-forsaken place?" she reproached him. "Oh, Josef, if I didn't know you better, I would think you intended all of this!"

When Manoah had made the same accusation, Josef had deflected it smoothly. But such words from Marissa were a troublesome sign.

A lump in his throat, he proceeded carefully. "My lady," he managed to say, "you know I love Samson. . . . Why, I love Samson almost as much as I love . . . you."

Something in this pronouncement raised the hair on Marissa's neck. Whether it was intuition or a spiritual prompting that pricked her, she stopped in the path and turned suspicious eyes upon her companion.

"What did you say?" she whispered.

"I . . . I love you, Marissa."

Josef's head was bowed as he repeated this. He knew his words rang hollow—though, after all these years, he did not understand why.

Recoiling, the Jewess wrapped her shawl tighter. There was a cool breeze blowing across the hollow where the brook ran, but no cooler than usual. It was not the breeze that made her skin bristle.

Suddenly, the mystery of recent days took on clarity. She knew, as she surveyed Josef's pinched face, that the source of her pain lay behind his pea black eyes.

Stifling a cry, she turned and ran for home.

Never would she open her door to Josef again. Though she go to her grave husbandless and childless, she would rather die than submit herself to him.

TWO

*J*osef sat in the parlor of Mardok's home, fidgeting with his tasseled sleeves. Many a time he had sat here, waiting to meet with the wealthy Philistine, but never on an errand such as this.

In the past, his visits had been most cordial, and the results had been profitable for both of them. They had spoken of trade and contracts and had struck lucrative deals time and again.

But today, Mardok would have nothing pleasant to say, and the prospects for an ongoing partnership were bleak indeed.

When the potbellied Philistine entered the parlor, his expression verified Josef's fears. He was red-faced, and though he had thought long on this encounter, his anger was still fresh.

"So," he began, not even extending a hand in greeting, "you have much to answer for. Tell me, best man, where is your groom?"

As Josef knew, Samson had not returned to Timnah since he delivered the thirty tunics. His escapade in Ashkelon had been broadcast throughout Palestine, and since then he had retreated to his parents' home, keeping a low profile and working in the fields beside Manoah. A warrant was on his head, but to this point the Philistines had honored Zorah's feudal boundaries, leaving Samson alone so long as he remained there.

"Surely you know he dwells with his father," Josef replied. "He is likely quite afraid to come back here."

"Ha!" Mardok scoffed. "Afraid? Are we speaking of the same fellow? The last I heard, he murdered thirty men with his bare hands! Why should he be afraid?"

This was a valid point. Josef fidgeted with his sleeves again and cleared his throat.

"Why did you curse my daughter with this freak?" Mardok raged. "You have always done well by my family. What good did you think could come of this?"

When Josef gave no answer, Mardok grew angrier yet.

"You are responsible for this misery!" the Philistine snarled. "As Samson's best man, it is your duty to see that he fulfills his vows! Will he be a husband to my daughter or won't he?"

Though Josef had not spoken to Samson since the wedding feast, his role as best man carried great weight. Even so, he doubted that the groom would take his advice any longer—and certainly Samson had not confided to Josef any of his intentions.

"I am sure he means to do right by Jezel," Josef wheedled. "At heart Samson is a good man. Give him time. He will return."

"Time?" Mardok bellowed. "That is just the point! My daughter runs out of time!"

Perplexed, Josef shook his head. "Come now, Mardok. Samson will make good on his promise. But even if he does not, Jezel is a young woman with her whole life ahead of her. She will surely find another—"

At this, Mardok drew close, fists clenched, and he bent over Josef until his breath was hot upon the Jew's face.

"You do not understand!" he spat. "Jezel is with child! Samson's child! Time is of the essence, and you would do well to take your duty seriously!"

Stunned, Josef sat rigid beneath the Philistine's fist. One false move and the big man would take out his frustration on the bony Zorahite.

"I see," Josef peeped. "We *do* have a problem." Mardok's fist was only inches from his hooked nose. Staring at it wide-eyed, he swallowed hard. "As you say," he squeaked, "I have always done well by your family. In this matter it shall be no different. It is my duty to bring Samson to his senses, and so I shall."

Another tense moment passed as Josef quivered beneath Mardok's grilling gaze. At last, the Philistine heaved a sigh and lowered his fist from the little man's face.

Once again, Josef's master salesmanship had scored a victory. As always, his convincing tone and utterly sincere expression had won the Philistine's heart.

"Very well," Mardok conceded. "You are a good man, Josef. Jezel would have done better to marry a man half as good as you."

It was an honest compliment, but not meant to be taken literally. What Mardok did not realize is that it posed a tantalizing suggestion, sweeping through Josef's crooked heart like the light of vengeful providence.

If he were to marry Jezel, what problems could be solved! What wonders of retaliation would be his! Not only would Jezel have a husband, not only would her child have a name, but Josef would win a victory over Samson that would make the taking of Marissa a paltry satisfaction by comparison!

So what if Marissa had rejected him? He would have won the *wife* of Samson, and his firstborn child!

So quickly did this delicious scenario form itself in Josef's conniving brain that he felt his head would burst. Barely was he aware of the words that pushed forth from his own dry throat.

"Do you mean it?" he said.

"Mean what?" Mardok asked.

"That I would make a good husband for Jezel."

Blankly, Mardok stared at him. When he saw that the little fellow was serious, he gave a nervous laugh.

"Well . . . you know . . . you are a good man, Josef. I only meant . . . "

"It is a matter for discussion," Josef reasoned. "If it would help your daughter, I would consider it!"

Flabbergasted, Mardok sank down into a chair. "What about Samson?" he stammered. "You just said you would bring him back."

"That I did," Josef agreed. "I did say that. But perhaps your suggestion is a better course."

Had he really suggested this? Mardok wondered. Head spinning, the Philistine leaned back and watched the tiles swirl along the ceiling.

"Samson is a fine fellow," Josef went on, allowing no time for reflection. "But he is unpredictable. I never knew just how unpredictable until this sorry situation. I assure you, I am more than willing to do my part in making this up to you. If marrying your daughter would be any consolation, I would set aside personal scruples . . . er, plans, to do so."

For a moment the ceiling tiles stopped swirling. Mardok got a grip on himself and looked Josef squarely in the eye.

"Funny little man!" he laughed. "How you play with my mind! My daughter *is* married. Would you make her a bigamist?"

Chuckling with him, Josef slapped his thigh and countered quickly. "It seems Samson has forfeited his right to her, if you wish to find a loophole."

"A loophole!" Mardok repeated.

"Of course," Josef reminded him. "When you gave Jezel to Samson, did you not impose a condition upon the marriage?"

Mardok thought back, and when he lit upon the matter, he sputtered in amazement, "So I did! I told Manoah that his son must live in Timnah!"

With a shrug, Josef nodded.

"You *are* a clever fellow!" the Philistine hooted.

"Does that make me good enough for Jezel?" the little man teased.

"Good enough!" Mardok howled. "More than good enough!"

THREE

*F*or seven long months, Samson stayed with his parents and worked the fields beside his father. Harvest time had arrived once again, and if ever his help was needed on the family farm, it was now.

But over the weeks following his rampage in Ashkelon, his anger had turned to a deep, unrelenting depression. Never would he understand Jezel's betrayal with the riddle. If she had only come to him honestly, stating her predicament and asking for his help, he would have gladly told her the answer. Instead she had shamed him.

Mostly, however, he had shamed himself. To this day he could scarcely believe that the legend of his actions in Ashkelon was true. Though he had performed the deeds with his own hands, it seemed but a dream—a horrifying dream.

Samson had stayed close to home all these months. He had not gone to visit Peniel; he had avoided the sight of Marissa. He was a wanted man and must not set foot outside his home territory, but it was not this that kept him in seclusion. It was the disgrace of being who he was that confined him.

Ironically, the very actions that were a personal horror had made him more of a local hero than ever. In fact, the story of his revenge against the Philistines brought people from all over Israel to his obscure village, hoping to catch a glimpse of the "man of iron."

That was the name he had acquired among his country-men. The Israelis had never discovered the secret of the Philistines' dark metal. Without it they remained in hopeless secondary status, as far as military technology was concerned. But now they had their own powerful weapon—the miraculous strength of Samson. And they touted it among themselves, dreaming that such power as his might one day save them from their oppressors.

They had even started to call him a "judge," placing him in that select caste of characters who had raised Israel to her highest levels, spiritually and politically.

But he was, for now, an unseen judge. He did not embrace the title, for he considered himself anything but spiritual. He still wore his hair in the seven Nazarite locks, but he had failed to keep his vows time and again and felt hypocritical even looking the part.

To Samson's way of thinking, he was so far removed from the God of his youth that redemption was a gift beyond his grasp. He was not a hermit like those at Mahaneh-dan. Still, he retreated farther each day into a shell of seclusion, working the fields with his eyes to the ground, crawling off to bed each night having spoken to hardly a soul.

It was Rena who finally intervened. She had been glad when her son returned from his prodigal stint in Timnah. Now, though, she saw that her dream of Samson once again integrating into the Jewish community was pure fantasy. As time went on, she knew that something . . . anything . . . must be done to rouse Samson from his grave of despair.

No one disapproved more of Samson's marriage than his aged mother, but if returning him to Jezel would resurrect him, she would stoop to even that.

She went to him one day, finding him at lunch beneath his father's fig arbor. It was noontime, the hottest hour of the day, and he rested there from a long morning of wheat harvest.

Manoah's share of the annual yield came from a cooperative field. Each day Samson worked alongside other farmers' sons, all of whom were tan and strong like himself. But at noon and during each break, the usually sociable Nazarite went off to sit in the shade of this tree or that, always alone.

As Rena came upon him she tried not to show that her heart ached for him. Behind her on a tether was a small, flop-eared goat, a kid of her prize ram.

"When you go back to your wife," Rena said to her son, "give her this goat as a gift from me."

"A gift?" Samson marveled. "But, Mother, why should you give Jezel a gift?"

Rena tied the goat's lead to a fig branch and sat down beside Samson. "Your father and I gave your bride a paltry wedding gift. Perhaps we can win her favor in this way."

Astonished, Samson laughed. "Why would you want to win her favor?" he asked. "Surely there has never been a worse daughter-in-law! Besides, I have no intention of returning to Timnah!"

Rena studied his fretful eyes with motherly compassion. She knew it was risky for him to reenter Philistia, but she also believed he was the loneliest of men, and that only the love of his wife could restore him. Though the elderly mother would have preferred her son had chosen Marissa—or any Jewess—as his bride, he had married Jezel. Now Rena easily read the longing of her son's heart.

"You are Jezel's husband," she argued. "Can you think to leave her a widow in her prime?"

Casting the situation in this perspective was face saving for Samson. To see himself as magnanimous would make it more comfortable for him to go back.

Still, he had his pride.

"She has her father and her good looks," he said with a smirk. "She will do well without me."

Rena, sighing, pressed him. Placing a finger to his chest, she prodded as though to pierce his stubborn heart.

"Do it for yourself, then!" the old woman insisted. "You love her, Samson. You are dying without her."

MARDOK STOOD upon the rooftop of his sprawling house, staring wide-eyed into the street below. Scarcely could he believe what he saw: his daughter's wayward husband was passing through the crowded marketplace.

Yes, Samson was coming, and upon his face was a look of meekness and beneficence such as Mardok had never seen him wear. When he further noted that Samson carried a young goat in his arms, his pulse sped anxiously. Turning from the balustrade, he hurried down the rooftop stairs and headed for Jezel's room.

Where was Josef when Mardok needed him? The Zorahite had gone from Timnah on yet another business trip, leaving the seven-months-pregnant girl alone as soon as he had married her. Now Mardok must face Samson's wrath without so much as a helping word from the new groom.

Huffing and puffing, he chased down the gallery, calling for his two daughters. "Jezel! Zerah! Quick! Come here!"

The young women emerged from the chamber, Zerah still holding the brush with which she had been coiffing her sister's golden curls. "What is it, Papa?" she asked. "You look like you've seen a ghost!"

"Samson!" Mardok exclaimed, pointing his chubby finger toward the street. "Samson is coming!"

At this, Jezel gripped her swollen belly. The very sound of that name still caused her heart to trip. She loved Samson, but she knew he must not see her now.

"Come, Zerah," Mardok insisted, grabbing the younger sister by the arm, "you must greet Samson with me. Jezel, you stay in your room! Under no circumstances are you to show your face downstairs. Mind what I say!"

Within seconds, Samson's knock was heard at the door, and a servant was admitting him to the courtyard.

Jittery as a fat cat, Mardok descended the stairs, a bleak smile stretched across his lips. Behind him came the bewildered Zerah, trying to hide herself against his wide back.

"Well, Samson," Mardok greeted. "So you are alive, after all."

"Alive, with a warrant on my head," Samson replied. "I should not be here, Mardok. But I must see Jezel."

With this, the Israeli set the goat on the courtyard floor. "This is a peace offering," he said, "from my parents and myself. Now let me see my wife."

Mardok chuckled nervously. "We did not hear from you for so long, Samson," he croaked. "We did not know what to think."

"I am here now," Samson replied. "I have no use for your people or your ways. Only let me see my wife."

When the Philistine stood squarely on the bottom step, as though protecting the stairway, Samson glanced up to the gallery. "Is Jezel in her room?" he asked.

"You cannot see her now," the father-in-law said. Quickly he pulled Zerah around in front of him.

"Take Samson to the parlor," Mardok told her. "And fetch the wine."

Growing suspicious, Samson shook his head. "I will have no wine," he said. "I will go in to my wife, in her room!"

Putting forth a hand, Mardok stayed him. "That would not be wise," the Philistine warned. Then, with a tense laugh, he shrugged. "I really thought that you hated her intensely," he lied. "So, when we did not hear from you, I . . . gave her to your best man."

This was announced so matter-of-factly that one would have thought Mardok had bartered a head of cattle.

But the words sliced through Samson like knives.

"You what?" he cried. "You *what?*"

"Now, now," Mardok replied in a syrupy tone. Reaching up, he patted Samson on the cheek and turned him toward the parlor. "Things are not so bad. You may not care so much for Jezel as you think. Look," he whispered, pointing to Zerah. "Is not her younger sister more beautiful than she? Please, let her be yours instead."

Zerah, who led the way to the parlor, cast a wary glance over her shoulder. She sensed that her father was up to no good, and in humiliation, she glared at him. Then she saw him push Samson after her—and she melted.

Was not Samson the most handsome man on earth? Zerah had always thought so. She had suppressed envy toward Jezel for the catch she had managed. If Samson could be her own, she would accept the "humiliation" of what her father was doing.

Bending seductively over a tea table, she picked up a carafe of wine and filled a goblet for the Israeli. She approached him, fawning and smiling, lifting the cup to his lips.

As Samson watched her, outrage surged through him. Pushing her hand away, he slopped the wine down her dress and turned again for the stairs.

"Jezel! Jezel!" he cried, bounding up the steps.

Barely had he reached the gallery before a half-dozen of Mardok's menservants were upon him, pulling him backward.

Holding him tight, they wrestled with him as he called again and again for his wife.

They were dragging him across the court toward the street when the door to Jezel's chamber cracked open. Defying her father, the pregnant woman stepped into full view.

"Samson!" she shrieked, her arms outstretched. "I love you!"

At this, all movement ceased. The menservants gazed up at her, still holding Samson but wondering how to proceed. Samson stared at his wife, taking in her appearance, and his eyes widened in astonishment.

The pregnant girl stumbled toward the stairs. She had nearly reached the court when Mardok snarled bitterly, "Take him away!"

But Samson would not be squelched. Straining against his captors, he stared wildly at his beloved.

"Whose child do you carry?" he cried. "Is it Josef's or mine?"

"Take him away!" Mardok repeated. "Go, Samson, or I'll call the authorities!"

"Whose child is it?" Samson growled, spitting venomously at his father-in-law. "You owe me that much!"

"I owe you nothing!" Mardok shouted. "You forfeited your right to Jezel and to all that is hers when you left Timnah!"

With this, the man of iron was thrust out of the door, left to beat upon it vainly. At last, stepping back into the street, tears coursing through his beard, he lifted a fist to the unheeding wall.

"This time no one will blame me!" he cried, his voice pushing through the doorway and echoing in the marketplace like a trumpet. Facing the awestruck townspeople who now gathered about the house, he declared again in strident syllables, "No one will blame me when I avenge myself upon the Philistines!"

FOUR

Samson huddled in a cave above the vineyard where he had wrestled with the lion. He had come to this place in dejection, not willing to return home, yet not knowing how he would avenge himself against his enemies. All evening long he sat in the mouth of the mountain hole, listening to the songs of the Philistine reapers in the fields below and gritting his teeth.

What he would give to silence them! What he would give to subdue the entire land, so that never again would a heathen voice be raised in laughter and never again would a Philistine face mock him!

As the pagan songs rose on the night air, so did the smoke of a hundred stubble fires where the fields were being burned off, and the smoke of a hundred campfires where the reapers and harvesters partied. Like a million fireflies, sparks of chaff from the winnowing baskets danced into the darkness, chasing the reapers' laughter.

In Jewish fields, this very night, there would be no women on the threshing floor. The job was a manly one and was accompanied by much jesting and drinking. It was improper for women to intrude upon such scenes.

But in Philistia, women worked side by side with the men and consequently partook of the same merriment. Pagan threshing floors were the site of lewd excesses that would have caused a decent Jew to blush.

As Samson observed from his high station, he could not see much of what went on below. But the sounds and the songs that reached him on the air told a full enough story. Imagining what transpired, he clenched his fists, and that part of him that still longed for God fired his desire for holy retribution.

The flames of his own little campfire flickered in his eyes, repeating the spark of anger that flashed there. Holding forth a stick above the flames, on which was skewered a skinned rabbit, he turned it over and over, pretending the rabbit was a Philistine.

Then the Philistine became Josef, and Samson's hand trembled so that the stick bounced up and down amidst the flames.

"It is *you* I should hate," he snarled, "you little weasel! You are as detestable as any Philistine!"

Plucking the small, scorched carcass from off the stick, Samson eagerly drew it to his mouth and, with his teeth, pulled the flesh from the bones.

"In fact," he mumbled, "I hate you all—Josef, Jezel, Mardok . . . all of you!"

Even as he said this, however, his heart was pricked. For he knew that, of the three, he could not utterly hate Jezel. To hate her would be to hate the child she carried. And for all he knew, that child was his.

Quivering, he poked the stick into the fire and tossed the rabbit bones into the bushes. He must clear his mind. Hate would consume him if he did not get control.

With a sigh, he curled up in his cloak and tried to sleep. Even the revelers below grew quiet, many of them swooning from too much drink. At dawn they would rise for another day of work, but it was well past midnight, and even the rowdiest must rest.

Samson did not dream this time as he lay above the vineyard. He was fully awake as he imagined Josef and the others dwelling among the cliffs, in burrows, propagating like rabbits. Orgiastic scenes, not unlike the ones on the threshing floors, swept across his closed eyelids, and with a lurch, he sat up, wondering again whose child Jezel carried.

But more than the question roused him. There was a sound in the bushes, a rustling, sniffing sound.

Tucking his cloak about him, he cocked his head and listened. Yes, there it came again, the scuffle of some wild creature rummaging in the undergrowth.

It could not be a lion. A lion would have come at him without any warning.

Standing softly to his feet, Samson reached out and pulled back the clump of leaves that concealed the creature.

What he discovered was not one, but two animals. Scruffy and lean, a pair of jackals hunched over the remains of the castoff rabbit. With their narrow noses, they sniffed for any flesh remaining on the bones, and with their long ears laid back, they warned one another not to take an unfair portion.

Samson was fascinated by their ravenous feasting. Neither of them realized a man was present, until the Zorahite, struck by an idea, parted the bush and leapt upon them.

"Aha!" he cried. "So you want rabbit, my fine foxes!"

Grasping the two astonished dogs by the tails, he dragged them toward the fire, tying them together by their tails. Then, plucking a brand from the ashes, he tied it between the jackals' tails and then released them, sending the dogs streaking like fireballs toward the valley floor.

"Go!" he cried. "Run through the fields and the vineyards! Fetch the Philistine rabbits! There are more than enough for you!"

JACKALS WERE well known for their eerie, penetrating howl. Most nights of the year, people of the hills and deserts went to sleep by the jackals' howl, the high, lonely call issuing down the wadis and vales from desolate dens.

But for days now, the cries had been more penetrating, interrupted only by long periods of ominous quiet.

Samson was on a rampage, storming up and down the hills of Palestine, ferreting out the habitations of the wild dogs, turning the snarling creatures tail to tail and tying blazing branches between them. Night after night he struck, sending his fiery, yelping avengers through the standing grain, or-chards, and groves of the Philistines, until in the path of the deadly inferno, there was hardly a field suitable for harvest.

And night after night, Jezel observed the orange sky that heralded her husband's crusade.

"See how he loves me!" she often whispered to her sister. "He would destroy the earth to have me!"

"Do you honestly believe Samson will return for you?" Zerah questioned.

"Of course," Jezel insisted. "Why else does he work these wonders? When all his enemies have been conquered, he will rule Philistia. He and his son," she said, rubbing her belly.

FIVE

A week into Samson's fiery stampede, morning burst upon the streets of Timnah in a rush of pounding hooves and shouting soldiers. Like avenging phantoms, police from the Pentapolis pushed through the dawn, charging into town and beating on the doors of every house. Demanding entrance, they turned rooms inside out, looking for the one who, witnesses said, was responsible for the holocaust in the Philistine fields.

But Samson was not there. "This is Mardok's doing," the townspeople told them. "He gave Samson's wife to his best man, and because of that this evil is upon us!"

Storming Mardok's house, the police found no sign of the Nazarite. And when Mardok could tell them nothing more, they set his house ablaze, just as Samson had done to the country round about.

Having achieved a measure of justice, and hoping Samson would take warning, the police departed again for the coast.

By evening, as the ruins of Mardok's estate still smoldered, the streets of Timnah were vacant, all the houses dark as tombs. Terrified citizens had fled to the hills, and if there were living souls still dwelling here, they were all in hiding, waiting until they were certain the king's militia were gone for good.

But through the city gate this evening, one brave soul dared to venture. Or perhaps he was only ignorant of what had transpired here, and not so brave at all.

Soon enough, he would discover that his wife and father-in-law were dead within the ashes of the fallen mansion.

Josef had been away on business when this unspeakable thing had happened. Therefore, as he rode into Timnah this night, he was unprepared for the village's deathly stillness, and for the smell of smoke that hung heavy in the air.

In horror, he came upon the ruins of the mansion. Dismounting, he tiptoed across the hot pavement, numbly picking his way through the rubble. Covering his nose with his mantle, he tried not to choke on the acrid vapors of charred timbers and molten bronze fixtures. As he stumbled over the debris of once-glorious furnishings and wove past the remains of food-laden tables and smoking tapestries, he managed to find the collapsed staircase that had been central to the house.

"Jezel!" he cried. "Mardok! Where are you?" Slumping to his knees, he scavenged through the fallen waste for a sign of life.

"Lord God!" he groaned. How he hoped the family had escaped!

Surely this was Samson's doing! Josef had seen the fires in the hills on his return from the coast, and he had heard rumors of the wildman's latest rampage. Surely Samson had learned of Mardok's betrayal and had come here to take back what was his own.

Yes, that was it! Josef reckoned, standing up and kicking at the rubble. Samson had taken Jezel, probably to Zorah. Most likely, Mardok and the others had gone free, and only the house had fallen.

With a shudder, Josef turned for the street, thinking to mount his horse and speed away. This was not a safe place for him; Samson doubtless was looking for him. And he knew the strongman would have less mercy on him than on the family.

But just as he reached the blackened door, a peculiar sound called him back. Shuddering and catlike, it came from the vicinity of the staircase, the plea of some hapless creature trapped beneath the wreckage.

Josef would have turned from it, not caring to look upon the death throes of some unfortunate pet. But the cry was persistent, giving way to pathetic whimpers that were much too human.

Swallowing his fear, Josef returned to the center of the house and, following the call, came to a heap of roof tiles. He hoped that the stench arising from the pile was not that of burning flesh.

Fist tight against his stomach, he bent over and removed the tiles one by one from a mound beneath, until, to his horror, he unearthed an arm.

Instantly he recognized the silver, snakelike coil that braceleted the wrist, and falling back he gasped, "Jezel!"

"Oh God! Oh God!" he wept, lifting tile after tile in frantic quest. Yes, it was his wife, his and Samson's! And beside her, in the ruins, lay her father and her sister.

"Samson! You freak!" he bellowed, as he uncovered the three burned and battered corpses. "What have you done?"

Scalding tears fell from his eyes, mingling with black smudges on his arms and hands as he unearthed the tragic family. Truly they were dead, each one of them—crushed by the house when it collapsed in the fire. But still Josef heard helpless whimpers, beckoning through the ashes and rubble.

Gingerly, he removed the last of the litter from Jezel's skirts, and as he did, he found a crimson stain upon her legs. A pool of blackened blood oozed from beneath her, and turning her over, Josef let out a cry.

There, in the hollow of her groin, a small creature wriggled, blood-covered and caked with ash. To its navel was still attached the umbilical cord that had once fed it with its mother's life.

Aghast, Josef stared upon the raging babe, whose crinkled face and screaming mouth demanded help. Josef could barely take it in—how had the child survived? Even with Jezel's body to shelter it from the falling rubble, it was, surely, a miracle that the babe was alive. Reaching forth a shaking hand, Josef dared to touch the tiny form.

Instantly, the wee one opened its bleary eyes and, seeing a figure above it, ceased crying.

But only for a fleeting moment. Immediately it began to rage again, flailing its feeble arms and turning its head this way and that to nuzzle at its mother's cold thighs.

"Oh Lord!" groaned Josef. "Oh Lord!"

Reaching for the knife he kept within his belt, he drew it out, quickly cutting the cord and severing the infant from its lifeless host.

Josef knew now that Samson had not destroyed this house. Never would the Nazarite have slain the mother of a child he knew might be his own.

Despite his churning stomach, Josef managed to lift the bloody babe in shaking hands and, inspecting it, found it to be a boy. Wrapping it in the lap of his cloak, he drew it to his chest.

So, he thought as he peered into the infant's desperate eyes, *this is the son of the hero of Israel!*

"What shall I do with you?" he whispered.

His first thought was to find Samson, to deliver the child to its father, where it belonged.

But that thought sprang from the part of him that had been the strongman's friend. As his eyes traveled from the babe to the dead mother, then to the fallen Mardok, he thought again.

He was the only one who knew the truth, the only one who knew, for certain, whose child this was.

Gripping the babe tightly to him, he stood up and turned for the street.

Jezel was dead, and Marissa had rebuffed him. But he had the Nazarite's child.

As long as he did, he still had power to bring his rival to his knees.

SIX

Samson raised himself up from a restless night's sleep and peered above to a blaring autumn sun. Across the golden orb dark-winged shadows passed, and he shielded his face as though they would swoop toward him.

Crying out in fear, he huddled against the ground, emerging, as if drugged, from an exhausted slumber. As he came to himself, he heard the shriek of hawks high above, and he knew the shadows were not Philistine spears.

Pushing himself up, he studied the rock spread out beneath him. Having run all day from the region of the Philistines, he had at last entered Israeli territory. He had hiked to this place at dusk, hoping its desolation would provide a measure of security.

There was no shelter here. He had been obliged to sleep in the open, and there was no soft place for a bed—only this tablelike rock, spread across a ridge of shepherd hills.

But it did not matter, for he could not have been comforted, even in a palace.

Thoughts of his dead wife and her tormentors had robbed him of all peace. Even now, the memory of Jezel and the thought of the agony she must have suffered filled him with anguish.

Yes, he knew of her fate and the fate of her household. The news had reached him in the hills the next day, though no

Philistine or Israeli knew his whereabouts. It had met his ears on the evening breeze that bore hillward the harvesters' party songs. The demise of Mardok and his daughters had become a matter of rejoicing in the few unburned fields of the Philistines, the subject of campfire jests and loud hilarity. Samson, who hid out in the autumn hills, had heard the news immediately.

And just as quickly, he had taken action, striking ruthlessly and slaughtering many within the camps of the Philistine reapers.

Now he was a good day's distance away from Zorah—far enough, he hoped, that his return to Israel would not endanger his parents. Surveying the tableland to which he had come, he found that the flat ridge was only the bottom stair of a jagged badland. On every side, steep rock cliffs ascended to the sky, pocked with caves and fissures. Somewhere to the east was the great Salt Sea, the dead end of the River Jordan. Most of the shepherd hills, of which this ridge was a facet, were rounded and gentle. But this was Etam, the famed "hawk ground" of Judah, a site as unwelcoming as the sea it bordered.

Scanning the cliffs, he saw everywhere the reason for the place-name. Huge hawks' nests filled nearly every nook and cranny of the rock walls. Had Samson come here ready to die, he soon would have been carrion for the birds of prey.

But he was not ready to die, and he believed it was good strategy to come to hawk ground. Shepherds avoided this place not only because their flocks would have no sustenance here, but also because their lambs would be fair game for the broad-winged predators. They also avoided the grasslands at the foot of the hawk home, so Samson could stay here indefinitely without being discovered.

Here he could renew himself. And plot his next move against the enemy.

Stretching flat upon his back, he let the warm air that ascended from the Salt Sea spill over his bare arms and legs, and he reveled in the sunlight that stroked his torso. This simple act somewhat alleviated the ache of his heart, as though the sun's rays diffused the pain.

He almost fell asleep again, his energies drained by grief and anger. But he dare not do so, as the searing sun would utterly deplete him. Looking about for a place of shade, he saw a cleft in a distant rock, against the cliff face. With effort, he stood up and headed for it, his tongue burning with thirst.

Inside the narrow cave it was cool and musty. But there was no water. Upon his belt was his wine skin, recently filled at a stream as he had traveled through Judah. Eagerly he drew the spout to his parched lips and drank, trying to be frugal.

For the first time in many days, there was no enemy to fight, no Philistine on whom to take revenge. Though it was only morning, the cool of the cave wooed him to slumber. And Samson curled up within the rocky womb like a child unborn.

How long he lay in this fetal position, he knew not. The sun had arced over the earth more than once and might have passed over the sleeping Samson yet again, had the sound of many voices and the tramping of many feet not wakened him.

"Samson!" came a thunderous call. "Samson! We know you are here! Come forth!"

Jolted awake, Samson opened his eyes and peered toward the slit of light that marked the cave door. Had he only dreamed that a thousand voices called him?

No. There it came again, the command of countless tongues, demanding his emergence.

Stepping to the mouth of the cave, he looked out, blinking at the sight of three thousand men lining the rock slope that led toward the valley. Though arrayed in battle gear, this was no Philistine army. The men who confronted him were of his own people, each done up in whatever armor he could find.

Many wore turbans rather than helmets and carried staffs rather than spears, looking very much the peasants that they were.

Scanning the faces of those who glared up at the cave, he recognized them as Judahites from the nearby hills. Here and there he saw merchants and tradesmen with whom he and his father had done business.

Creeping forth, he stepped into the open day and raised a hand in hesitant greeting.

"Brothers!" he hailed them. "What brings you here?"

The spokesman of the company, a general of sorts, stepped to the fore and cried, "Don't you know that the Philistines have entered Judah? They have spread out across the valley!"

No, Samson did not know this.

"What can I do to help?" he stammered.

"*Help?*" the general laughed scornfully. "You are the *cause* of our distress, Samson! Not our *savior!*"

At this, all the troops hooted, shaking their weapons and surging forward, ready to take him. But their commander called a halt.

Then, confronting Samson again, the general sneered, "Do you also not know that the Philistines are rulers over us? What is this that you have done? You have brought their wrath against your own countrymen!"

Though feeling quite sheepish, Samson tried to appear dauntless. Lifting a fist, he shouted, "As they did to me, so I have done to them!"

Again the crowd hooted, barely heeding their commander's call for silence.

"And as you have done to them," he snarled, "so they will now do to us in turn! Unless . . . ," and here he paused, daring Samson to defy him, "unless you turn yourself over to them!"

The Nazarite's heart drummed. He knew he had no choice but to do whatever the soldiers of his own people demanded.

"My brothers," he choked, "how can I do this? Would not each one of you have taken revenge? My wife and her family were killed by the enemy!"

But no one was moved by Samson's misery.

"You have been called a judge in Israel!" the general replied. "Yet you have brought imminent destruction upon your people! We have come down to bind you, so we may give you into the hands of the Philistines! Will you resist?"

Samson looked at the ground, his shoulders slumping.

With a sigh of surrender, he pleaded, "Swear to me that you will not kill me yourselves."

At this, the force moved up the slope as a body, three thousand out to capture one unresistant man.

Securing Samson's wrists behind him, the commander answered, "We will bind you fast and give you into their hands!" Then, so that all the men could hear, he added, *"We* will not kill you!"

The army laughed in derision as they led the hunched captive toward the valley.

What need would they have to take Samson's life? In handing him over to the Philistines, they would be sealing his fate without drawing a drop of his blood.

SEVEN

*V*ictors' parades were usually awesome spectacles, glorifying the conqueror and his nation with loud marching bands and displays of captives, booty, and spoil.

But the march of the Israelis from Etam to Lehi, where the Philistines waited, was hardly awesome. Though the soldiers of Judah had fulfilled their commission, they had taken no booty and had in tow only one pathetic captive. Nor were they displaying him as evidence of their nation's might, but rather as evidence of their submission to the enemy.

They had been told to capture Samson, to bring him to Philistine justice, and they were complying.

Samson had been their hero. Now he was their hostage. He had been a legend in their homes and about their fires. Now he was their loser. Though he had single-handedly ravaged Ashkelon and the vineyards of Timnah, he was now the symbol of his countrymen's weakness.

As Samson plodded behind his captors, he kept silent. He had begun this journey weary and thirsty, and the Philistine command post was yet miles away. No one offered him a drink of water; no one let him rest. When the three thousand stopped for a break, Samson was forced to stand and was allowed nothing to eat.

His kinsmen were not content to make him their sacrifice. They must humiliate him in the process. Mocking, they accused him of hypocrisy. How dare he claim the title of a Nazarite? Since when did Nazarites mingle with pagans, drinking from their cups or marrying heathen women?

Nazarites were supposed to abstain from strong drink and from touching the dead! Yet Samson was guilty of all these infractions. He had made a name for himself as a reveler, a companion of Philistines. And he had slain hundreds of men, set foxes ablaze, and smeared himself with blood!

As Samson trekked toward the valley, he kept his head down, offering no self-defense.

He knew he had made grave mistakes. He had broken every vow he ever made. He should not have succumbed to the wiles of the Philistines, to Jezel and her sumptuous beauty. He should have revered his parents and the ordinances of the Nazarites at Mahaneh-dan.

Yet the contradictions which had always driven him would not let him take full blame for his present condition.

The tangle of compulsions that had always motivated him was neither fully evil nor fully good. Because it was neither, it was a conundrum that would have driven a lesser man insane. And today, as Samson plodded beneath its weight, he asked himself, not for the first time, just why he had been so perversely designed.

Had he been a pagan, he would have attributed the riddle of his nature to the whimsy of the Fates, to the mocking humor of heartless gods. He would have attributed the contradictions of his drives to unseen, battling forces who cared nothing for his soul, but only for their own, endless competition.

But Samson was not a pagan. He believed in the God of Israel. It was this belief that would neither let him take full blame nor acquiesce to the Fates for the mess he was now in.

Somehow he sensed, in the very core of him, that his own failings and sins were but a secondary catalyst in the drama he played out. Somewhere, above and beyond his own part in the drama, there was a larger scene—one so large and so vast that those on the earthly stage could catch only glimpses of its entrances and exits, openings and closings.

As Samson dragged his feet along the dusty tabletop of Etam and descended with his captors toward the green plain of Judah, his head swirled with the immensity of such thoughts. Shrugging, he chuckled privately and sardonically.

"Fool!" he muttered. "The sun has robbed you of good sense! Only the mad think so nobly of themselves! You are a sinner, a common, back-alley sinner. God is not hoodwinked by grandiose rationales!"

Yet as he plodded past highland vineyards, he was reminded of the great lion who had set upon him outside Timnah, and his fists clenched with the memory of the supernatural strength that coursed through him that night. Yes, he had broken his Nazarite vow, enduring the blood of the slain cat. But had not *God* brought the cat to him, and had not *Adonai* given him strength for the kill?

He had been wrong to ignore his parents' wishes, to take to his sanctified breast the love of a heathen woman. Yet from the wedding and the riddle of the honey-laden lion had sprung the incident of Ashkelon, and the Spirit-motivated drive to ravage the Philistines. It had not been Samson's own strength that wreaked devastation on the coastlands. It had been the hand of God, and it had simply been Samson through whom God wielded that hand.

As the wide valley of Judah opened before the marching army, Samson lifted his head, feeling the cooler breeze of the green, surrounding hills. But the plain before him, most pleasant at other times, was today a fearsome spectacle. Spread across the harvested valley, replacing the camps of the reapers, were now numberless tents and machines of war. Incredibly, the entire army of the Pentapolis, the five cities of the coast, had come out against this one, lone man, and tens of thousands of troops, arrayed in gleaming armor and bearing weapons fashioned of iron, rose at the approach of his Judahite captors.

Not only was the Philistine machinery and weaponry magnificent, but the troops were, on the average, a head taller than the men of Israel. It was, in fact, customary among the Israelis to refer to their enemies as giants, so much larger did they seem. In truth, it was not unusual for true giants to be born among the Philistines, for their ancestors had intermingled with the colossal Anakim race.

But as Samson gazed upon his enemies, it was not only fear that seized him. Just as his personality often seemed divided, so did his emotions. With the fear came a tangential feeling: a surge of disgust and an overwhelming desire for revenge.

In cruel humor, the army of the Philistines hailed him. Mocking and laughing, they shouted, "Hero of Israel! Where now is your strength? Welcome, terror of Timnah! Zealot of Zorah!"

With this, they moved out from their hundred camps and rushed toward the highway. They had made a bargain with Judah, that they would take Samson peaceably. And so their swords were sheathed, their spears lowered.

But their jeers and taunts continued, until Samson's ears burned, and his blood coursed hot through his veins.

Now, the Judahites had bound Samson very tightly with two new ropes when they had taken him from Etam. Round and round his wrists and up his arms they had wrapped the fetters, knowing his unnatural strength. So secure were the bonds that they were willing to stake the success of their mission on them.

This moment, however, as the jibes of the Philistines singed his ears, the strongman felt a jolt of white-hot heat shoot through his forearms. Then the smell of smoke arose behind him, where his wrists were tied.

Wheeling about, he felt flames dart from the binding hemp. In an instant the ropes had been consumed, falling from his arms in a pile of ash.

His captors cried aloud, falling back at the manifestation. Samson, drawing his arms before him, gazed at the fallen fetters. "My God!" he shouted. "You *are* with me!"

As he looked about for a weapon, the song of the Nazarites welled from his soul: "The Lord is a man of war! The Lord is his name!"

The weapon he found did not suit his Nazarite calling. It was the remainder of a dead creature, the jawbone of a donkey, lying in a field. But it was convenient, long, jagged, and sharp.

Running for it, Samson picked it up in his broad fists and began to swing it over his head. Racing down the highway, he dove straight into the ranks of his mocking oppressors.

A shriek of revenge and unearthly power filled the valley as Samson slashed away at the stunned soldiers. Armor and iron were no match for the divinely appointed jawbone, and soon their seemingly impenetrable protection lay in sheared heaps at the feet of the terrified Philistines. Man after man fell, until entire squadrons writhed in bloody piles about the fields.

Still Samson moved on in unflagging vengeance.

Those who remained ran for their lives, but there must have been a thousand who fell that day, as the Judahites watched their hostage prove once more to be a hero.

By noon, Samson stood beneath the blazing sun, the valley littered with the corpses of his enemies, himself covered with their blood.

As the army of the coastland retreated toward the west, he once more lifted the crude weapon over his head, filling his lungs and blaring like a trumpet,

"With the jawbone of a donkey,
Heaps upon heaps!
With the jawbone of a donkey
I have killed a thousand men!"

Then wheeling about, he faced his mesmerized captors, the ones who had once called themselves his people, and he flung the jawbone into their midst.

Stalking away, he kicked at piles of carrion strewn in his path.

"Heaps!" he laughed. "Heaps and heaps!"

PART

FOUR

❧

The Gate Stealer

ONE

*W*hen Samson left the fields of devastation where he had slain the thousand Philistines, he headed obliquely back toward Zorah, so close to swooning that he only vaguely knew where his feet took him.

He had had no water to drink since he had left Etam as the Judahite army's prisoner. In his rambling journey he passed by streams and fountains, but he did not have presence of mind enough to drink from them. Ultimately, his staggering trek took him full circle, back to Lehi. And when, two days later, he collapsed upon the very plain where the enemy had met its demise, he was close to death.

When he awoke on the third day, his tongue was so swollen, his lips so parched, that despite his delirium, the craving for liquid burned him like fire. Lifting bleary eyes to the sun, he managed to pray, though his words were a croak rather than the tones of a victorious warrior.

"O Lord," he rasped, "you have given great deliverance by the hand of your servant! Now shall I die of thirst and fall into the hands of the uncircumcised?"

Strewn still about the field where he had fallen were the bloating corpses of his vanquished enemies. So dreadful had been his retribution that the Philistines had not even returned to bury their dead.

Just now, though, one coming upon the scene could not have told the difference between Samson and one of his victims. Only when a small tremor shook him did he sit up and through dry, tortured eyes seek the source of the shaking.

The rumbling seemed to emanate from a hollow over in the hills of Judah. Curious and desperate, Samson hoisted his great frame from the earth and stumbled toward the quake.

Within a leafy grotto, where a seasonal spring had gone dry, a fissure split the ground and a small fountain spewed forth from the rocks.

Throwing himself down upon the jagged ridge, Samson eagerly gulped the cold water, cupping it in his hands and showering his face with its refreshing spray.

As he did, tears mingled with the water, and rocking to and fro, he praised the Lord upon his knees.

"Truly you are with me!" he cried. "You never have abandoned me! I called upon your name, and you answered. This place shall be called En-hakkore, 'the fountain of him that prayed'!"

SEVEN FULL days did Samson remain at En-hakkore. Not since his visits to Mahaneh-dan had he felt so close to the Lord.

All during that week, he was granted solitude. No harvesters returned to reap the blood-soaked fields. No Philistine warriors returned to seek revenge, or to retrieve the bodies of their fallen ones.

As though he were a youngster again, he recalled the songs taught to him by the Nazarite monks, and he sang them lustily, long into the dark hours. After bathing in the spring, he let his unshorn hair dry in the autumn sun. And after running his fingers through its tangles so that it was smooth and manageable, he parted it into the seven locks of his sect.

Somehow, Jezel and the horrors attending that relationship now seemed very distant. The more he devoted himself to prayer, the less power her memory had over him, until at last he could envision her face only with great effort.

By the seventh day, Samson was consumed not by thirst, nor by lust, but by a desire such as he had never known: he longed with all his being to catch a glimpse of God Almighty.

All that morning and afternoon, Samson reveled in the privacy of his grotto. When evening came, eager anticipation gripped him.

Perhaps he heard the footsteps before the expectation over-swept him. Whether the sound sparked the hope, or the hope was instilled by a higher power, he cocked his head toward the valley road.

Yes, someone approached his bower!

He did not know if the evening shadows played tricks with his eyes, but it seemed someone now stood at the leafy entrance to his retreat. He remembered stories of the patri-archs, how the angel of the Lord had greeted them and spoken with them at various times in their lives. He knew that Adonai had taken the form of a man for such appearances.

Although the silhouette within the green frame was of slighter build than he would have expected, he bowed his face to the ground, a cry of praise issuing from his heart.

"Lord!" he groaned. "Have mercy on your servant!"

But the voice that returned his salutation was surely not that of God Almighty! High and nasal, it wrenched him from his ecstasy.

"Samson," it replied, "I was told I might find you here."

Squinting against the pale light, the Nazarite was outraged.

"Josef?" he cried. "You traitor! How dare you come here?"

Leaping to his feet, the strongman would have taken the weasel by the throat. But Josef announced, "Hear me, Sam-son! I bring word from the Pentapolis!"

"Word from your bosom friends?" Samson snarled, pushing him out of the bower. "I would as soon kill you as look at you!"

"I—I understand . . . ," Josef stammered, nodding and holding up his hands. "And no one would blame you! But, Samson, let me explain."

Growling, the Nazarite moved past him, standing in the open and facing the little squirrel, whose back was to the grotto.

"You were once my dearest friend!" the big man shouted. "But you have become my worst enemy! Worse by far than the most wicked Philistine!"

Storming down the slope toward the highway, Samson turned east, ready to head for Zorah. But Josef cried out behind him, "What I did, I did for you, my friend! Mardok would have given Jezel to another, but I saved her for you. I married her," he insisted, "so that you could have her again, whenever you chose to return!"

Stunned, Samson stopped dead in his tracks. In the core of his being, he knew Josef lied. What power this fiend had to twist his heart, he did not understand.

Wheeling about, he faced him, his breath coming in short, heady gasps.

"Josef . . . ," he groaned.

"It is true! Believe me," the conniver pleaded. "Did I not introduce you to Jezel? Why would I have done so if I wanted her for myself? But enough of that for now. We must make haste!"

"Make haste?" Samson whispered, his head reeling.

"For Gaza," Josef sighed impatiently. "The lords of the Pentapolis wish to meet you there . . . to discuss a treaty."

TWO

Samson lay upon his back, staring up at the pagan emblems embossed on an enamel ceiling. Moonlight glanced off of the sea beyond Gaza's city wall and illumined the glossy tiles, so that the faces of long-haired sirens and water goddesses arrayed upon them returned his gaze with sensuous smiles.

Like a love song, the sea whispered from the shore, rocking his mind with ebbs and flows. An autumn breeze flirted with the chamber's gauze curtains.

Lifting his head from his satin pillow, Samson drew the bedsheet across his loins and turned to the woman who slept beside him.

He was not certain of her name. Josef had introduced her when he brought him to the wallside inn, but her name had been the least important of her features. Though Samson had not anticipated the bountiful services he would be given upon payment of his night's lodging, he had not refused them.

He had not even noted the amount of money Josef placed in the woman's hand when he registered him in this place, so captivated had he been by her red-haired beauty.

All the way to Gaza, Josef had spun cunning words. Though Samson was determined to resist them, he could not entirely refute them. How did he know but that his old friend had indeed meant the best for him? Jezel was lovely, and some new beau would have come courting very soon.

As for the child she had carried, it was apparently Josef's. The footloose Jew would not have married a woman encumbered with another man's child. Therefore, Samson put all thoughts aside that the baby might have been his own.

Josef's story was well reasoned. He had married the daughter of Mardok to reserve her for Samson. What else would a decent best man have done? And since he was only fulfilling his obligation as a husband, he could not be blamed if she became pregnant in the bargain. Indeed, if Jezel had carried Josef's seed, and the child died with her, there was a dimension of tragedy to the tale that made deep questioning inappropriate.

By the time they reached the capital, far from entertaining doubt, Samson pitied Josef—and the old cords of affection tightened about his heart.

Neither was it Josef's fault that Samson had succumbed to the scarlet woman who lounged beside him. If she had spoken fetchingly to Josef, the skinny Zorahite had the strength to resist her, and likely he slept with a clean conscience down the hall. But he was a better man than Samson, and when the ruby wonder knocked upon Samson's door, it had opened to her. The wine she offered, as red in the cup as her lips were red, had easily bought the Nazarite's kiss and his caress.

Though she slept, Samson's shifting on the bed caused her to stir. Drowsily she turned, so that her face was toward him. Feasting upon her supple beauty, Samson let his eyes drift across her body.

Long and glorious she was, like so many of her Philistine sisters. She put him in mind of Jezel. Though she was not so amply endowed, she knew how to move, and even in her sleep she seemed to practice seduction.

The grotto and the holy longings it had inspired now were very far away. If a phrase of a song or prayer pricked him, Samson put it quickly from his mind.

Reaching forth a hand, he rested it gently on the concave of the woman's waist. In response, she awakened, smiled up at him, and drew him to her perfumed bosom.

THREE

*T*he council hall of Dagon's temple rang with a hundred voices. The fire in the center pit cast the shadows of mighty men against the stone walls, its light darting between their wild gestures like a frantic moth.

Josef, who was *not* asleep in the wallside inn, stood at the head of the crowd, waiting for the chief councillor to bring order.

"This fellow was best man at Samson's wedding!" the men shouted. "How can we trust him?"

"He is an Israeli!" they hooted. "A citizen of Samson's own town! Why should he side with us?"

Josef remained quiet upon the stage where the five princes of Philistia, the "seranim," sat. Though his face was pinched and white, he maintained his composure. He knew he took his life in his hands, coming here. He also knew the reward, if he was successful, would be well worth the risk.

Calling for silence, Bariath, the leading prince, arose and confronted Josef. A full cubit taller than the diminutive Israeli, he glared down upon him with contemptuous eyes.

"You say you have brought Samson with you from Lehi," he snarled. "We have called our leaders out from their homes by dark of night to hear you. You know the penalty for misrepresenting yourself?"

Josef did not know the specific punishment, but he could well imagine. "Yes," he gulped. "I tell the truth, Your Excellency, I have brought Samson to Gaza."

Bariath, who well fit the legends of the Philistines' gigantic ancestors, scrutinized the tiny but forthright man. The Israeli tried not to let his eyes wander over the glinting studs of the hard leather vest that covered the prince's chest and came within an inch of his own hooked nose. Nor did he study too closely the hardened biceps that pushed out against Bariath's tunic sleeves.

Though Bariath represented the secondary capital of Ekron, which lay within the vale of Sorek, bordering Danite territory, he was chief of the Philistine captains. Having won notoriety in war and fame for his cold-blooded interpretation of Canaanite law, he was feared by friend and foe alike. His comrades on the bench, the seranim of Gaza, Ashdod, Ashkelon, and Gath, rarely contested his opinions on any matter, and so he ruled Philistia virtually single-handed.

Peering down upon Josef from beneath blond, bushy eyebrows, the giant took a deep breath and turned to address the assembly.

"Lords of the Pentapolis," he hailed his fellow princes, "and men of Philistia! Samson has ravaged our country for nearly a year! Whether this Jew speaks the truth or not, it would be wise to follow up on his story. If Samson has come to Gaza, he trespasses on the sacred streets of our blessed god, Dagon! We must make him our prey and our quarry!"

Here and there a warlike cheer arose, but the great Aryan was disappointed by the manifest lack of enthusiasm.

"Are we men or mice?" he roared. "Shall we hang back while Samson assaults the holy temple?"

Of course, the memories of the strongman's escapade through Ashkelon, and of his rampage through the unreaped fields of Timnah, were still fresh. The most recent devastation of the troops in Judah was too much to put aside.

As the councillors hesitated, one man dared to step forward.

Siloam of Gerar was not one of the five princes. His small city was not one of the league that made up the Pentapolis. But he was the highly respected manager of the iron smeltery and sword factory that had made Philistia a leading military power.

"Bariath of Ekron," he challenged, "you speak easily of going against Samson. But if he has once more invaded our homeland, and if he is accompanied by this shrewd comrade, do you not fear he has planted other infiltrators amongst us? Do you not suppose that Josef is a spy, and that soon others will follow, until the Jews discover the secret of our strength?"

No one present doubted what Siloam meant by "secret of our strength." For generations the Philistines had guarded the formula for smelting iron, which they themselves had wrested from the vanquished Hittites. Were the world at large to have that formula, Philistia could itself be vanquished.

Murmuring fearfully, the crowd consulted together, nodding their heads and considering the dire possibilities.

At this, the five princes surveyed Josef with renewed suspicion.

"Hear! Hear!" the prince of Ashdod cried, arising from his throne. "Siloam is a wise man! How do we know that Josef of Zorah is not a spy?"

Refusing to be caught up in the frenzy, Bariath mulled over the words. Approaching Josef once more, he snarled, "You hear the accusations! So tell us, why *have* you come to Gaza? And why are you willing to betray Samson to us? Is he not the hero of Israel?" Then, spitting upon the floor, he shouted, "No one is more to be despised than a traitor! Are you a traitor to your people, Josef?"

Falling back, the little Jew swallowed hard and tried to answer. Though his response was well rehearsed, it was barely audible.

Donning his most humble and innocent of faces, he replied, "Good sir, I am no traitor. I, above all men, love my people. It is for this reason that I deliver Samson into your hands."

Pondering the inscrutable answer, the audience fell silent.

"Explain," Bariath sighed. "You are no traitor?"

"Indeed not, sir!" Josef asserted. "It is true that at one time Samson was a hero in Israel. But now the people mock him, for his bloodthirst brings shame upon our country. I have the backing of my government in this matter," he lied. "You would do us a favor, gentlemen, to rid us, and yourselves, of this blight!"

For a long while the council chamber was quiet, as the men digested Josef's smooth defense.

The fire at the center of the room crackled hellishly, casting demonic shadows against the walls as Bariath called for an accounting.

"I suppose," he hissed, "you want nothing for your services, Josef? You are willing to reveal Samson's whereabouts . . . without reward?"

Stunned, Josef felt the blood drain from his face. No matter what he answered, he would be a fool. And so he said nothing, shuffling his feet against the stony floor while hundreds of eyes observed his unease.

"Pay him!" Bariath cried, turning from the weasel and spitting once more upon the pavement.

At this, the treasurer of the assembly rose from the front of the congregation and held forth a small purse of gold.

When Josef did not reach for it, the clerk tugged at his hand and opened his palm.

The little bag seemed, to Josef, unusually heavy for its size.

FOUR

*B*ariath sat in his suite in the military hall of Dagon's temple. In no place other than the palace of the king himself were there more luxurious quarters. But how Bariath wished he could go home to Ekron, to sleep in his own bed!

All this foolishness about Samson had given him a headache.

It was at least a comfort that he had brought his mistress with him from Sorek Vale. At the first word of the strongman's latest move, he had mounted his horse and ridden through the gloaming to the seacoast capital. Following him in her own carriage was his ravishing attendant—and when the council meeting ended, he was pleased to find her waiting for him in the apartment that was his home away from home.

Just now, the woman ran her hands over the tense muscles of his shoulders, massaging them with long, penetrating strokes. Delilah was good at many things. But she was most expert at giving massages.

Almost as soothing as her even, persistent touch was her mellow voice, with which she knew how to woo Bariath into a delicious state of near oblivion.

Leaning over him as he sat hunched upon his stool, she let her raven tresses drape his naked torso.

"Relax, Bariath," she purred. "Never have I felt such knots in your neck. You are too good a man, my love, to carry so many burdens."

As she spoke, her words were accompanied by the movement of her warm and supple hands.

But Bariath wished, just this once, that she would not speak. He did not want to think of his problems. Especially he did not want to rehash the events of this evening's meeting.

Usually, he was grateful to have Delilah for a sounding board. She was his best friend, as well as his personal courtesan. Although she was not monogamously his own—she spread her affections amongst a number of high political figures and was paid handsomely in the process—she was more often with Bariath than with any other man. And she entertained him whenever he wished, even if it meant she must cancel previous appointments.

The arrangement between Bariath and the woman was unspoken but unquestioned among those who vied for her time. As for Bariath, though he did not like to think of "his woman" with anyone else, he accepted her "indiscretions" as part of her charm, as well as her means of support. It not only made her all the more attractive to him, but released him from any undue sense of responsibility for her.

All that considered, she was indeed his best friend. And he coveted his hours in her presence as much for the chance to speak of his daily challenges as for the physical therapy they afforded.

Nevertheless, tonight he preferred not to talk. For the ordeal of the meeting and the conundrum of Samson had left him utterly frazzled.

As Delilah moved her hands from Bariath's neck to his head, she poured a vial of ointment through his blond curls and worked the healing oil into his temples with small circular motions.

"So," she cooed, "is it true? Has the crazy Israeli come to Gaza?"

Barely did Bariath hear her soft question, so close had she brought him to sleep. But through the cottony haze of near slumber, he perceived her voice and, without resisting, grunted a reply.

"Indeed!" Delilah mused. "Samson in Gaza!"

Had Bariath been more alert, he might have noticed a thrill in her tone. With his eyes closed and his head bowed, he did not see her face brighten at the thought of the strongman's proximity.

For a while she said nothing more, lost in private fantasies of what the hero of Israel must be like. There was, for Delilah, no guilt connected with such thoughts. From her perspective, the commitment between herself and Bariath was quite superficial.

Of course, she was too wise to confide her imaginings to her lover. Men, she knew, were inordinately possessive when it came to the women they had known. And so she would be discreet as she fished for further information.

Cleverly, Delilah cloaked her interest with a question regarding Samson's betrayer. "The one who revealed him to the council . . . ," she cooed, "is he an Israeli spy?"

"Umph," Bariath mumbled, his chin resting on his chest. "A weasel," he snorted.

Tilting her head back, Delilah continued to massage her lover's temples, while her mind raced excitedly.

"Did he divulge Samson's whereabouts?" she inquired.

At this, Bariath opened his eyes and managed to sit up, straightening his shoulders. Delilah, sensing his irritation, turned quick attention to his neck muscles. When he instantly relaxed, she proceeded with more caution.

"Such silly Jews they must be," she sighed, "to come against mighty Bariath!"

Assured of his lady's devotion, the Philistine breathed heavily, nearly drowning in slumber. Since Delilah seemed concerned for his welfare, a buffered approach snared him with hardly a prick of notice.

"So the council lies in wait?" she guessed. "Where are they stationed?"

To her great delight, Bariath answered without a quiver of resentment. But as the truth came forth, it was a mixed blessing.

"They lie in wait beside the city gate," he snored, "beneath the wallside inn."

So limp was the Philistine from Delilah's pampering that he did not realize his mistress had ceased her ministrations. Caught away by the revelation he had just given, she forgot her duties, her hands lying listless upon his shoulders.

"Mariah . . . ," she hissed.

So, Samson was lodging at the house of her chief rival! Most likely he slept, even now, in the arms of Mariah, the notorious red-haired madam of Gaza Inn!

Flaming jealousy shot through Delilah's dark eyes and her tall body tensed arrow straight.

Only the thought of Mariah had power to incite envy in the seductress. For years she and the scarlet innkeeper had vied for the same clientele. And though all the men assured Delilah that there was no contest, that she was by far the more beautiful and more practiced of the two, the competition was nonetheless keen.

Delilah knew there had been times when Mariah had been chosen over herself. Rare though those times had been, they had never been forgotten and had piqued the women's rivalry to ever-higher scales.

Seething, Delilah inadvertently dug her claws into Bariath's shoulders, and when he lurched awake, she gasped.

"Oh, oh, dear Bariath!" she cried, leaning forward and planting gentle kisses on his back. "Come. Lie down," she cooed. "You have had a bad dream."

Wincing, Bariath clutched his offended shoulders, wondering how a dream could be so real. When his lady took him by the hand, he obeyed like a small child.

"Come," she purred, drawing him to the couch. "Lie with me."

Soon his head was cradled on her soft breast, and he slept without thought of the council or the Israelis.

But as Delilah ran her long fingers through Bariath's golden curls, her own thoughts were an inferno.

She had never laid eyes on Samson, but she had wanted him since the day he first stormed through Philistia. Now that Mariah had him, her desire was more than womanly fancy. It was the fire of challenge—a challenge she would embrace with suffocating relish.

FIVE

Samson rose from the bed in his wallside room and walked to the window that overlooked the city square. Far to the center, blocks away, the balustrades and rooftops of Dagon's temple caught the light of the moon.

At the sight, his drowsy face lost its color and a spear of shame shot through his heart.

"Lord God!" he groaned quietly, gripping the window ledge. "What have I done?"

Turning about, he gazed upon the sleeping Mariah, whose dreamy smile told, even in slumber, the ecstasies of the evening spent with the "hero of Israel." But her smile was no comfort to the one who had enjoyed those ecstasies with her. Guilt, fresh and pungent, spilled through his soul, shriveling his spirit with its rancid perfume.

Was it only yesterday that he had enjoyed another type of ecstasy, one far to be preferred to the transitory sensations of lust fulfilled? He had reveled in the love of the Lord and had sworn, this entire last week in Adonai's presence, that he would serve him forever.

But now . . . now he had once again proven his unworthiness. He had succumbed once more to his greatest weakness, the wooing lips and scented neck of a heathen woman.

"Lord God!" he whispered again. But his heart and mind could formulate no further words to express his misery. He

155

was a Nazarite from birth, dedicated to the Lord's service. Yet he seemed incapable of overcoming his frailties.

Yes, he had broken every other commandment of the order of Mahaneh-dan. He had drunk strong drink. He had slain hundreds and thousands of men and had smeared himself with the blood of the dead, both animal and human. He had eaten and frolicked with pagans.

But each of these transgressions had been precipitated by involvement with an ungodly female. Though he could not blame anyone but himself, he would have avoided strong drink, except that it had been offered by a seductive hand. He would not have rampaged through Ashkelon, had he not been tricked by a lying woman. And he would not have gone to war, except to avenge her death.

Just now, as he stood silhouetted in Mariah's window, the only thing that distinguished him as a Nazarite was his peculiar hairstyle. His face burning, he fingered the seven braids that fell across his chest.

"Had I a pair of shears, I would cut you off and cast you from me!" he groaned, tugging at the dark locks. "I am not worthy to bear your mark!"

He spoke too loudly. The woman stirred upon the bed, and Samson froze. The last thing he wanted was for her to awaken, to call him to her as she had done before. Though the thin sheet that draped her body revealed enough to arouse him, he had no desire to be with her again.

Scornfully he castigated himself. His lack of appetite was not due to any spiritual greatness on his part. His all-too-familiar longings would ensnare him soon enough. They had been temporarily satiated. That was all.

How he wished he was like Josef! Josef, who was apparently free of such temptations. Or who, if he experienced such inclinations, was stronger than they.

But as soon as Samson thought of his little companion, a twinge of resentment followed. Why, since Josef knew his shortcomings, had he brought him to this place?

The more he considered this, the more the details of the previous evening came clear in his mind.

He remembered that Josef had addressed the harlot by name. In fact, when they had arrived at the inn, he had asked for her specifically. "Mariah!" Samson muttered. That was what Josef had called her. He knew her and had thrust her into Samson's path!

Responding to her name, the woman awoke, rubbed her eyes, and smiled deliciously at Samson.

"Yes, love?" she replied. "What are you doing? Come back to me."

Holding out a hand, she beseeched him, but Samson backed toward the window. In the hope that there might be a stairway leading from the chamber, he scanned the wall outside. Gladly would he have leapt to the street, were he not a full three stories from the ground.

It appeared that if he were to escape her, he would have to bypass the bed, exit though the chamber door, and then find his way through the halls of the inn to the main entrance below.

Madly he started past her, ready to do just that. But she was standing now, sidling toward him.

Flashing shame-filled eyes upon her, he turned again for the window, prepared to leap through it like a cornered animal.

But this time, when he scanned the street, he noticed something he had not seen before.

In the shadow of the city wall, ranging to either side of the Gaza gate and clustered all about the inn door were armed men. At the towers beside the gate tops there were more guards than usual. And every eye was trained upon the inn, its door, its windows, and its rooftop.

At once, he knew their purpose. The fact that none of them had seen him as he stood plainly in their view was some quirk of fate. But he knew he must not risk further exposure, unless he meant action.

"Josef, you fiend!" he snarled through gritted teeth. Wheeling about, he pushed past the surprised Mariah. Beyond the bed was the chamber's other window, the one facing the sea. Grabbing his loincloth and his cloak, Samson wrapped them about his naked frame, then glowered at the woman.

Mutely she watched as he reached for the window ledge, flung himself outside, and hung there, surveying the glacis of rubble and rock that surrounded the base of the fortress.

It was a long way to the ground, further than from the chamber to the street inside the city. But he could not hesitate. Releasing his grip, he trusted himself to gravity, hoping that the rough wall against which he slid would help break his fall.

Though he landed in a heap of pain, he managed to stand. He was scraped and bloody, but otherwise he was whole. Limping toward the gate, he stood for a long while beneath the moonlit guard tower.

As he brought his hard breathing under control, Samson studied the road that headed north along the wall and then veered east from the sea. He knew his enemies focused on the inn door and on the windows that faced the city square. He could try to make a run for it, hoping no guard would see his flight up the highway.

But this was risky.

His only other option was to confront his enemies, and this too could mean death. There was no jawbone handy, as there had been on the plain of Judah. He had no weapon in his belt. But he did have his bare hands, which, in the case of the lion at Timnah, had served him admirably. If he was going to die, he might as well take a few Philistines with him.

Surveying the gigantic gates, he noticed the camel-tall doors that were hinged in the center of them. Each evening when the larger gates were shut, the city allowed the smaller doors to remain open long enough for dawdling merchants to enter or exit just before curfew. So long as the greater gates were closed, there was general safety from invasion. But at curfew, even the smaller doors were barred from the inside and defended.

Glancing above, Samson saw that his presence was thus far undetected. Though he doubted God much cared for his sin-ridden prayers, he nonetheless sighed a quick one and took a deep breath.

With a mighty groan, he threw himself against the camel doors. They were eight inches thick, constructed of hard oak and strapped with iron bars, but they creaked and echoed his groan. Towering five feet over his head, they would not have quivered at the touch of a lesser man. But under Samson's power-packed heave, they began to rattle.

Before the men inside the walls were aware of what transpired, the heavy black hinges connecting the doors to the larger gates started to bend.

Seeing the progress he made, Samson was spurred to greater effort. With one potent lunge after another, he smashed his brawny shoulders against the oak boards.

An incredulous cry ascended from the street, and the name of Samson rang through the marketplace. The clatter of shields and spears told the invader that his foes gathered now directly behind the doors.

But he did not pause in his battering assault. As his enemies threw their collective weight against the doors, he only pressed harder, until the hinges moaned and snapped.

With one more mighty lunge, he threw himself against the buckled bars, and a desperate shout assailed his ears as the doors fell inward, crushing a dozen Philistines.

Hesitating only long enough to find a handhold, he grasped the doors and hoisted them skyward, ripping the doorposts out of their footings and balancing the colossal structures against his knees.

The Philistines who had avoided the toppled doors looked on in speechless amazement as the titan of Israel turned about, braced the gates against his buttocks, and then hoisted them to his back.

Paralyzed, Samson's enemies watched as he carried the gates away, striding like a mythical god up the seacoast highway and vanishing into the mist of the eastern plain.

Marissa's Dream

ONE

*I*t was unheard-of for a woman to visit the Nazarite camp at Mahaneh-dan. There was no code barring women from the monastery, but any Jew or Jewess knew the inappropriateness of such action.

The fact that Marissa took it upon herself to violate the ban was evidence of her desperation.

She had had a dream. Though she had not seen Samson for eight years, she thought of him daily. And it was not unusual for him to appear in her dreams. Usually the visions were sad or plaintive, sometimes bittersweet, reflecting the emotions that went with each thought of him. But last night's dream had been a nightmare.

In her sleep, she had seen Samson in the clutches of some terror, being swept away by some life-threatening plot.

Samson had certainly been in danger many times since he had left her. Yet she had never been tormented by a nightmare to that effect.

These days, Samson held a position of honor. Since his feat at Gaza, he had returned to great acclaim in Israel and soon thereafter had been officially designated judge among his people, for they had viewed him as such for several years. With his headquarters in Hebron, city of the patriarch Abraham, he was more protected now than he had been in his carefree youth.

After uprooting the Gaza gates, Samson had actually carried them on his back through forty miles of country and had erected them atop a high hill overlooking the very fields where Father Abraham had tended his flocks generations before.

Since that day, he had been heralded as God's chosen vessel, the one ordained to guide Israel through this generation. After a half-century of being a flock without a shepherd, Israel now had its champion, its spokesman for the will of the Lord.

Inspiring his brethren to faith in God, he had proceeded to build up the armed forces and had leveled repeated blows at Philistia, raising Israel to the region's lead position militarily and economically for the first time in centuries.

Samson's legend was heralded far and wide, so that he was an international champion.

But Marissa, who had not heard from him since his marriage to Jezel, was more attuned to him than anyone.

And she had had a terrifying dream.

It was spring in the Zorah hills. Just as Samson and Manoah had done when the boy approached his thirteenth birthday, Marissa picked her way across the swollen streams that ribboned the highlands. Unlike those travelers, however, she had no one to talk to, and only her fearsome dream spurred her on.

What if the old monks refused to admit her, refused to hear her story? Or what if, upon hearing it, they passed her off as a woman more foolish than most?

She would have gone to the priest of her hometown, had she thought he could advise her. But in the priest's eyes, Samson was beyond threat, a blessed governor, protected by the Lord.

And she would have gone to Rena and Manoah, respecting their wisdom, except that she did not want to cause them worry. Manoah's health had not been good of late, and anxiety would only exacerbate his problems.

The only other people who knew Samson's spirit were the hermits of Mahaneh-dan.

It was sunset when Marissa descended the last hill before the camp. As she caught her first glimpse of the little compound, she knew why Samson loved it here.

The hivelike huts were pink in the glow of the sultry evening, and from their rounded tops spiraled curls of smoke, carrying the aroma of simple meals across the vale. From Samson's accounts, she knew that vespers would soon be called, and the monks in their white, hooded habits would emerge like ghosts from their abodes.

She knew also that Samson's mentor, the beloved Peniel, dwelled in a cave on the far slope. That is, if he was still alive.

He had been a very old man when Samson first came here. He had tutored the growing Israeli until he reached twenty years of age. Perhaps he had since passed away?

Marissa's one hope of acceptance in the camp was that Peniel was still here and that he would remember her name. Years ago, Samson had spoken to him of their plans to marry. And hadn't Manoah gone to the old monk in distress and anger when Samson chose instead to wed the Philistine woman? If the elder remembered those conversations, he would surely remember Marissa's name.

Tiptoeing down the hill toward the quiet hollow, Marissa kept her eyes on the caves. Would Peniel be the first to emerge for the evening meeting? Soon she saw that he would not. Somewhere in the hamlet a bell was ringing, calling time for vespers, and from the huts came the many praying hermits who dwelt apart from the elder.

Dare she hail one of them? If the meeting started before she was noticed, her introduction would be even more awkward.

Yes, she must put feminine scruples aside. She must make herself known quickly. Samson's safety was at stake.

"Sir!" she cried softly, catching the ear of one hooded fellow as he stepped forth from his hut. "Sir, I would see Master Peniel."

Stunned, the hermit, apparently a young novice, stood up and stared at her. "You—what?" he stammered. "Woman, who are you?"

When she stepped closer, so that the light of his hut fire lent a radiance to her face, he seemed to tremble. Likely he had not seen a woman, certainly not one so beautiful, since he had cloistered himself in this place.

"I must see Peniel," Marissa insisted. "I have heard he is a prophet. Perhaps he is also an interpreter of dreams. I have had a dreadful dream, and only Peniel can help."

PENIEL was still senior adviser of the Nazarite camp, but he had not attended vespers for several days. A week before Marissa's appearance, he had taken to bed, surrendering to frailty and advanced age.

A stiffening pain in his joints had come upon him with increasing severity in recent months, causing his already crippled leg much torment. For some time, the younger monks had come for him each evening, bearing him to vespers upon a stretcher. Now even that mode of transport was too uncomfortable.

Still, though he was very weak, he managed to host his female visitor congenially. While the novice who had first seen her had not laid eyes on a woman for many months, Peniel had neither seen nor spoken to a female for more than half a lifetime. To have such abstinence rewarded with such beauty, so close to the end of his earthly journey, seemed a gift from God.

"So," he sighed, smiling at her across the cave fire, "you are the fair Marissa." He handed her a clay cup of spiced tea, and she smiled back as she took it.

"I am pleased that Samson mentioned me," she said. "But that was a long time ago."

This wistful comment pricked Peniel's heart. Apparently Marissa had never fully recovered from Samson's rejection.

In a corner of the cave, the novice who had introduced her listened in. Obviously smitten by her beauty, he hesitated to depart, hoping that Peniel would think it best to have a third party present.

"What do you think?" Peniel chuckled, waving him off. "Is a crippled old fellow like me compromised by a lovely lady's company?"

Blushing, the novice bowed and backed out of the cave, leaving the two to themselves.

"Never mind him, my dear," Peniel went on. "You may speak frankly to me. Why have you come? Has it to do with Samson?"

At the sound of that name, Marissa began to weep. "You will think me a fool," she confessed, "but I still pray for him daily."

Leaning toward the fire, Peniel studied her intently.

"A fool?" he asked kindly. "To pray for the governor of your people?"

Marissa drew a deep, shuddering breath, then gazed into the flames.

"Or do I detect more than patriotism in your concern for Samson?" the old man queried.

When Marissa bit her lower lip, blinking back more tears, Peniel nodded. "You have never ceased to love him, have you, my child?"

"They say you are a prophet," Marissa sighed. "So you have read the contents of my heart. But I have not come to speak of love. I have come because . . . "

Hesitating to divulge her purpose, she grew silent.

"You have had a dream," the old monk guessed.

Marissa glanced up in amazement. "How do you know this?" she cried. "The novice did not tell you! I was with him when he announced my visit!"

When Peniel only stroked his beard, looking very much the sage, Marissa sighed, "I suppose you know my dream without my telling you!"

"I do," Peniel declared. "Not because I am a great sooth-sayer, but because I, too, had a dream, just last night. I shall be surprised if we have not been troubled by the same vision."

"Then you have seen it?" Marissa marveled. "Was Samson ensnared?"

"By a woman's hands," he acknowledged.

Suddenly the nightmare flashed fresh across her mind. It *had* been a woman's hands that held Samson in an iron grip, alternately stroking him and strangling him. Recoiling, Marissa cried, "Yes . . . yes. Then I am not just a jealous female! Samson is endangered by—"

"By his own appetites," Peniel filled in.

To hear the truth so plainly put came as a shock. Marissa looked at the floor, embarrassed by the man's forthrightness. Fearing he had offended her, the old fellow crept near and placed a hand upon her shoulder.

"I am sorry," he whispered. "Samson broke your heart once upon a time, and I fear he could do so again." Then he paused, closing his eyes as if seeking direction. When he reopened them, he stared straight at her. "But my dear lady, you must know that he has always loved you!"

Shaken, Marissa pulled away. "Do not torment me!" she pleaded. "To believe such a thing will make me forever his captive!"

"And you have not been captive until now?" the old monk challenged.

Marissa had not come here for this. Were the elder not so endearing, she would have slapped him.

Instead, she retreated into silence, and Peniel proceeded.

"In a corner of the dream," he recalled, "there was another entity . . . a serpent . . . do you remember?"

Jolted by the memory, which had flown away upon waking, Marissa groaned. "Yes! I do remember! How could I have forgotten? The eyes of the snake . . . they were the eyes of someone I know!"

She needed to think hard to identify the snake and its beady eyes, but then one name came to her. Josef. He had dogged Samson's steps for years, introducing him to Jezel, leading him to Gaza. All this Marissa knew from reports attending Samson's every move.

Peniel did not ask her the snake's name. Whether or not he already knew it, his focus was on the lady at his side.

"The Lord has given you this vision," he insisted. "He brought you here for confirmation. If you and Samson are bound together, as I believe you are, then you must go to him. Warn him, Marissa, of the danger yet before him."

Astonished, the woman gasped. "Me? But, why . . . "

"Who else?" he asserted. "Had the Almighty meant for me to go, he would have given me strength to do so."

As the task was laid before her—the ordeal of solitary travel, the fear and joy of seeing Samson, the potential for fresh rejection—she could only ask one thing.

"Will warning him be of any use? Will it give him strength to resist temptation?"

At this, Peniel only shook his head. "Even a prophet has his limitations," he answered. "Samson was always a riddle. But you are an open book. Love is calling, and if you do not heed it, you will be forever the most miserable of women."

TWO

*T*he day Marissa left Zorah for Samson's capital at Hebron, her journey brought her into company with many other travelers along the north-south highway skirting Israel's hilly spine. In this fact there was some comfort, for Marissa had never traveled so far from Zorah, and being on her own was frightening.

Not that Hebron was a great way from her hometown—it was a mere day's journey through easy country. But it was always risky for a woman to travel without a companion. If she hung near caravans and families that passed this way, she would be safer from the bandits and highwaymen who ruled the roads.

She kept her face veiled and her head covered with her mantle. The less people saw of her, the better. And she wore a simple homespun dress. Though she would have preferred that Samson see her, after all these years, in an elegant gown, she must not bring attention to herself during the journey.

A seamstress, Marissa had fine scarves and dresses in her closet, for her trade, like most every other Israeli merchant's, had flourished under Samson's administration. Fabrics of all kinds—silks from India, cottons from Egypt—were now readily available. And so Marissa marketed, and wore, more costly goods than she had before.

In the years since she had last seen Samson, she had been a busy, industrious woman, and generally happy. Though she had never married, she enjoyed the company of village children and filled her days in service to her community.

While thoughts of Samson and the memories that word of him called forth sometimes pricked her heart with sadness, she never imagined she would risk so much to see him. Now, spurred by a force beyond herself, she traveled, one foot in front of the other, toward an unknown destiny.

As she hastened down the highway, she spoke to no one and certainly did not divulge the purpose of her pilgrimage. All about her were people of various rank: poor folks going to Hebron to seek financial assistance; wealthy merchants overseeing pack trains laden with handcrafts and produce; crimson-robed men from the coast; and nobles of the Philistines, who still liked to think of themselves as overlords of Israel.

Had she known that not far behind her there traveled another woman full of dreams about the strongman of Hebron, she would have cringed. But while she was innocent of this fact, she found herself moving faster and faster, as if she were in a race—for Samson's heart and soul.

THE GOLD trim of Bariath's iron-framed carriage caught the sun in a flash as the conveyance sped down the highway, overtaking Marissa and leaving her far behind.

Many handsome vehicles had passed the Jewess as she made her way toward Hebron. Heedless of pedestrians, the passengers simply expected them to move aside, and so they rarely slowed down.

Such was the case with this vehicle, and though Marissa identified it as Philistine, she could never have guessed that the couple who rode within, concealed by drawn curtains, were the chief prince of the confederacy and his ravishing mistress.

Had she known, she would have feared all the more for Samson, thinking that Bariath could mean him no good.

As for the woman at his side, Marissa would have thought little of her. She was very beautiful, but she was Bariath's consort. The Jewess would not have suspected that she desired Samson for reasons of flesh and pride as much as Marissa desired him for reasons of love.

Nor did Bariath know the plot brewing in Delilah's mind.

Ever since the harlot had heard tales of the strongman, she had longed to meet him, to see how easily he might be won. Now that Mariah, the hostess of Gaza Inn, had been his lover, Delilah knew no end of jealous agitation.

When Bariath had invited her to come with him on this peace-seeking mission, she had not revealed her eagerness. But the invitation was, she believed, a boon from the gods.

Selecting from her wardrobe her most seductive gown and putting in a full day on her cosmetics and coiffure, she had carefully prepared for the visit.

Many a Philistine noble had fallen with one glance at her beauty. And Delilah had deduced that though Samson was strong, he apparently had a weakness for beautiful women. If she passed before his gaze just once, she would surely captivate him.

Unlike her paramour, Delilah did not travel to Hebron to seek help for her fallen nation. She did not care that Samson had humiliated her people. She did not care that he had set the uprooted gates of Gaza upon a high hill in Judah, or that they now formed the entrance to his own judgment hall.

Delilah planned, when she met the gate stealer himself, to do some thievery of her own.

For Bariath, the cause of this trip was not a happy one. Philistia smarted from Samson's economic and military blows, and he had been sent to seek a treaty.

The Philistine was quiet as he traveled. Delilah knew he brooded, and that he wished for her to coddle him, to tell him that, though he must humble himself before his enemy, he was still the bravest and the mightiest of men.

But her focus, just now, was not on Bariath's needs. Drawing aside the curtain of her carriage window, she peered up the highway.

That must be Hebron in the hazy distance.

Placing a long-nailed finger to her lips, she smoothed the berry-stained wax that reddened them.

She hoped Samson liked scarlet. It had always been Mariah's color, but now Delilah had claimed it, painting her cheeks, her lips, and her nails with crimson and donning a wine red gown.

She was after blood, and she looked the part.

THREE

*W*hile the judges of Israel had all served the same purpose—to lead the nation back to God after times of spiritual wandering—their life-styles were as diverse as their personalities and reflected the needs of the nation at various periods. Some judges were itinerant, moving from place to place as they were needed; some dwelt in caves, the people seeking them out for advice; some were primarily military heroes; and others were philosophers, enshrined in holy houses.

Samson's calling led him from a hermitage to the town's gathering place, and on to the battlefield. He had lived in caves and houses. Now he dwelled in a chateau above the clean, white city of Hebron.

On the brow of the Hebron hill, the Israelis had built a fine home for their new judge. Prestigious and commanding, it doubled as judiciary headquarters of the nation, and in its receiving hall, Samson heard cases that were brought before him.

Today he had passed judgment on three matters: the rights of a farmer to an unpaid percentage of his wares consigned to a merchant; the rights of a young girl to receive child support for her baby from the family of her recently deceased husband; and the rights of a soldier's widow to receive support from the state.

But this evening was the beginning of the Sabbath, and there were no more hearings on the docket until the day of rest was past.

Samson paced the airy porch outside his private chamber. At the far end of the house, cooks bustled in the kitchen, preparing the evening meal and enough food to see the residence through the holy day.

For the judge, this was a time of quiet reflection.

As so often happened when he was alone, his thoughts traveled over the events of his life. Shame marked many of such private moments. Of course, there was gratitude and pride for the ways in which the Almighty had seen fit to use him . . . but the women of his life, their faces and forms, never failed to dart through his ruminations. It was with bittersweet sadness that his mind increasingly turned to Marissa, the lost love of his youth.

Through all the years and all the vagaries of his distorted choices, she had retained a stubborn hold on his heart. Truly she was but one of many beauties who had turned his head. But his love for her went beyond the carnal. Her smile, which he had never forgotten, reflected the content of his deepest soul. For it manifested love for God.

Indeed, in Samson's mind, Marissa and the Lord intertwined until they were almost inseparable. When he worshipped Adonai, he often recalled the Jewess. And while memories of other women left him feeling unclean, recollections of Marissa, though tinged with regret, were always elevating.

He had passed many years now as judge at Hebron. In all that time he had maintained his integrity, scrupulously adhering to the Nazarite vows he had taken as a boy. The sullied reputation that had dogged him had been replaced in the people's hearts by his capable administration, and by the legends of his heroic deeds. As his confidence in God's presence had grown, so had his wisdom. And this, added to his natural boldness, had made him a capable governor.

But his exalted position was often a lonely one.

He wore no crown, for there was no king in Israel, and his was not a royal station. But neither did he wear the simple habit of a monk, or the homespun tunic of a farm boy. He had become accustomed to the embroidered robes and fringed mantle that designated him the people's prophet-justice.

Nevertheless, there was little comfort in finery when he longed for a soothing human touch and the cheerful voice of a heart-mate. What he would give if only he could go back and reconstruct the past! He had had everything a sane man could want when he had Marissa. He had been on his way, even then, to becoming a leader in Israel. And he had had Marissa's promise to be his bride, his life companion.

How different his story would have been, had he only followed the plan of God, and not his own lusts!

Breathing deeply of the cool air that reached him from the Maritime Plain, Samson gripped the porch rail and lifted his eyes to heaven.

Shaking his head, he contemplated the riddle of that very confession. Had he not been led astray, would he ever have gone against the Philistines as he had? Would war and revenge have boiled in his veins if he had never experienced the slippery seduction of his enemies?

Not for the first time in his life, tears of frustration welled in his eyes as the puzzle of God's ways with him—and of his own ways with himself—remained a hopeless heap within his heart.

His was the age-old question of how the will of God and the freedom of human beings could be compatible. He dared not accuse the Lord of tempting him to sin; Samson knew he was responsible for his own mistakes. Yet he also knew that when all was said and done, the Almighty had been in charge of his life since before he was born.

Had Peniel been here just now, Samson would have filled his ears with these questions. If Marissa were here, he would have poured out his heart to her. As leader of Israel, he could not voice his doubts to just anyone, and so he swallowed them in silence, day by day.

Reaching up, he brushed a stray lock of his never-shorn hair away from his brow. Though he had strayed shamefully from his youthful vows, it was a consolation to realize that the mark of a Nazarite was still upon him.

He remembered how bemused Marissa had been when he had returned to Zorah for his bar mitzvah party, and she had beheld his new coiffure. That night, he had taken her in his arms and promised her that, though he must serve the Lord as a Nazarite, he would one day make her his own.

Closing his eyes, Samson leaned against the porch rail, feeling the Hebron breeze blow through his braids. "Oh, Marissa," he sighed, addressing the air, "if I only had another chance to right things . . . to keep my vow to you. . . ."

But as always, the reply was the same. Vacant, empty night. Marissa was lost to him forever. Never had he dared to question that; never had he gone seeking after her, nor had he summoned her to appear before him. Likely she belonged to another long since. Even if she did not, she would never want to see the one who had hurt her so deeply.

With his head bent, Samson turned from the rail. Supper would be arriving soon in his chamber—wineless, meatless, in keeping with his ordination. But just as he was about to leave the view of the city lights, a disturbance at the entrance to his estate drew him back.

Someone desired admittance to the hall of justice.

Briefly, he looked toward the Philistine gates that marked his headquarters, watching the guards shake their heads and their spears.

"Who would be here at this hour, and just before Sabbath?" Samson asked, addressing a servant who placed a food-laden tray upon his table.

"I will see, sir," the servant replied. "Likely some beggar from the streets. I will send him away."

Darting another look toward the gate, Samson nodded.

Then he stopped short, for he had caught a glimpse of the latecomer—and it was no beggar who pleaded with the guards. It was a woman, tall and comely, her mantle fallen back from her head as she talked.

Surely his eyes deceived him! The visitor seemed a phantom of his most recent reveries, the image of the willowy Marissa.

Throwing up a hand, he called his servant to a halt.

"By all means," he commanded, "go to the gate. But do not send the intruder away. Bring him here that I may rebuke him."

FOUR

Samson paced his chamber, his food growing cold and untasted upon the dinner tray. If he was correct, if the woman at the gate was Marissa, the love of his life would be standing before him momentarily.

Fidgeting with his wine red robe, he glanced in the mirror that hung upon his wall. Marissa had never seen him dressed this way. Would she approve? She had loved the more rustic lad she had known as a girl. Samson was now a prince among his people, decked in finery. Marissa might be put off by such adornment.

Nervous, Samson cocked his ear toward the hallway. Any moment he would hear her footsteps. Reaching for the clasp of his robe, he unhooked it and drew off the luxurious garment. The long tunic he wore beneath it was elaborate enough, with its intricate, embroidered border. And the pendant about his neck was a more than sufficient mark of his rank.

Stowing the robe in his closet, he cleared his throat and turned with trembling hands for his dinner tray. When the woman was announced, he would be calmly eating, reclining upon his upholstered chaise.

Barely had he struck this pose, a cluster of grapes suspended between his fingers, when a rap at the door announced her coming.

"Enter," he called, attempting a stern tone.

When his servant opened the door, it was with some hesitation. As Samson had expected, he did not thrust the intruder to her knees, as he might have done a scroungy beggar.

"Your holiness," the servant stammered, "this is a most unusual thing. This . . . woman . . . claims to be a friend of yours. The guards were at a loss to turn her away. She requests . . . *insists* that you will want to see her."

Glancing up, as if to say he had no time for such silliness, Samson saw that the caller had placed a veil over her face upon entering the palace. Only her dark eyes showed above it, shaded by her mantle. And they were lowered, so that they did not meet the gaze of the prophet-judge.

"A woman?" Samson barked. "I know no woman!"

This claim was calculated not to wound Marissa, but to assure the servant of his good reputation. Of course, it was also a convenient way to tell Marissa he was alone in life, that no female companionship graced his existence, and that all the degrading folly of the past had been put behind him.

When she fleetingly lifted her eyes, he knew she understood, and he thought he saw the glint of tears along her lashes.

Look at me again! he longed to cry. *Oh, Marissa, I know who you are, and I love you!*

But his restraint was impeccable, and though he yearned to clutch her to him, he maintained his composure.

"Very well, sir," the servant replied. "I shall send her away."

Clearing his throat again, Samson placed the grapes on the tray, and leaned forward. "Certainly," he agreed. "But as long as she has gone to such trouble, let us hear what she has to say."

Facing the woman, the servant commanded, "Speak, as the judge has said. Who are you and what have you to say for yourself?"

Now Marissa, who had been on the road all day, who had climbed to Mahaneh-dan, who had suffered a dreadful dream and had come here despite great trepidation, was near fainting. To be standing now before Samson, the dream of her life, to see him not as the boy of her youth, but as the legend of her people, kingly in attire and position, caused her head to spin. Placing a shaking hand to her throat, she tried to keep from swooning, but the room swam, and her knees quivered.

Suddenly all strength escaped her, the chamber grew dark, and she slumped to the floor.

With a gasp, Samson lurched from his lounge and reached for her. He had not meant to be cruel. Had he been cruel?

"Leave us!" he barked at the servant. "Send for the physicians!"

Not questioning the propriety of leaving the judge alone with a female, the servant hastened to comply. As Samson bent over the woman, his breath came shallow and quick, his heart beating like a bird's.

"Dear lady!" he groaned, lifting her in his arms. With utmost gentleness he carried her to his lounge and laid her out like a cherished doll.

It was still possible that this was not at all Marissa. But he would not believe it. Daring to touch her veil, he lifted it ever so cautiously from her face. And when he looked, for the first time in years, upon her incomparable loveliness, a tear splashed from his cheek to hers.

Instantly all of his longings to care for and protect her rose within him. Gazing upon her lips, he longed to kiss them.

But he dare not!

Instead, he lifted one small hand in his and stroked it lightly.

Still the feel of her soft skin moved him fearfully. She was in a swoon. She would not know that he raised her fingers to his lips and brushed them with a kiss.

But the sound of rushing feet rang down the hallway. The servant and the doctors were coming.

Standing up, Samson moved toward the door, wiping his eyes with the back of his hand.

"She has not recovered," he said with detachment. "Find a room for her and tend her until she does."

"Yes, sir," the physicians answered.

When they approached her couch, however, Samson remembered the veil and wished he had replaced it over her face.

Feigning nonchalance, he quickly explained, "She said I would know her, but her face was covered. Indeed, she is a girl from my village, but I have not seen her for years."

═══ FIVE ═══

*M*arissa was resting in a guest chamber, having recovered from her faint. The doctors had insisted she must remain quiet, that the judge could see her in the morning. But she could not sleep.

She could not put from mind the sight of Samson. Always, to her womanly eyes, he had been the most beautiful man on earth. But she had never seen him surrounded by luxury, garbed in finery. How he glowed! More so, even, than in his youth!

But he was not only wealthy and powerful. He was the man God had always intended him to be, the spokesman of Adonai to the people of Israel. And his physical glory was enhanced by that divine ordination, so that he was not only the strongest of men, but seemed the embodiment of the Almighty himself.

Marissa gazed up at the intricate tiles of the palace ceiling and wondered how she could have come here. Yes, it had seemed important that she do so. But she felt so foolish now.

Had Samson recognized her? Had he laughed when he did?

Sorely, now, did she regret that she had worn such a simple, homespun gown. She had done so out of practicality, knowing the highway would be dusty and the traveling risky. But she certainly could have made a better choice, something more colorful, more . . . endearing.

Sighing, she turned her head upon her pillow, blushing with shame. What difference did it make what she wore? Samson had been the companion of women far more beautiful than she. He had surely forgotten her long ago.

And now, what an entrance she had made! Fainting upon the judge's floor! If he had forgotten her, he would never do so again. From now on, when Samson thought of Marissa, it would be with a sneer.

But, she scolded herself, had she come here to impress him? Wasn't this a journey of ministry, and wasn't she here to bring Samson warning?

Choking back tears, Marissa sat up on the couch and looked about for her satchel. Perhaps she had been mistaken about this entire venture. Perhaps her dream and her search for reassurance at Mahaneh-dan had been the product of buried longings. Her heart had tricked her mind, contriving an excuse for her to come here—and creating this entire foolish escapade!

Well, she would not be foolish any longer. She would slip quietly from the palace, under cover of night, and she would go home. If God did mean to warn Samson, he could do so without her aid.

At last she spied her travel bag beside the door, where the servant had put it. And her sandals were beside the bed.

Quickly she slipped the shoes on and stood shakily to her feet.

On tiptoe she approached the door, listening a moment for sounds in the hall. As she placed her hand upon the latch, however, she did not know that another listener stood just as quietly outside her chamber, wondering if he should awaken her.

When she cautiously pulled the door open, she took a sharp breath, for the silent visitor was visible through the crack.

"Marissa?" Samson whispered. "I should not have disturbed you."

Controlling her shaking hands, the woman peeked out at him. "I am sorry," she stammered. "I have intruded. I will go quickly."

With this, she opened the door further and thrust her bag into the hall. Avoiding Samson's gaze, she pushed past him, not knowing which way to go, but hoping for an exit.

"My lady!" Samson called to her. Pursuing her down the hall, he grasped hold of her wrist, turning her about. "Where are you going?" he cried. "And why have you come?"

With a shuddering sigh, Marissa looked at the strong hand that held her, and wrenched her wrist vainly. "Let me go, my lord," she pleaded.

His heart burning like a coal, Samson studied her plaintive face. Stubbornly did she resist his gaze, but as he held her arm tight, he lifted her chin with his free hand, forcing her eyes to meet his.

When they did, she trembled, for his expression seemed to reveal things she longed to know.

"How can you leave?" he groaned. "How can you come so far . . . after so long . . . only to leave me now?"

For what seemed an eternity, the two stood locked in silent fascination, silent agony, gazing upon one another. Neither spoke a word, but all words of love were communicated in their transfixed faces.

At last, Samson broke the trance, raising his hand from her chin and tracing the curve of her cheek with his forefinger. Closing her eyes, Marissa pressed her face against his open palm, her lips parting in a sad smile.

Overcome, Samson could deny his feelings no longer, and with one sweep of his arms, he enfolded her, drawing her to his bosom and claiming her lips with his own.

Again and again, softly and sweetly he kissed her, drawing her passion from her in a stream of tears. And when she pulled away, he drew her close once more, holding her head between his hands and kissing the teardrops from her face.

"Oh, Marissa!" he cried. "Tell me you have come to redeem me! Tell me you will stay!"

Sobbing quietly, the woman buried her head upon his shoulder. "Master," she pleaded, "I have indeed come to redeem you. But not this way . . . not like this."

Then she raised her chin, determined strength in her voice.

"I have come because God sent me," she asserted. "I have had a dream, my lord, and Peniel sent me to you."

Astonished, Samson took in her words. "A dream?" he asked perplexedly. "What kind of dream?"

"A dream of warning," she announced.

Stepping back, Samson studied her fervid expression.

"Very well," he said. "Sit with me, and tell me of this dream."

Marissa brought her swirling thoughts captive to her mission and looked intently at the prophet-judge.

"In this dream there were three figures," she began, "yourself and two others. I saw only the face of one, and the hands of the other. The hands were those of a woman, beautiful but clutching, with long, sharp talons and stunning strength. The face was mocking, demonic, and full of hatred for you. The more the woman held you, the more did the demon laugh!"

Amazed, Samson gazed at the floor, a chill working up his spine.

"Do you know who these characters were?" he asked.

Fearfully, Marissa proceeded. "The hands . . . the woman . . . I know not. I did not see her face. But the mocker, I know."

Before she spoke his name, it echoed in Samson's spirit.

"Josef . . . ," he whispered.

Suddenly, Samson's soul shrank within him, his stomach tightening with memories of regret.

He knew, now, that Marissa perceived Josef's part in all his personal failings. She knew that Josef had introduced him to Jezel, that Josef had led him to the house of Mariah. All Israel knew these things, as did all Philistia.

"But . . . ," he faltered, "that is behind me. The sins of the past are put away, and I have not seen nor spoken to Josef since I came to Hebron. Why would God so warn me now?"

Marissa ached for him, hearing the pain in his voice. When he searched her gaze, begging for understanding, she had never felt so helpless.

"I cannot say," she replied at last. "I do not know all the ways of God. But Peniel, also, had this dream. And so you are twice warned."

Incredulous, Samson shuddered. "Peniel?" he gasped. "Not only you?"

"That is right," Marissa whispered.

Numb, Samson stood up and paced the hall. Was he, in truth, still vulnerable? Had he grown so little that his old demons still had power? Turning about, he studied Marissa with helpless yearning.

"But *you* are here!" he cried. "God sent you, my angel! He must still love me, a little!"

Reaching forth a beckoning hand, Marissa wept, "Oh, Samson, he loves you greatly! This warning is for your salvation, not your condemnation. Heed it, and you will be wise!"

With a quiet sigh, Samson nodded. Of course, she was right. He *would* heed the warning.

Truly, God loved him. As he gazed upon his best friend and her beseeching gesture, he knew she was a living testimony to that love.

Drawing near, he raised her to her feet and held her hands in his.

"So, dear lady," he whispered, "is this all you came to say?"

Giving a nervous smile, Marissa stammered, "I have given you God's message."

"So you have," he replied. "But what of *you,* Marissa. Have you spoken all your heart?"

When she avoided his gaze, he squeezed her hands gently. "Say it," he breathed softly in her ear. "Tell me you love me."

Breaking, she leaned into his embrace and raised her lips to his.

SIX

*T*he evening that Marissa arrived at Samson's
headquarters, another set of visitors also paid a call. They had
entered Hebron hours before the woman of Zorah, for they
had passed her on the highway, leaving her in the dust of their
churning carriage wheels. But they had waited to approach
the palace, waited until dusk when their silent passage along
the terraced moat would go unnoticed.

Nor did they ask entrance to the judge's house. They did
not speak with the guards outside the gates, but only waited
quietly, observing the opulent residence from a cautious distance, each recognizing that the palace had been built upon
the strongman's legendary status. And, too, Bariath and Delilah viewed, with flashing Philistine eyes, the very gates that
had once stood guard over Gaza.

Until this very moment, Delilah had cared nothing about
the uprooted gates. Though they were a humiliation to her
people, she was far too self-absorbed to be troubled by national shame. The account of Samson's triumph at Gaza had
only reinforced her desire for him.

But though she knew well the story of Samson's mighty
feat, the superhuman grandeur of it did not fully impress her
until she saw the gates in this setting. As she tried to envision
one man bearing them upon his shoulders, trudging over

forty miles of hilly terrain to erect them on this mount, her mind was boggled.

Gripping the sill of the carriage window, she cocked her head back and gazed at the mammoth bars and crossbars of the doors, scanning the width and height. She had never laid eyes upon the Israeli hero, but at this instant, as she surveyed the miracle wrought by his strength, she was madder than ever for him.

Indeed, her mouth watered, and she raised a hand to dab her lips. Straightening her coiffure, she scanned the palace walls on the remote chance that Samson might even now be standing at some window.

But as she dreamed private dreams of him, her consort, Bariath, was devastated.

"This is worse than I had thought!" he snarled, as they passed beneath the shadow of the looming doors. "The gates are at the very forefront of the judge's compound!" Knotting his fist, the chieftain pounded his knuckles into his thigh. "To think that I have come to kiss the villain's feet!" he spat. "I should be here to draw the sword!"

Delilah glanced sideways at the Philistine. "Of course, my lord," she whispered. "All in good time."

SEVEN

*I*t was the afternoon of the third day. Marissa had returned early in the morning to Zorah, not by foot, but in a regal conveyance appointed by Samson. And she had left the judge's palace arrayed in fine clothing, her carriage laden with gifts for herself and his aged parents. About her neck was a gold chain, a betrothal gift from her beloved.

Yes, Samson had sent her away to prepare her wedding trousseau. In a few weeks, he would be going to Zorah to whisk her back to Hebron as his bride.

Today, as the judge considered the events of the night, he could scarcely believe how suddenly all the desires of his heart were being fulfilled. Last evening, he had been a forlorn soul, longing for the touch of a woman he had not seen for years.

Now she was his.

Everything was his, it seemed. He was the spiritual adviser to God's chosen people. He lived in uncommon luxury, and he would soon possess the girl of his purest dreams.

On top of all this, he had received word that the Philistine chieftain, Bariath, and his mistress had arrived in Hebron, and that they desired to see him. For Bariath to come here without armed guards, and in the company of his consort, must mean he was on a diplomatic mission. Finally, after years of Israel's dominance, Philistia was anxious for peace.

As Samson sat in his receiving hall, he tried to put thoughts of Marissa aside, to prepare himself for what could lead to a political summit. All morning he had met with his advisers and accountants, and they had briefed him on Israel's fiscal strengths and weaknesses, her armed forces, and the contents of her storehouses. On his lap, just now, were scrolls of figures and facts compiled by his councillors, regarding the state of the nation.

If Bariath wished to discuss rebuilding relations, Samson must be as informed as possible on Israel's current condition.

Though the judge had rescheduled his docket of cases so that he might have time to prepare for this meeting, he could have spent a week in consultation before he absorbed all there was to know. When his clerk announced that Bariath waited in the hall, he quickly rolled up the figured scrolls, placed them in their wrappers, and wiped his sweaty palms upon his robe.

"Send him in," he replied.

Samson had never seen Bariath, but he had heard that he was a man whose physique matched his political power. He was not surprised when the chieftain half filled the doorway to the stateroom, his tall, muscular frame and shock of blond hair testimony to his Aryan ancestry.

The fact that the great warrior bowed as he entered assured Samson that he was, indeed, here on a mission of peace. Still, the judge was cautious as he addressed him.

"Come forward," Samson hailed him. "Greetings in the name of the Lord."

At this, Bariath drew nearer, standing erect and drawing one arm across his chest in salute. "Greetings in the name of Dagon," he returned.

"You have come a good distance," Samson said. "From Gaza? You must be weary."

The seemingly polite remark was a pointed reminder of Samson's feat of bearing the Philistine gates all the way from the coast. But the chieftain took it graciously.

"We did not come here from Gaza," he replied. "We came from Sorek Vale, where we dwell."

"You have brought family, then," Samson acknowledged.

"I have," Bariath answered.

At this, Samson nodded toward the court clerk. As he summoned Bariath's companion, Samson ran over in his mind details from the scrolls he had just put aside.

So far, the encounter was going smoothly. The judge's confidence had never been greater, and he offered Bariath a seat at a long table as a servant poured three goblets of wine.

"The Lady Delilah," the clerk announced, leading Bariath's consort into the room.

Glancing up, Samson felt his breath catch in his throat.

He had known what to expect of Bariath. He had known he would be a giant, intelligent of eye and commanding of presence. But he had given no thought to the Philistine's companion.

Now, as he beheld the courtesan, her tall, ample figure draped in scarlet, her ruby gown robed by a cascade of ebony curls, his body tensed.

Suddenly, Marissa's warning dream flashed to mind, and Samson recoiled from the woman's outstretched hand.

"Delilah?" he repeated coolly. "Greetings in the name . . . "

But it seemed it would profane the name of the Lord to mention it in this woman's presence. So, with a stiff bow, he simply led her to the table.

PART

SIX

❧

The Devil's Journey

ONE

*J*osef leaned forward on his horse, pressing into the wind. His eyes were squinted against the grit that blew up from the highway, but the scowl upon his face had been imprinted there long before this unseasonable journey.

Drawing his mantle over his cold nose, he glanced behind him at the wagon that was usually laden with goods to trade. This trip to the coast was for personal business, and he carried no merchandise to sell. In the wagon were a sack of small tunics, a few loaves of bread and slices of cheese, and a skin or two of milk. Besides these there was only one other bundle, a young child wrapped in a wool blanket and asleep upon the wagon floor.

It was not yet winter, but the autumn wind crossing inland from the sea could chill the bone. Normally, Josef would never have made such a journey—but he had reached a point of desperation.

For seven years he had borne the responsibility of raising the boy who rode in the jostling cart. He had let the world, and the boy himself, believe that he was the lad's father and that the child had been born from his marriage to Samson's ex-wife, Jezel.

For a while, that deception had been Josef's secret triumph, a private vengeance against the strongman.

When the boy had been a baby, Josef had found it easy to enjoy the secret without it impeding his life-style. The child was kept in the custody of nursemaids at Josef's villa in the Zorah hills. Once weaned, he had been passed between a number of governesses, and for all of his short life, he had dwelt away from the public eye.

But, lately the boy was less a passing pleasure and more a burden, demanding Josef's time and attention as he grew older. Decisions must soon be made as to his schooling and his future, decisions with which Josef did not care to be troubled.

Not that the boy was a difficult child. He was, in fact, a quiet lad, with a meditative and compliant spirit. Regarding this, Josef had often been amazed, for his mother had been anything but spiritual, and Samson, his true father, was a volatile character. Perhaps he took after Samson's parents, Rena and Manoah, who were among the gentlest folks on earth.

But only Josef would have made this connection, for he alone knew the truth of the boy's ancestry.

Indeed, so lovable was the child that even the hard-hearted Josef had suffered over what to do with him. He had decided to find him a new home, for he was too selfish to care for him any longer. When he realized that he could not dispose of him in Israel without bringing public censure upon himself, he decided to go into Philistia.

Foreign children were a welcome commodity there. He would not sell the lad. Rather, he would pay handsomely for some Philistine family to take him off his hands. What they did with him from there, whether they made him a slave or adopted him as their own, he would never need to know.

Still, the boy *was* a delightful child, and Josef was not so devoid of conscience as to take this journey lightly.

He could have waited until spring to transport the lad. But in the spring business would pick up, and he could not risk interference with his trade.

Yes, this was best. When he returned from the coast, he would tell his fellow Zorahites, with tears in his eyes, how bears had set upon them along the way, and how the boy had been torn asunder. He would ask the priest to pray for him in his grief, and like the murderous brothers of Joseph of old, he would show the townspeople one of the lad's little tunics, ripped and splattered with blood. Only Josef and God would know that the blood was not the boy's, that Josef had slain some bird or beast to spatter the garment.

All of this he rehearsed in his head while the sound of the wagon's wheels, grinding through the cold air, kept him from falling sleep.

He and the lad would be in Gaza just before sunset, and they would take lodging at the house of the harlot, Mariah. Surely she would have leads to help him dispose of the child.

This would not be the first time since his appearance before the Philistine council that he had lodged at the inn of the scarlet-haired woman. For nearly a year following the incident of the gates, he had stayed clear of Philistia altogether. Some of the seranim still suspected he had colluded with Samson when the strongman brought shame upon them. In fear for his life, Josef had been wise to avoid the land of Israel's enemies.

But, in time, he had again ventured into alien territory. Now that Samson had established himself as governor of the Jews, repeatedly shaming Philistia on the battlefield, focusing Israel's trade on other countries, and humiliating the confederacy in the international marketplace, any Jewish merchant who could afford the stiff tariffs on trade with Philistia was welcome within its borders.

Hunching his shoulders against the cold, Josef glanced behind him at the sleeping child. How innocent he was to the evils of the world! How innocent to the future about to be cast upon him! Scarcely could Josef believe himself capable of what he was about to do.

Sometimes he hardly knew himself. It seemed he was two people. In a faintly lit corner of his soul sat the Josef of his childhood, a phantom huddled beside a dying fire of goodness. Surrounding and crushing that small ghost was the Josef of today, whose heart never beat but with the pulse of resentment and hate.

Much too strong was the Josef of the present. The feebler part, containing what little remained of conscience, grew weaker with each passing day.

For years, the only force for good in the man's life had been the child who now slept in the wagon. Though he had been Josef's unwitting captive, and though Josef had never really loved him, he was a reminder of more innocent times; his sweet voice and dark-eyed smile were like barbs that pricked the Israeli's hardened heart whenever he was near.

Josef was glad the boy was sleeping. If he were to rise up, if he were to speak a word, the man's stony soul might shatter. The wagon would turn about and this dastardly errand would be terminated.

Lifting his whip, Josef spurred the donkey that pulled the cart. Once he reached Gaza, all hesitancy would cease.

His perspective was always clearer whenever he crossed the border from Israel to the land of the Gentiles.

TWO

The boy rubbed his eyes and looked up at the night sky. Through a haze of sleep he had heard Josef call his name.

"Dan," the call came again. "Dan, we are here."

At his young age, the boy could not appreciate the nobility of his own name, bestowed upon him when Josef had found him in the rubble of Mardok's house. His surrogate father had often told him it was the name of one of Jacob's sons, the name of the tribe of Israel of which they were members. But Dan had not yet learned to fully appreciate his people's history.

Josef had selected the name because it would appear devout to do so and would win the merchant approval among his fellow Jews. All Dan knew was that the times Josef had used his nickname, Dani, were the few times he had felt valued.

Tonight, as Josef lifted him from the wagon and stood him on his feet, he did not call him Dani.

"Papa," the boy said, yawning broadly, "I'm sleepy."

"I know," Josef said, taking him by the hand and trying not to look him in the eye.

"Are we in the city?" Dan asked, his gaze traveling up Gaza's high enclosure.

"In a moment we will be," Josef replied, leading him through the gate. Behind them rumbled the wagon, and the donkey gave a steamy snort in the cold air.

"Where will we stay?" Dan asked. Patting the donkey on the nose, he said, "Where will Flop-ear stay?"

At this, Josef jerked on the boy's arm, impatiently pulling him down the avenue.

"You will be warm. Both you and Flop-ear will be fed," he answered.

This did not satisfy Dan's curiosity, but he could tell Josef was in a sour mood, and he pressed him no further.

Momentarily, they came to the stairway leading to the wallside inn. As Josef unhitched the wagon and tethered the donkey to a post, the street rang with the noise of the closing marketplace. While merchants and housewives hurried home for the evening, rowdies began their tavern-hopping.

No longer drowsy, Dan clung to Josef's cloak and looked about him with wide eyes. Everywhere were lights and loud groups of jostling people. He had never seen such vivid garments as the women of Gaza wore, nor had he ever seen folks behave so strangely, laughing and joking, embracing and fighting. Quickly he moved up the stairs with Papa, hoping for sanctuary in a quiet room above.

When they reached the top step, however, they found anything but quiet. Entering the hotel, they traded the glow of street torches for a smoky yellow haze, and the cold night for the sticky humidity of many bodies.

As they had traveled, Dan had buried his nose in a warm blanket. Now he shielded it against an acrid odor wafting through the room on cloudy puffs.

He knew about alcohol, but not about opium, a substance imported from a continent away. He did not understand that only the wealthy indulged in it.

But he did understand that he had never before seen so much gold, in rings and bracelets and pendants. Nor had he seen adults reclining together on pillows, laps, and bosoms, as these did.

Clinging to Josef, he greeted the scene before him with bewildered silence. Why, he wondered, had his papa brought him to such a place?

Then his focus was grabbed by a most peculiar creature, a red-haired woman dressed all in scarlet, with blood-red lips and ruby fingertips. Sidling up to Josef, she smiled a snakelike smile, and Dan darted behind his papa, peeking out only to see if the creature was real.

"Dear, dear Josef!" the siren cried. "Where have you come from on this dreary night?"

Yes, she was real. But surely very wicked! Did Papa actually mean for them to lodge in this place?

Trembling, Dan hid in Josef's cloak and listened as the man made arrangements for the two of them to stay the night.

"You brought a companion, Josef?" Mariah crooned. "Why I never knew you to travel with a woman!"

At this, Mariah's patrons laughed hilariously. Scrawny Josef had often been the brunt of jokes, as the women of the inn draped themselves about him in cruel humor.

Ignoring the raucous crowd, Josef drew Mariah aside and whispered to her.

"What?" she shrieked. "A child? Josef . . . how could you?"

He should have known Mariah would be so indiscrete. Suddenly the crowd grew quiet, riveted upon him.

Face crimson, Josef reached behind him, pulling Dan into the yellow light. Astonished customers stared at the boy, women drawing their slack-necked gowns closer to their chins, and the men flashing angry eyes at Josef.

"This is no place for a child!" Mariah hissed through gritted teeth.

"I know . . . I know," Josef replied. "Only one night. Tomorrow I will find a place for him . . . I mean for us." Glancing sheepishly at the boy, Josef felt his face grow redder than ever.

"Mariah," he went on in pleading tones, "you are my only friend in this city. The only one who can help."

At this, Mariah's interest was piqued. Never before had Josef enlisted her aid in his personal business. Waving to her clients, she bid them resume their merrymaking.

"Help?" she repeated, opportunity in her tone.

Dan overheard Josef's reply, but he did not know what it meant.

"You will be well paid," he said, satisfying her unspoken inquiry. "It is a delicate matter . . . most delicate."

THREE

*D*an sat up on the narrow bed Josef had provided in the most luxurious suite of Gaza Inn. Always the wealthy Josef stayed in these quarters, but never before had he brought someone with him.

Likewise, it had been years since Josef took advantage of the services provided by the inn's women. Unlike the other male clients who frequented Mariah's hotel, he stayed here only because it was conveniently located near the market-place and brought him into company with travelers from throughout the region. He had found it to be a rich source of business contacts.

He enjoyed the company of the red-haired hostess, much like one thief enjoys the company of another. He did not respect her, nor was he attracted to her. He simply found in her a kindred soul, one whose selfish and designing character was similar to his own.

This evening Mariah was present in the suite's parlor. She sat upon a cushioned stool, feasting on grapes and cheese and quaffing house wine, while Josef paced the chamber to and fro.

Dan, his dark eyes even wider than they had been in the lobby, cocked his head toward the parlor. If he listened closely, he could pick up some of Papa's words as the thin man passed back and forth before his slightly open door.

Josef had waited until Dan was asleep before summoning Mariah. The boy had dozed soundly once his head hit the pillow, but Josef did not know that the woman's high-pitched cackle had wakened him.

How long the two had been talking, Dan did not know. But when Mariah laughed, Josef rebuked her and quickly peeked inside the lad's chamber. Lying very still, Dan had appeared to be asleep. But once the conversation resumed, he lay awake in tense silence, catching every word he could.

"You told me you had a son," Mariah teased, "but I never expected one so handsome!"

"He is a comely lad," Josef agreed. Then in a morbid tone, he added, "I am quite devoted to him. That is why this decision comes so hard."

The boy, who leaned so far that he came close to falling off the edge of the bed, could not see Mariah's skeptical expression.

"Come, Josef!" she hooted. "When have you ever made a decision contrary to your own wishes? If you choose to unload the boy, it is because that is what you *want* to do!"

Dan took a sharp breath and clutched the bedcovers to his chest. Did his ears deceive him? Had Papa brought him to Gaza to give him away?

As he eavesdropped, he began to tremble so violently he feared his papa would hear the clattering bedpost.

But Josef was so self-absorbed, he only wheeled on Mariah and growled like a trapped animal, "Very well, my lady. You know me too well to be fooled."

Then, with a groan, he said, "I shall tell you something I have never told a soul, a secret that has been a blessing and curse for seven years." Tense silence followed, until he sighed, "Perhaps if you know the truth, you will want to help."

The two listeners, the woman in red and the boy behind the door, hung on the small man's words, one out of evil curiosity and the other because he knew his future depended on the next syllables.

"Dan . . . is not my son," Josef hissed. "I found him in the rubble of Mardok's house only hours after he was born! His mother, her sister and father lay dead in the ashes, the only people on earth, beside myself, who knew the truth."

As Josef walked to the street window, gazing out but seeing nothing for the shadow over his soul, Mariah leaned over his frail shoulder. "And what *is* the truth?" she asked.

With a shrug, Josef turned to her. He knew she had guessed the answer, since he had married the Nazarite's abandoned wife.

"Samson," he croaked. Then with more force, "Samson! He is the boy's father!"

Dan lurched upon the bed, causing the frame to creak, but Josef heard neither this nor the little squeal he suppressed.

To the sound of Samson's name, Mariah had her own reaction. Samson was the only man who had ever spurned her after spending a night with her. Never had she forgiven him, hating him since the day he left with Gaza's gates upon his back.

As much as Delilah desired to have him, Mariah desired revenge against him. In fact, had she known that Delilah was envious, she would have laughed. She would not have wished Samson on her worst enemy, which, it so happened, Delilah was.

"Amazing!" she cackled. "Josef, you are amazing! You have carried this secret all this time? But why?"

The man glared at her with livid eyes. "You could never understand!" he cried. "No one will ever understand what it was like to grow up in Samson's shadow! To admire and hate him for who he was and . . . what he had!"

Pushing Mariah aside, Josef paced again. "Always he was strong and I was weak! Always he was the hero and I the scorned. When we grew older, girls flocked about him, but looked on me with contempt!"

Mariah moved toward Josef as he continued to rave. "Hush, friend," she whispered, pointing toward the bedroom door. "The boy . . ."

At this, Josef's face went white, and he tiptoed to the door, his heart drumming. To his relief, Dan appeared, once more, to be asleep. The man did not see the tears that sheened the lad's smooth cheeks.

"He has not heard," he sighed. Then, in a softer voice, but full of self-defense, he continued. "Samson is not as smart as I. This I always knew. At least, he is not as clever—"

"Not as devious?" Mariah interpreted.

"Very well!" Josef snapped. "I began to turn the tables when I got him married to Jezel. That was my idea, you know! And the beginning of Samson's downfall!"

If Mariah was surprised, she did not show it. "Ha!" she scoffed. "Some downfall! Samson is now the most powerful man in Israel and Philistia! More powerful than Bariath and all the seranim put together!"

Josef's face burned, and if eyes could wield knives, Mariah would have been cut to shreds. "The final battle has not been waged," he growled. "The war between Samson and myself is lifelong and will not be finished as long as we both have breath!"

Mariah drew her shawl about her shoulders, warming her goose-bumped arms. "And what of Samson?" she retorted. "Does he know of this war? It seems it has all been your secret. What satisfaction is there in knowing what you know, when Samson is oblivious to your hand in it all?"

"I have never been one to promote myself," Josef sniveled. "I have been content with private victories. My choicest revenge has been to raise Samson's son as my own, having what he would have wanted most in life and keeping it for myself!"

Mariah glanced toward the bedroom door. "You speak of the child as though he were chattel!" she said marveling.

"He has served his purpose," Josef sneered. "Now it is time to move on."

Incredulous, Mariah shook her head. "What do you wish of me, Josef? Why have you come here?"

"You know more people in Philistia than anyone," he replied. "You know people from distant places. Surely among them there is someone who could use a child. Someone who could take him far away . . . "

As Josef rubbed his lanky hands together, his small, black eyes sparking, Mariah recoiled. "I am no slave-monger!" she spat. "You have come to the wrong place!"

At this, Josef placed a hand on his throat, as though offended. "Slave?" he sighed. "How can you suggest such a thing? Surely you know a family . . . a merchant or tradesman who could apprentice him . . . even adopt him?"

Mariah's head spun. "Perhaps . . . ," she said. Then, astonished at herself, she snarled, "No! I want no part of this, not for any sum!"

Josef knew she was headstrong, but he had not expected such nobility in this woman.

Recalling that only one man had ever brought her down, he altered his approach. "So," he hissed, "should I return the boy to Samson? Would you have me enjoy the momentary pleasure of letting Samson know the truth, only to have him reclaim the prize?"

Mariah was dumbfounded. If anyone hated the Nazarite as much as Josef did, it was she. Did she want Samson to have the desires of his heart?

Suddenly, she saw the whole venture in a new light. As she thought about it, she could sympathize with Josef's sense of triumph as he had kept the boy all these years. As much as she resisted it, she found herself sifting through names of people who could use a child.

In a voice barely more than a croak, she conceded. "Very well. I will think on it." With this, she exited the room.

Josef was left to himself as she hastened down the corridor. He did not expect to hear from her until morning, thinking that she would lie awake all night pondering prospects.

But only moments later she returned, rapping stealthily on the door.

As he let her in, she wore a steely countenance. He could not know that as she had fled down the hall, she had passed the very window where Samson had escaped—the window where he had leapt to the ground, before tearing the gates from their posts; the window that always reminded her of his humiliating departure and the scornful way he had pushed her from him.

Now Mariah paced the chamber, rubbing her hands together just as Josef had done. She saw the chance to get her own revenge on the strongman, and she was determined to make that revenge as sweet as possible.

"What would hurt Samson more than knowing we have his son?" she hissed. "What would hurt him more, even, than the boy's death?"

Josef stammered, "I don't know, Mariah. What?"

"For the boy to serve Samson's enemies! The *god* of his enemies!" she declared. "For the boy to serve in the very temple of Dagon!"

His spine tingling, Josef was suddenly as horrified by her intentions as she had been by his.

"The temple?" he stammered. "But . . . the boy . . . he is a Jew!"

At this, Mariah turned on the weasel, her aquiline nose set squarely before his hooked one.

"Jew?" she challenged. "When did Jewishness ever sway you one way or another?"

FOUR

*J*osef held his head in his cold hands, pressing his throbbing temples with his fingertips. It was not like him to overindulge in wine and spirits, but he had spent the past three hours sitting before the fireplace of Sorek Inn doing just that. And his body, unaccustomed to such abuse, was reacting painfully.

Strong drink was supposed to help one forget. Yet Josef would never be free of the disbelief and horror on little Dan's face when his "papa" had delivered him to the priests of Dagon's temple. The child's one plaintive cry still echoed in Josef's ears. Beyond the single utterance, the boy had remained silent as a lamb led to slaughter, making no sound as the man he had known as his papa abandoned him.

That had been four days ago. Now Josef faced the ugly fact that the freedom he had hoped to gain by unloading the boy had been a mirage. As he had turned for home, pursuing business along the way, his heart had been burdened with guilt such as he had never known.

Still, he might have recovered had he not learned of Samson's upcoming wedding. Despite the guilt it brought, the fact that Samson's son now served in a pagan temple was a succulent victory. Even so, Josef found himself unable to really enjoy it in the face of one all-consuming fact: Samson was about to win Marissa once and for all.

Moving his fingertips from his temples to his ears, Josef tried to stop the sounds of gossip and drunken hilarity that spilled across the room. Philistine soldiers, who had recently entered the inn from the wintry night outside, were deep into sarcastic banter.

"I thought the ladies of Gaza Inn were more to Samson's taste!" one hooted.

"They say this woman of Zorah is a virgin!" laughed another.

"Perhaps a real woman is too much for him!"

"Mariah was. I hear he leaped from a third-story window to escape her!"

On and on the jokesters went, outdoing one another with ribald humor. With each reference to Marissa, Josef's heart quivered.

Shrinking inside himself, he gazed dejectedly into the fire, waiting for the wine to work its numbing magic. Zorah was only a half-day's travel away. Only a few days ago he had looked forward to returning home after putting little Dan behind him. But now Josef dreaded setting foot in Zorah. Not only did Dan haunt him like a phantom, but the knowledge that Marissa was forever beyond his reach cut like a knife.

Unable to endure another word of the soldiers' cruel quips, Josef staggered to his feet and headed for his gallery room. Perhaps wine-soaked slumber would deaden his tortured mind.

But just as he started up the stairs, conversation at the far end of the table grabbed his attention once again.

"Is it true that Bariath took Delilah with him when he went to Hebron?" someone asked.

"Indeed!" came the reply.

"To meet Samson?" another voice marveled.

*Ooh*s and *ahh*s followed this, as the men imagined the vamp working her magic upon Israel's hero.

"Bariath must be a fool!" someone suggested.

"No fool," another objected. "Bariath knows how to bait a hook!"

As Josef stood on the bottom step, a tingle of wicked speculation ran up his spine. He had heard of Bariath's mission to Hebron. He had even heard that his mistress had accompanied him—but the possibilities this posed had never occurred to him.

Shaking his head, he reasoned with himself. How likely was it that the Nazarite would fall again to a seductive Philistine female? Not even the vulnerable Samson could be so slow a learner!

When the rowdies at the table confirmed his thoughts, he headed up the stairs.

"Word is that our lady was ill-received in Samson's palace," one of them reported. "The judge hardly spoke to her the entire time Bariath was there."

"Ha!" another responded. "Could the harlot of Sorek be losing her touch?"

Certainly, Josef thought, plodding toward the gallery, *the gate stealer has had enough of Jezels and Mariahs. He has Marissa and would never be such a fool as to lose her twice.*

FIVE

*J*osef's donkey leaned against the stable wall at Sorek Inn, seeking shelter against the morning chill. His ears perked up when Josef came for him. Despite the cold, it would be better to travel than to stand still within this dreary barn.

But the master's voice was, itself, chilling, and while the donkey could not interpret the sinister look upon his face, he sensed in Josef a most peculiar change.

"Come, Flop-ear," Josef grumbled, harnessing him and leading him forth. "We will be home soon."

No one who knew the Israeli would have recognized him. Shriveled and bent, he was a mere shadow of the man who had gone to Gaza only days before. In the interval since he had delivered Dan to the priests of Dagon, something preternatural had left its mark upon him, draining his physical powers, yet infusing his decrepit spirit with an elixir of evil strength.

This morning, when Josef had arisen from his rumpled bed, he did not don the face of a pious Jew. He did not rehearse the story he had planned to tell his fellow Zorahites about the "death" of Dan and the "wild beast" who had supposedly set upon them in the mountains. For the first time in his life, he did not care what the Jewish community thought. It was quite unimportant to appear righteous in their eyes.

At some point in the night's long hours of wrestling with conscience, Josef's spirit had crossed a line. At some point in the testing darkness, all struggle had ceased. The faint light of goodness that remained within his soul was at last snuffed out, and the poor little phantom that was his better self curled up and died within its narrow corner.

Today Josef was a new man. Not better, but more dauntless. The despondency that had taken him to bed was now vanquished. He did not know how he would triumph, but the final chapter had not yet been written. He was determined that Samson would yet be outdone, and he would be victor.

As Josef hitched his donkey to the wagon and loaded his belongings in the back, he congratulated himself on a successful trip. When he had gone to Gaza, only the child had occupied the cart. On his return, Josef had managed to buy enough wares from Philistine merchants to pay for his journey in resale.

Even in his worst state of mind, he was a shrewd businessman, and already he made mental notes as to where he could turn a profit with the goods.

Just as he was about to mount the seat of his cart, however, a flurry of activity at the inn gate caught his attention.

Shielding his eyes against the blinding winter sun, he studied a group of Philistines who followed a golden carriage into the yard. Whoever arrived had apparently traveled through the night from some distant place. Their opulent vehicle and the reception they were getting told they were people of some importance, and Josef watched in curiosity as the newcomers stepped out of the cab.

He instantly recognized the chief of the seranim, Bariath. Never would he forget the man who had questioned him before the Philistine council the night he betrayed Samson into their hands.

Though Josef had taken advantage of the Philistines' need for trade with Israel and so felt it safe to return to Gaza, he had purposed never to confront Bariath again.

Quickly he pulled his mantle over his face for fear he might be recognized.

Doubtless Bariath was returning from his trip to Hebron. Josef watched the carriage door, expecting that Delilah would soon emerge. He had heard that she was a beauty, but never had he imagined just how ravishing.

As she stepped forth, giving her hand to the blond giant, Josef clutched the edge of the wagon. When she stooped beneath the small portal, her long black tresses caressing the folds of her scarlet cloak, he drew a sharp breath. Despite her heavy coat, Josef could see she was a woman of fine figure, tall and well endowed.

Her face was uncommonly gorgeous, with full, ripe lips and a haughty chin, and though her dark, painted eyes avoided all others, she held every gaze in a captive trance. Tossing her head as though to say she cared nothing for anyone's admiration, she passed through the yard with a quick stride, pulling all the men in her wake.

Only Josef remained outside, hesitant to join the crowd. For a long, cold moment, he stood beside the stable, telling himself that it was foolish to linger. He must be going to Zorah, and he must not let Bariath see him.

But he, like the others, had been hypnotized by the flashy vamp. Perhaps, if he kept his mantle close to his face, he could step inside long enough to hear a report of Bariath's journey. The Philistine chief had, after all, just come from seeing Samson, and Josef could benefit from news of their mutual enemy.

Creeping through the hotel lobby, Josef peered into the pub. The Philistine soldiers and numerous inn customers clustered around the fireplace, asking Bariath about his encounter with the Israeli judge.

Eager were they to know if the journey had been successful, if Samson had agreed to lower embargoes, and if there was hope for a renewed Philistine economy.

"We made progress toward a treaty that will heal Philistia's wounds," Bariath replied. "But we have only begun. Formal negotiations will be resumed next month, when Samson comes to Sorek Vale!"

Astonished, the crowd murmured excitedly. This was the first they had heard of an upcoming conference. And it would be held here!

Josef, likewise, was amazed.

But then, it made sense to continue the talks closer to Zorah. Samson would be going there for his wedding.

As the people continued to ask questions about Israeli forces, trade decisions, Philistine goals, and the like, Delilah kept a cool back to the crowd. Facing the fire, she seemed lost in thoughts all her own. When she did turn around to remove her heavy cloak and drape it across a chair, her face was pensive, her lips pursed in a malcontented pout.

No one asked her why she was so quiet. Word had preceded her: the Israeli had given her an icy reception. Nobody dared test her patience by inquiring into the matter.

Delilah was known for her quick temper. She was a pampered woman, used to having her way if only by force of her charms. If someone had been so presumptuous as to shun her, it should not be spoken of.

Not that the gathering ignored her. Her mere presence defied ignoring. The men simply kept a respectful distance, letting her fondle her unhappiness in private.

Josef, however, was riveted to her. While his ears picked up the give and take between Bariath and the crowd, his eyes dwelt upon Delilah in his own private reveries.

His was not a lustful attraction. Not that he was immune to such feelings, but his energies had for so long been consumed with revenge against Samson that all other desires had atrophied.

No, it was not lust that burned in Josef's eyes; Delilah was of interest in direct proportion to her usefulness against Samson. And as Josef studied her, he sensed she could be a key to his endeavors.

Like everyone else present, he knew that Delilah's withdrawn attitude, her sulking self-pity, was the result of Samson's rebuff. Apparently the Israeli judge had the power to make her miserable.

Which could only mean one thing: Delilah desired him.

Josef straightened his hunched back and pulled away from the entry, leaning for a moment against the lobby wall. A crooked smile worked across his lips, and he gave a secretive snort. *Of course,* he thought, rubbing his chin with his spindly fingers, *Delilah has been smitten by Samson. She is a woman in love, a woman scorned.*

Yet she was a powerful person. In all of Philistia, Israel, and perhaps the world, there was no woman more beautiful. Josef quivered to think of the impact she must have had on the woman-loving Samson. Indeed, that must have been the reason for Samson's cool response to her. She had the power to move the judge of Israel, and he had stayed as far from her as possible during Bariath's visit.

With a tingle of scheming delight, Josef peeked again into the pub. Delilah still kept her sad gaze to the floor, and Josef knew how she felt. He had spent a lifetime nursing wounds inflicted by Israel's strongman.

Reaching for the purse that hung from his belt, Josef pulled forth a silver coin. Quickly he placed the money on the clerk's counter and made a reservation for one more night at Sorek Inn.

"Will Bariath and his lady be staying here?" he inquired.

In surprise, the clerk replied, "Staying? Why, sir, my lady lives here!"

Delighted at his good fortune, Josef turned for the gallery stairs. He would make himself comfortable in his room, and later he would introduce himself to Delilah.

SIX

*B*y the time the inn served its midday meal, the meeting with Bariath had concluded and most of the customers had departed.

When Josef emerged from his room, he stepped to the gallery rail and peered into an empty dining hall.

Delilah was nowhere to be seen. But the fire still burned bright, and he decided he could wait beside it until she appeared.

As the clerk had told him, Delilah lived at the inn, probably in some sumptuous suite on the top floor. She would surely come downstairs before long. And even if it were evening before she did, Josef would be patient.

It was not long after he had seated himself, however, that his anticipation was realized. The sound of a woman's voice, sending a chambermaid to fetch a pot of tea, drew his attention to the gallery. As a young girl hastened down the stairs toward the kitchen, she was followed by her mistress, the glorious Delilah.

"Hurry now!" the lady commanded. "I am freezing!"

When Delilah reached the dining hall, she paused at the foot of the stairs, rubbing her hands together and glancing about the room. Obviously, she had hoped to be alone. The sight of a solitary customer warming himself was a disappointment.

Seeing that she was turning to go again, Josef stood up.

"My lady," he called, "do not leave on my account. I will not be staying long. Please," he said, gesturing to his own chair, "you may take my place."

Delilah blew on her blue fingertips. With a toss of her head, she complied, sighing something to the effect that when she had napped upstairs, her maid had let her chamber fire go out, and she was sure to catch her death of cold.

"Thank you," she said, pulling the chair close to the flames and sitting down. "I see we entertain a gentleman at our inn."

Josef, receiving the compliment graciously, gave a broad smile and made the comment an entree for further conversation.

"And I see that my friend, Samson, has entertained a true lady."

At the mention of Samson's name, Delilah was visibly shaken. Drawing back, she looked Josef up and down, wondering just who he was.

"Samson?" she stammered. "How do you know him?"

Josef gave a casual laugh. "I dare say, I know Samson better than anyone on this earth knows him. We grew up together in Zorah and have been companions through the years."

The little Jew rocked back and forth on his heels as he proclaimed this, his hands locked behind him in a humble pose.

"Of course," he sighed, "I have not seen much of him since he went to Hebron. Sometimes he seems to ignore me."

At this, he glanced sideways at the woman, hoping to read empathy in her face. Indeed, she had turned toward the fire, her gaze hardening into a frown.

"But then," he went on, "I know he is a busy man. How did you find him, my lady? Was he his old warm self?"

Josef could not have dissected Delilah's heart more quickly had he used a knife and scalpel. Reaching for a lock of long, dark hair that tumbled down her breast, the woman twisted it over and over in anxious fingers. When it was nearly a knot, she lifted hot eyes to her inquisitor.

"Your judge," she said, "is a cautious man. Bariath and I could have expected nothing more than the time and interest he devoted to us."

"Ah," Josef said with a nod. "Then you were well received. I am glad. For I have known Samson to be aloof with strangers. Why," he chuckled, "sometimes he is even aloof with me, and I have known him all his life!"

If Delilah had resisted her growing affinity for this little man, her resistance now weakened.

As the chambermaid brought a steaming pot of tea from the kitchen, Delilah told Josef to pull up a seat, and soon she was pouring him his own cup of brew. Waving the maid off, Delilah focused full attention on her guest.

"You are from Zorah?" she asked. "What is your name?"

Josef dared not reveal too much about himself. Doubtless the woman had heard of the weasel who had betrayed Samson to the council, and who had been guilty by association when the strongman tore Gaza's gates from their roots.

"Yes," he hedged. "I am a native of Zorah and have known the judge's family for years. Can we hope to see peace between our countries, my lady, since your brave visit to Hebron?"

He knew that he had hooked her. The question was a ruse. She was no more interested in discussing politics than he.

"I am surprised that you describe your friend as you do," she responded. "As I think about it, I *could* say he was standoffish. But I assumed he was exercising political caution."

Hearing this, Josef choked. "My dear lady," he said, clearing his throat, "I should be most disloyal if I spoke my heart freely. But I will say this much: if Bariath alone had visited him, he might not have been so aloof."

As though unaware of the impact this comment would have on the woman, Josef smiled wanly.

Blood rushed to her cheeks, and Delilah raised a quivering hand to her hot face. "Sir," she lisped, "what do you mean?"

"I speak out of turn," he apologized.

When the woman pressed him, he shrugged. "I am only assuming that for Samson, the presence of a woman as beautiful as yourself was cause for fear."

"Fear?" Delilah marveled, her eyes wide like the cup she held. "Why should the great Samson fear one woman?"

"I *do* overstep my bounds!" Josef confessed. "It is not good to say more."

When a sideways glance revealed the lady's disappointment, Josef sighed a deep sigh.

"Very well," he muttered. "This and nothing more. Samson is not a proud man, dear woman. He struggles, you see. He struggles with himself and with his past. He knows his weaknesses, all too well. He is not a proud man."

With this, he stood up from his seat, seemingly determined to betray nothing else about his old friend. But he knew that he had planted just the right seeds. He was sure that Delilah, as well as all the world, was aware of Samson's past indiscretions. Josef believed he had given the woman enough food for thought, and as she pondered his words over the next days, he had no doubt they would produce the desired results.

"Really, I must be going," he announced, picking up his satchel and backing toward the door. "I am honored to have made your acquaintance, my lady."

"Delighted, I'm sure," Delilah called after him. And then with a quizzical expression, "Shall we see you here again?"

"Perhaps, perhaps," Josef said, bowing and hastening for the exit.

As he turned about, however, a great shadow filled the doorway, blocking his passage. Looking up, he saw Bariath looming over him, and with a gasp he pushed past him.

It seemed the Philistine had not recognized him. As he sped across the courtyard, Delilah cried out, "Bariath, you must meet my friend!"

But Josef had already untethered his donkey and was heading for Zorah.

"What a funny little man," Delilah mused, joining Bariath in the lobby. Leaning out, she watched the guest's quick departure and shook her head. "What a funny, fascinating little man."

PART SEVEN

Samson
and Delilah

ONE

*A*lthough Marissa was a seamstress, there was no long mirror in her cottage shop wherein customers might view themselves in her handmade gowns. The slabs of polished copper that royalty were privileged to hang in their halls and bedchambers for viewing themselves were unknown in common households.

Today the seamstress used a small hand mirror, raising and lowering it to view her appearance at different angles. She relied on the word of Rena and several women friends who had come to view her in her wedding dress.

"Oh, Marissa!" the younger women cried. "Your mother would be so proud to see you! How old were you when she began making this gown for you?"

"I was just a girl," she replied, twirling before them so that the linen fanned out from her long legs in brilliant waves. "She purchased the fabric from an Indian merchant and used to sit before the fire many a night embroidering it."

The women knew that Marissa's mother died not long after her bas mitzvah. They also knew that the daughter had taken up the task of working on the gown herself from that day on.

"How glad she would be to know that you will marry Samson!" they declared. "What a prize you have won!"

At this, they giggled like young girls and embraced Rena, the groom's mother.

The bride-to-be stopped her spinning, lifting her hands to her flushed face. "He *is* wonderful, isn't he?" she sighed.

As if her heart would burst for joy, she took a deep breath and turned for the window, casting her gaze up the highway that wound out of town toward Hebron.

Every day for days now, wagons filled with food and wine for the wedding and gifts for the bride had arrived in the village, sent from the judge's palace.

Visitors from all over Israel had reserved rooms in the town's small inn. The oasis outside the village would be the campground for hundreds of pilgrims, and most of Zorah's citizens had booked spare rooms for renters.

The festivities that would accompany this wedding were the talk of the region, and everyone for miles around, commoners and aristocrats alike, looked forward to the gala event.

"Will Samson be arriving much before the wedding?" Rena inquired.

"Only the night before," Marissa said, taking the old woman's hand. "He will be going to Sorek before he comes here, for his second meeting with the Philistines."

All of Israel had heard of the strides Samson was making toward peace with the Philistines. Since Bariath had invited him to continue their peace talks, Samson would probably enter married life heralded not only as a mighty judge and warrior, but as the greatest diplomat in many a generation.

Starstruck, the women gathered about Marissa, gazing with her up the road. "You are about to be the wife of the leader of Israel!" one of them said. "How we will miss you when you move to Hebron!"

Turning to them, Marissa gazed fondly upon each radiant face, especially Rena, who was like a mother to her. "I will come home often!" she promised. "Zorah will always be my home."

Embracing, the women stood in a silent huddle, until Marissa pulled back, tears glistening upon her face. "Be happy for me, dear sisters!" she said with a smile. "All of you are wives and mothers. In only one week, I also shall have a family, the husband I have always wanted!"

TWO

*W*hile Marissa and the town of Zorah made preparations for the wedding, another woman and another town were preparing for Samson's coming as well.

It had been a month since Josef had sat with Delilah beside the inn fire, revealing to her the nature of Israel's judge. In all that time, she had scarcely passed a waking hour without turning his words over and over in her mind.

Tomorrow Samson would confer with the mighty men of Philistia—beneath her very roof. If only Delilah might get him alone, she could use the keys Josef had given her to unlock the strongman's heart and draw him to herself.

Meanwhile, she was obliged to entertain her paramour, Bariath. She knew she must be careful, once again, not to let on how she thought of Samson. But if she used her wiles to best advantage, Bariath would actually end up facilitating her efforts.

With the patience of a female spider, Delilah had spent the past weeks spinning a cunning web. At first the only threads of that web had been the bits of information Josef had given her. Then, as the time drew closer for the judge to visit Philistia, the snare had taken firmer shape—and the spinner had grown ever more certain that her intended victim would fly directly into it.

Clever spider that she was, she had reserved a place for Bariath in her web. He would be the unwitting doorkeeper, the one to lead Samson into the trap and spread it wide before him. And all the while, he would think he did himself a favor.

Quietly Delilah laid out her plot, never saying a word to Bariath of her intentions. Tomorrow the trap would be tested, and everything depended on how she handled the intervening hours.

Bariath came to her this evening in a merry mood. He looked forward to tomorrow's conference, believing that it would be the turning point for Philistia's economic future. If he could make the right concessions, if he could get Samson to lower trade embargoes and establish a military moratorium, he would be hailed the savior of his country.

It was this very goal that Delilah must undermine if she was to achieve her own. She must make Bariath doubt that his plans were best for Philistia and for himself.

"What is this I feel in your shoulders, my love?" Delilah cooed as she ran massaging fingers over Bariath's muscled back. "My love is not tense, but neither is he relaxed," she deduced. "Ah, Bariath, you are full of anticipation, full of excitement."

"Right, as always," Bariath replied, turning over on the bed and facing her as she bent above him. "You read my body like most women read a face or a voice," he said, drawing her to his bosom. "Yes, I am excited! Tomorrow will be an historic day!"

At this, Delilah pulled back, sitting on the edge of the bed with a well-timed look of disappointment.

"What is it?" Bariath asked. "You don't agree?"

Delilah shrugged her shoulders and gave a wan smile. "I can understand how you would look forward to tomorrow," she said. "It is just . . . well, I can recall when Bariath would not have been so eager to give away his power."

Frowning, the giant sat up beside her. "Give up my power?" he grumbled. "I shall always be the most powerful man in Philistia!"

Delilah stood and walked to her dressing table, tinkering with the vials and potions arranged there. "In Philistia, yes," she replied.

Bariath bristled. "Delilah, I don't like your tone!" he growled.

The woman looked at the foot of the bed, avoiding his scowl like a pouting child. "Oh, love . . . ," she said faintly, "it is just that I remember better times. Times when you were content with nothing less than all the power in the world!"

Wounded, Bariath lay down again, placing his fingers upon his throbbing temples. "Can't you be happy for me?" he groaned. "Tomorrow we will gain for our country new prosperity. It is all planned, what will be said, and who will say it. All the chieftains are in agreement. We have fought Samson for years, all to no avail. What more can we do than we have done?"

With a sigh, Delilah shook her head. "Nothing, I suppose. You are right." Sitting at her table, she stared vacantly into her hand mirror.

"It is very sad," she added, "that no one knows the secret of Samson's great power. Strange, don't you think, that after all these years no wise man of Philistia's court and no priest of Dagon's temple has deciphered its source?"

Bariath turned over upon the bed, as if to shut out her jabs. "The Jews say it is the God of Israel who gives the man his strength!" he quipped. "Who can wrestle against an unseen god?"

This sarcastic comment alluded to the gulf of difference between Philistine notions of deity and the Jews' unique theology. Among all the nations of the earth, only the Jews believed in an invisible, all-powerful Creator. Every other race clung to deities of limited power, whose moods were more fickle than those of human beings, who could be wooed and placated, whose demands were often gruesome, and who were symbolized in idols of stone and bronze.

But Delilah was not put off by Bariath's reminder.

"How silly!" she snapped, wheeling on him. Leaving her little bench she joined him on the bed, glaring down at him with surprising contempt. "You know nothing can be that simple! Why, the ancient giants of Canaan got their strength from the milk and honey of the land. The titans of Greece drank from the waters of Olympus and grew mighty! Surely there is some tangible secret to Samson's power!"

Suddenly intrigued, Bariath thought hard on her words.

"All right," he conceded. "Say that there is such a secret. Who in Philistia would be wise enough to unravel it?"

Delilah had not expected the entrée to her next suggestion to come so easily. For a moment, she hesitated to answer.

"Don't you think, dear lady, that our priests and magicians have pondered your very question? I am certain they have spent many an hour dwelling upon this mystery!"

"Ah," the woman replied, punctuating the air with a pointed finger, "but have they ever gone directly to the source for their information? Has anyone in Palestine asked *Samson* the nature of his power?"

At this, Bariath drew back, giving a baffled laugh. "Have you lost your mind?" he cried. "You think Samson would be so foolish as to reveal such matters to his enemies?"

"His enemies?" Delilah rolled her eyes. "Of course not! But, to a friend, or to someone who seems a friend . . . perhaps."

Propping himself on one elbow, Bariath studied the schemer in bewilderment. "You know of such a person?" he asked.

"I think so," she answered. "At least I think I can manufacture one."

More confused than ever, Bariath listened, his heart a muddle.

Eagerly, she proceeded, giving him no time to quibble.

"You know Samson has a weakness for women," she said. "All Israel and all Philistia know this. If I had the chance, just once, to be with him . . . "

Bariath lurched upright. "What are you saying?" he shouted. "No, Delilah! I shall not allow it!"

Placing a hand on her throat, Delilah pretended shock at this reaction.

"Why, Bariath," she whimpered, "can it be you doubt my devotion? Surely, you can't believe I find the jackal . . . attractive!"

This last word was said with a shudder.

Drawing close, Bariath ran a hand down her long arm. "There, there," he said, "I am sorry. It is just that . . . you are *my woman,* Delilah. I have sat by, silent about your many indiscretions. But this . . . this I could not abide!"

Never in the history of their relationship had Bariath drawn such a line. Part of her was flattered, but another part knew it showed how vulnerable he was to her every wish.

"Why, love," she answered, "how sweet you are!"

Then, with a lift of the chin, she rose from the bed and walked again to her table, where she ran a gilded comb through her hair. In her mirror she could see her lover, lying long-faced upon the bed.

It would be only a matter of time before he reconsidered. Surely, even now he did so.

By morning, he would see the wisdom of her suggestion. And by tomorrow evening, she would be entertaining Samson in the very place where Bariath himself now reclined.

THREE

*B*ariath stood before the fireplace of Sorek Inn, sweating not from the heat of the flames, but from anxiety. Facing the long room, he greeted the seranim, their guards, and many attendants who assembled there, calling each by name and trying to appear enthusiastic. Behind him his clammy hands fidgeted, his fingers knotting and unknotting.

Just last evening, he had been eager for the day to begin. He had imagined hailing his fellow Philistines, the heads of the Pentapolis, with hearty salutes. Now that the hour had come, he was not the confident man who had knocked on Delilah's chamber door.

All night long, he had tossed and turned on the bed he shared with his mistress. She, seemingly asleep despite his thrashing, had made no further mention of a rendezvous with Samson.

But the idea had caused no end of torment for Bariath.

Could it be that Delilah's suggestion was a wise one? Perhaps the Philistines were giving in too easily to the dominion of Israel. Perhaps one more attempt should be made to undo the strongman.

But what if the setup failed? What if, despite Delilah's charms, Samson made no slip and nothing whatsoever was learned about his power? Could such an interlude interfere with the peace talks already begun?

And even if no harm came to the nation, was Bariath willing to allow his lady a night of passion with the legendary judge?

Over and over these questions had played through Bariath's head. When dawn at last arrived, the sleepless wrestler had greeted the day with swollen eyes and an aching heart.

His concern for Philistia, however, coupled with his weakness for Delilah's every whim, had set him on an irreversible course. Though he still struggled, he knew that the agenda he was about to lay out for the council would be a surprising reversal.

As his friends, decked in long robes and ceremonial turbans, took seats at the polished tables and hoisted goblets in salutation, he gave a stiff bow.

"Gentlemen! Gentlemen!" he hailed them, raising his hands. "This is a momentous day for our beloved country, a great day for the king and for Dagon!"

Again the goblets were lifted, this time to a round of cheers.

"At noon," he continued, "the judge of Israel will sit among us. The destiny of Philistia rises or falls upon what we do this day!"

With enthusiastic nods, the seranim showed their unanimity, not knowing that Bariath was about to turn their plans inside out.

As the huzzah tapered, Bariath shuffled.

"We have only a few hours to go over everything," the prince of Ashdod called out. "I, for one, want a rehearsal!"

"Hear, hear!" the others agreed.

"Very well," Bariath answered. "It is wise to go over matters for negotiation."

"Never shall we surrender Gaza!" the chief of that city declared.

"Right!" the others cheered.

"And the port of Ashkelon shall not be compromised!" cried the master of that region.

"The copper miners are eager for trade," said Siloam of Gerar, "but never will we reveal the secret of our iron!"

All of this had been aired before, through the weeks since Bariath had ventured to Hebron, and for months previous. "On these matters, we are all agreed," he replied. "We have stipulated which forts shall remain secure and which shall be open to the Israelis. We have discussed the need for wheat from Israel, and our willingness to trade glass from the coast. Each of you is to represent his own city and his own province in the matters pertaining to them."

Taking a deep breath, Bariath scanned the audience. Hesitating over what to say next, he was caught by a movement on the mezzanine, and glancing up, he saw that Delilah had appeared, standing in the shadows of the columns.

No one else had seen her, but he knew she listened to every word. He knew what she expected of him, and he swallowed hard.

"Now, gentlemen," he said with a dry throat, "I have a question for you. Are we satisfied that all of our options have been considered?"

Looking at one another, the men shrugged. "Options?" they muttered. "What do you mean, Bariath?"

Shooting another glance at the gallery, the governor ran his tongue over his lips. "I am only saying," he went on, "that as much as we want peace with Israel—and no one wants it more than I, gentlemen—let us be certain there is no hope of regaining our lordship over Palestine!"

As the audience murmured over this, shaking their heads in surprise and consternation, Bariath began reasoning with them in terms similar to those Delilah had used with him the night before.

"Just as the Israelis have sought in vain to know the secret of our iron," he said, "so Philistia has, for years, wondered what mystery lies behind the strength of Samson! If only we could solve that puzzle, we might be able to come against him."

This no one could deny. But what purpose was served in pondering the impossible?

"What is your point?" someone demanded. "We cannot afford meaningless conversation!"

"That is true," Bariath replied. "Neither can we afford to make concessions, so long as there is a shred of hope that the old Philistia can be revived!"

"Can you show us such hope?" another cried. "We would be happy to see it!"

Laughing, the crowd scorned Bariath as he tried to bring order. When Delilah emerged from the shadows, standing in full view upon the gallery, the audience was stunned to silence.

Never had they seen the famed temptress look so ravishing. Bedecked in a black velvet gown, her bodice sparkling with golden lace and slit to the waist with a criss-cross of narrow chains, she posed long and luscious upon the balcony. Her elegant figure was framed by a cape of wine red satin, and her shoulders mantled with tumbling curls. Each curl, in turn, was spun with gold, and between the curls were intricate braids, intertwined with fine scarlet threads.

Leaning against the rail, she dipped in a fleeting bow and then stood erect, creating an effect of sheer feminine superiority. At the sight, not one heart below beat in normal rhythm.

Hardly allowing her dark eyes to touch the crowd, she gazed across the room, permitting herself to be worshipped.

Many a man here had known her most intimate charms, and at the vision of her, they relived them. Certainly, most of the seranim had stayed with her on occasion, and though they were devoted to Bariath, they recalled vividly the magic of his woman.

Bariath, knowing this, had always solaced himself with the notion that, despite her "career," she was his. Now he was about to risk even that fantasy in the hopes of assuring her continued devotion.

Had he been sane, he would have realized the irony of such reasoning. But when it came to Delilah, he was far from sane.

"Gentlemen," he announced, "our lady, Delilah!"

In mass, the audience bowed, showing their unrivaled appreciation for the matchless beauty.

"You ask who has the power to entice Samson's secret from him?" Bariath cried. "When all the priests and magi of the king's court have failed, give the assignment to Delilah!"

Astonished, the men studied the vamp on the balcony. Why had they never thought of this before?

A thrill of whispers became a gale of applause. And the gale became an enthusiastic storm. Siloam stepped forward, the light of victory on his face.

"Good Bariath!" Siloam declared. "Many a fellow here has parted with a tidy sum for an hour in this lady's presence. Over the years, you have shared her generously."

Bariath received this with grace, trying not to cringe.

"And dear woman," Siloam went on, "for the sake of Philistia, we are willing to pay you a life's wages! Entice Samson, dear lady! See where his great strength lies, and how we may overpower him. Then we will each give you eleven hundred pieces of silver, each of us from the treasury of his own city!"

At this offer, Delilah faltered in her regal pose. Knees trembling, she gripped the rail. All she had wanted was Samson. To be paid to have him was beyond all expectation.

Regaining her composure, she tried to appear sacrificial. "You are kind," she said. "For Philistia and for the king, I accept your offer."

Then, turning about, she left the gallery, disappearing down the hall.

With hot eyes, Bariath watched her exit . . . and wondered if she would ever be his again.

FOUR

*H*ad anyone ever flown as high as Samson flew tonight? In the history of humankind, had anyone ever known the praise of men, the adoration of women, the favor of God, and the riches of this world as Samson knew them?

At this moment, seated at the head table of a banquet befitting a king, seated in the presence of his enemies and receiving their open adulation, he thought not.

The great feast, laid out on the gleaming table of Sorek Inn, was almost ended. It followed a day of what appeared to be the most successful negotiations two contending peoples had ever achieved. Although Philistia still bowed the knee to Israel, her seranim seemed overjoyed that Samson would shortly lift embargoes against them, and that the terms drawn up before he arrived had been largely accepted.

But not the least of Samson's personal satisfactions was the fact that by the end of the week, he would take Marissa, his bride, to Hebron, to dwell with him in the honor and luxury of his high station.

Were he not so wary of his enemies, it would have been easy, this night, to like them. Certainly they had been hospitable since he had arrived, even preparing a lunch in accordance with his Nazarite vows and offering him no wine to drink. All precautions had been taken to make him feel comfortable in their company, and it was evident that they had researched just what it meant to be a Nazarite.

As the feast ended, Samson felt it would do no harm to join them in a toast. This was surely a special occasion, and the Philistines were delighted when the Israeli lifted a cup with them.

Having lived among the Philistines, Samson knew that no feast was complete until music and entertainment had been offered. As the cups were lowered, a little band of pipers and drummers started up in a corner of the hall. Servants ran about the room, snuffing out candles and wall torches until the light was low and relaxing.

Feeling quite secure, Samson laughed and smiled with the others when a woman appeared, swirling and swaying before them in a flourish of veils and trinkets. Upon her fingers she wore little bells, which she clapped together in rhythm with the music, while bracelets and chains upon her arms and ankles made music of their own.

Her dance was modest, no more suggestive than that of the Jewish maidens who danced at bar mitzvahs and weddings. Her face was covered by one long scarf, suspended from a headpiece and revealing only her dark eyes. If she was as comely as her eyes suggested, she was a marvel.

Samson knew the dance was circumspect in deference to his presence. He knew, having dwelt in this culture, that the purpose of a Philistine dancing girl was to arouse the drinking revelers. It was a credit to the hosts, Samson thought, that they had instructed her to show restraint.

Happily, this part of the evening would soon end. Samson would retire to his room on the gallery and would sleep with dreams of Marissa. Tomorrow morning, he would rise for a few more hours of conference, and then he would depart for Zorah.

Taking one last sip of wine, he tried to engage Bariath in conversation.

But the chieftain had had much more to drink than he, and he seemed lost in the dancer's swaying gestures. The more Samson attempted small talk, the more Bariath directed his attention to the woman.

Little did this trouble the Israeli, until the dancer fixed her gaze upon him. Her eyes, staying with him regardless of the way her body turned, were haunting, and despite her discrete motions, her expression was blatantly erotic.

Samson distracted himself by listening to nearby conversations, by tapping his toe to the music, by studying the activities of servants who cleared the tables. But whenever he glanced up at the dancer, she was studying him with a provocative, maddening gaze.

"Is she not a wonder?" Bariath said at last, leaning close. "I count it among my greatest treasures that she is mine."

"Yours?" Samson laughed. "Does the lady Delilah know about her?"

Bariath was not offended by the question. Philistine chieftains were notorious philanderers.

"Does she *know?*" he hooted. "Dear fellow, that *is* Delilah!"

When Samson observed the woman in silent shock, the chieftain moved in closer. "She will be entertaining us privately when the feast is over," he said. "Dessert will be served in her chamber."

Unprepared for this announcement, Samson fumbled for a reply. "Your offer is kind," he managed to say. "But it has been a long day. Perhaps another time . . . "

"Nonsense," Bariath objected. "Delilah owns this inn, you know. We must not insult her hospitality."

Sinking into his couch, Samson pretended not to notice as the dancer spun and twirled directly before him. "You are most kind," he repeated, focusing on Bariath. "But I can stay no more than a few moments. I face a long journey tomorrow."

FIVE

*T*he lamps of Delilah's chamber were subdued, but the small huddle of revelers gathered about her table made lively conversation. As the evening wore on, Samson wondered why he had been uneasy about joining Bariath and his lady for this private hour.

When he arrived, he had found, to his relief, that he was not the only guest at the little finale. Two of Bariath's fellow Philistines were present, Siloam of Gerar and Baldod of Gaza. Just now, the four men sparred happily over a board game, which Delilah had set up for them. Small figures of black marble and white ivory challenged one another upon the inlaid squares of an alabaster slab. Carved in the shapes of soldiers and horses, they hopped about the squares as their masters chose, and at the moment, the team of Bariath and Samson was in the lead.

Off to each side of the board, a small pile of ivory chips, varying in value, represented the gains and losses of each team. As a side lost a holding, it placed a chip in the opponents' pile, and when it lost all of its chips, or when it chose to concede, the game would be ended.

Bariath and Samson smiled broadly as Baldod reached for the largest of his chips, ready to hand it over.

"But that chip represents Gaza!" Bariath hooted. "You swore you would never give it up!"

This was, of course, a teasing reference to the day's negotiations, wherein Philistia had retained its capital city, while Israel had taken rights to half the profits of the port city of Ashkelon.

Placing the chip in Bariath's pile, Baldod grimaced. But his laugh was good natured. "It is a good thing this is only a game," he chuckled.

During the contest, Delilah sat quietly beside her paramour. Samson, trying to pay her no mind, kept his thoughts to the board. But just now she leaned forward, studying the board and whispering tactics in Bariath's ear. As she did, Samson felt her gaze upon him and saw, from the corner of his eye, how her deep-cut bodice caressed her bosom and how her lips shone in the lamplight.

As he caught her vampish smile, the old uneasiness returned. He remembered how he had steered clear of her when she came to Hebron, and he felt it best to continue now with the same policy.

"Baldod," Samson quipped, "if you care to relinquish a port or two with that chip, I'll be happy to take them."

"The game is not over," the prince replied, setting up the figures for another round.

At this, Delilah rose and crossed the room, bringing a carafe of wine to the table. "Dear Baldod," she soothed, "I am certain Samson will be as considerate of you tonight as he was at the conference." Pouring cool red liquid into the prince's goblet, she glanced at the judge. "You don't really want his old chips, do you, Samson?" she teased. "From what Bariath tells me, you are reasonable as well as powerful."

This was the first time since Samson's arrival in Sorek that the woman had spoken to him. In fact, her appearance at supper in a dancer's veil had been his first glimpse of her since she had visited Hebron.

"I am pleased that my reputation precedes me," Samson answered.

But Delilah had only begun to make her approach. "And honorable, too," she cooed. "Why, most men of your achievement will take whatever they can get, even if it belongs to someone else."

Looking up, Samson wondered if he was the only one suspicious of her meaning. When Bariath leaned back, stretching and yawning, and when the others only tinkered with the game pieces, he decided to say nothing.

Delilah sidled to his corner of the table, picking up his goblet and beginning to fill it. "Enough," he stopped her, raising a hand. "I shall have no more tonight."

Cocking an eyebrow, she set the cup down and turned to Bariath. As she ran her hands over her lover's shoulders, he again gave an enormous yawn, and the other men, as if on cue, did the same.

"Shall we finish the game in the morning?" Bariath suggested. "I will see you to your rooms, gentlemen."

Relieved at the offer, Samson stood up, ready to head for the door.

"Not so fast, Samson," Bariath chuckled, taking him by the arm and seating him again. "I will escort my friends, and then I shall return for one last toast. Wait here for me."

Speechless, Samson watched the men exit, going numb as Bariath shut the door. Suddenly, without warning and against his better judgment, he was left alone with Delilah.

As she began to clear the table, there was a gleam in her eyes that made him shiver.

"So," she said, her voice low and suggestive, "we are a pair."

"Not for long," Samson corrected.

"Of course," she whispered, wiping the table with a damp cloth.

Where were her servants? Samson wondered. Surely Delilah did not normally do such menial tasks. Nervous, the judge watched the door and the yellow line of light at the floor, hoping to see a shadow, hoping to hear Bariath's footstep.

He did not see that Delilah watched his reaction, that she knew his fears and counted on them.

As if filling time, she made conversation. "I met a friend of yours the other day," she said.

"Oh?" Samson replied, slowly sitting down. "Who could that be?"

"Funny," she laughed, taking a seat across from him. "I never caught his name. I am certain I asked it, but he never said."

Barely hearing her, Samson drummed his fingers on the table, listening for Bariath's voice.

"He was from your hometown," she continued. "A peculiar little fellow . . . "

This Samson did hear, and it troubled him. Darting a wary glance at the woman, he focused on the description.

"Go on," he said.

"Oh, it is nothing," she demurred. "But I found him interesting because he spoke of you."

"He did?" the judge said with a shrug. "I hope he was kind."

"Most kind!" she assured him. "What a darling little man, and how he loves you, Samson! Why he told me things about you that only the closest brother could know." At this, she lifted a hand to her bosom, feigning modesty. "I don't know why he privileged me with such secrets," she sighed.

This last word troubled Samson more than the fear that it was Josef she had met.

"Secrets?" he croaked.

"Well . . . ," she rephrased, "let's call them . . . insights."

Standing, Samson paced the sumptuous room, glancing over and over again at the door. "Why should my lady care for 'insights' on a stranger?" he asked. "I can be nothing more to you than your lover's enemy."

Delilah held up a glass goblet and watched him through the scarlet contents.

"You are not our enemy any longer, are you, Samson?" she asked. "As of today, you are our friend."

"Very well," he muttered, running his hands down his cloak. "So what did the fellow have to say?"

"Only that you are not so gruff . . . so cold a man as you seemed at Hebron. You *were* cold, don't you know?"

Stopping his pacing, Samson bowed stiffly to her. "I never meant to be unkind," he said.

"Oh, it is all right." Delilah smiled. "The little man helped me to see why you were."

Bristling, Samson stood rigid in the center of the room. Josef's sinister face flashed to mind, and he almost heard him hissing in the chamber's purple shadows.

"Whoever this fellow was, and whatever he told you, he is a liar!" Samson spat. When the words were out, he knew how foolish they sounded.

"Why, Samson," Delilah countered with a pout, joining him in the dim light. "How can you know this, when you do not know his words? What he said was most flattering to me, and now I am disillusioned."

She had come quite close as she said this and now stood directly before him, so that if he looked down he would feel her breath upon his face.

"I meant no offense," he said evasively. Pulling away, he went to the window and gazed out upon the wintry courtyard. Dead leaves skittered across the pavement, chattering like gossips. "What exactly did he say?"

Following Samson to the window, Delilah pushed the shutters wide. "He told me that you fear beautiful women because you fear yourself," she said matter-of-factly. "He told me that you fear me because you do not trust yourself."

Scarcely believing her audacity, Samson snorted and pulled away again. "Do you believe every fool who tickles your ego?" he laughed. Walking quickly to the table, he lifted his goblet and drained it of its last dribble. "To you," he said, tipping it. "There's our toast. Good night, my lady."

Heading for the door, he almost made his exit, when Delilah called to him. "My lord Bariath will be unhappy if you leave," she warned. "Would you risk the peace talks to escape me?"

"Escape you?" he said marveling. "Have you laid a trap, my lady? In that case, I am wise to escape!"

Delilah grimaced, fearing that she had miscalculated. Resorting to bigger weapons, she looked at the floor, assuming a wounded aspect.

"See," she said, "it is as your friend said. You fear me because I am beautiful. Why is it that I can never be a man's confidant and not his plaything? Do you know how lonely that makes me? To never have companionship of mind with a man I respect?"

Turning her back, she appeared to tremble.

Never in a thousand years would Samson have thought he could pity Delilah. Yet it seemed he had hurt her, and he was sorry.

"Dear lady," he stammered, "I did not understand . . . I thought . . . "

"Oh," she sighed, "I know. We are two of a kind. Women have loved you for your . . . body. Just as men have loved me only for mine." Looking languidly at him, she purred, "And so we settle, don't we, Samson? We settle for people who are beneath us, who can never give us what we really need."

Listening to her, Samson was bewildered. Did she speak of his past? Surely so. For it could not be Marissa she referred to. Marissa was good and holy, the fulfillment of all he had ever longed for.

Lifting his chin, Samson gazed upon her with greater pity than before. "You speak well, my lady," he said. "I have been the victim of such people. But those days are behind me."

Wiping a glint of tears from her eyes, Delilah took a deep breath and smiled vaguely at him. "Truly?" she sighed. "Then you have found what I am still seeking. You go to Zorah to be wed, I hear. She must be an angel, your betrothed."

"She is," Samson agreed, not seeing the spark that flew from the woman's eyes.

"I am happy for you," she lied. "To have a woman of great beauty, and greatness of soul . . . is an honor and a blessing."

As she spoke, she drew near again, and before he knew it, she was toe to toe with him. All this talk of Marissa seemed out of place in her presence. As Delilah lifted her tear-stained face, he struggled against the feelings she aroused.

"Tell me," Delilah pleaded, pulling his hand to her cheek, "does your lady reach every facet of your heart? Is she your equal, my lord, in every way?"

"She is," Samson said weakly.

But Delilah persisted, raising his fingers to her lips and letting his reluctant hand fall to the neck of her gown, where it rested, trembling upon her warm flesh.

"You are worthy of the best," she whispered. "Be certain you have it, Samson."

Groaning, Samson moved again for the door. "You do lay a trap, Delilah. I shall not fall into it!"

Moving swiftly, yet without seeming to hurry, she squeezed between him and the exit, her bosom heaving and her sweet perfume making him lightheaded.

Overcome, Samson wavered. As though he was carried by a fierce current against which his legendary strength was useless, he let his hand travel down her curvaceous side. As she held herself against him, he leaned his head down toward her. Then, with a groan of surrender, he pressed his lips to hers, feeding hungrily upon them like a man who had never before known a woman.

SIX

*I*t would be a lie to say Samson did not enjoy his night of folly with the Philistine vamp, Delilah.

From the moment he sensed Delilah's plot, he could have called a halt to the seduction. Foreseeing the consequences to himself, his pending marriage, and his people, he could have rebuked the temptation.

But once he took his first kiss, he was Delilah's captive.

Arising from her bed the next morning, Samson stumbled to the window, as though seeking someone to blame for his blunder. In the past, he could point to Josef. But Josef was not here, nor had he seen him for many years.

Samson knew that the little weasel had had a hand in this affair. He had undoubtedly laid the groundwork for Delilah's provocative presentation. But the Nazarite could have seen through her . . . *had* seen through her. Yet he had fallen. Some would say he had fallen in love; others would call it mere passion. Whatever it was, his heart was in danger.

Upon Delilah's dressing table was her hand mirror. Reaching for it, Samson raised it to his face and smirked at his own reflection. "Fool!" he muttered, his teeth gritted in a sneer.

What should he do now? Return to Marissa, take her pure hand in his and call her "wife"? Surely not! Could he return to Hebron and take up the sacred mantle, calling himself "judge and counselor"? Ludicrous!

"Shame is too good for you!" he rebuked the image in the mirror.

Just then, a knock on Delilah's parlor door jolted him. Returning the mirror to the table, he rushed to the bed and grabbed his clothes, which were strewn across the foot.

"Someone is here!" he cried, rousing Delilah. "Where can I hide?"

As he looked breathlessly about for a closet or nook to duck into, the woman sat up with a bemused smile.

"Love," she said, "what are you doing? It is only Bariath."

In wide-eyed terror, Samson groaned, *"Only* Bariath? Are you mad? Where can I go?"

Like a frightened jackal, the Nazarite was about to scoot beneath the bed, but there was not room for his massive frame.

Tickled, Delilah watched his scrambles.

"Calm down, Samson," she giggled. "Don't you think Bariath knows about us?"

The Israeli cringed. "He will have my neck!" he cried. As he scurried to get dressed, she pulled on her robe and went nonchalantly to the bedroom door.

"Come in," she called across the parlor. Leaving Samson to fend for himself, she greeted Bariath in the outer room.

His heart drumming, Samson pulled on his sandals, losing his balance as he did so and nearly falling on his face.

From the parlor he heard Bariath's voice. "Up so late, my lady? Go ahead and get dressed. We'll wait for you here."

We? Samson went numb. Bariath was not alone!

Samson cracked the door and peeked into the parlor. To his horror, Siloam and all the seranim were there, taking seats and chatting casually.

"Perhaps you should help the sleepyhead," Bariath told the woman, nodding to the bedroom door. "We should get started."

A shock ran through the Nazarite. Bariath *did* know! As Samson stood shaking behind the door, he noted that there seemed to be no disapproval in Bariath's tone. An edge of impatience, perhaps, but no discernible anger.

Just then, Delilah came to fetch the Israeli.

Finding him quivering in the shadows, she put her hands on her hips and shook her head. "Hurry, love," she sighed. "They are waiting."

"What?" Samson gasped. "They are meeting here? In your parlor?"

"It is convenient," she replied.

As Samson pulled on his vest, lacing it across his mighty chest, Delilah slipped up behind him and put her arms about his waist.

"You will be so happy you stayed with me! Bariath says that because we have gotten such a late start today, your conference will not be finished until tomorrow! Isn't that wonderful, love? We will have another night in paradise, you and I!"

"What?" Samson cried, wheeling on her. "You know that is impossible! I am due in Zorah!"

Downcast, Delilah pouted, fingering the belt Samson tied about his hard waist. "For your wedding . . . ," she whispered. "I know, Samson."

Not to be taken in again, Samson turned from her and secured his sandal straps around his muscular calves.

"But," Delilah sighed, "we have such a merry time planned for today! I have spoken with the seranim. They have agreed that we should mix pleasure with business. Oh, Samson," she flirted, "I have planned a grand game for all of us to play, just after lunch!"

Scowling, Samson shook his head and drew on his cloak. "I have no time for games, Delilah," he growled. "The conference will take no time at all, and I shall be on my way."

Holding him by the arm, Delilah pleaded, "You don't even want to hear about the game?" As she looked up into his averted eyes, she waited for him to soften. And when he turned her way, she fluttered her long lashes like a child. Images of their time together flooded his mind, and his emotions threatened to engulf him. He must not stay! Yet he could not risk offending Bariath and the others with a hasty departure.

"Very well," he conceded. "What is this game?"

Clapping her hands like a small girl, Delilah cried, "Oh, you will love it! It is something like the board game you played with Bariath and the others. Yet, instead of giving chips away, the loser gives something of his own, something of value. And instead of being played upon a board, it is played with real men!"

Despite his resolve not to be involved, Samson was intrigued. "Real men?"

"And women!" Delilah giggled. "Why, you might win me for good!"

His heart lurched, but he suppressed it. Heading for the door, he called, "Well, it is a shame I shall not be here for this contest. It does sound challenging."

As he stepped into Delilah's little parlor, he was greeted by the waiting seranim.

"Gentlemen," he said with a bow, "good day. Shall we get down to business?"

In the center of the parlor was the same polished table at which they had played the board game. It was uncluttered, save for a few scrolls on which were the terms agreed to thus far between the conference delegates.

Samson seated himself just as Delilah entered from the bedchamber. As the seranim bowed to her, she slipped up to Bariath, her lower lip trembling.

"What is it, my lady?" Bariath asked, taking her hand in his.

"I have tried to be a good hostess," she complained. "But Samson says he will not stay past lunch. I guess our little party is canceled."

Looking dreadfully offended, Bariath turned to Samson; his fellow seranim, appearing equally insulted, gathered about the table, glaring down upon the Israeli.

"Did our lady not please you?" Baldod asked.

"Has your time with us been unhappy?" Siloam echoed.

"Why . . . no," Samson stammered, amazed at their reaction. "Delilah has been . . . kind."

Glancing across the room, he saw that the lady stood with her head bowed, as though she would cry.

Was it possible he could risk all the progress made at the peace talks by simply skipping a party?

His throat dry, he fidgeted with the scrolls. "I suppose I can stay past lunch," he offered. "But no longer."

When the others applauded, and when Delilah's face beamed, he sighed with relief. Ignoring his fearful heart, he assured himself that he could resist Delilah for a few hours.

"This game," he asked, "what is it called?"

"Oh," Delilah said enthusiastically, "you will love it, Samson! It is called 'Who is the Strongest?' How can you lose?"

═══ SEVEN ═══

*T*hat afternoon, Samson was tested by his Philistine companions in a game that followed a set pattern of question and answer, trial and error, bondage and escape.

According to the rules, the Philistines had four chances to find out just how strong their opponent was. This, they said, was finding the "secret" of a man's strength. Each round of the game consisted of the challengers posing a question, wherein they asked the opponent if he might be bound by this or that so that he could not break free. The opponent had to decide when to allow himself to be bound as his challengers suggested.

Once a trial was accepted, the challengers would depart, and the opponent would be bound. Then, when the binder gave the cue, "The Philistines are upon you!" the challengers would reenter to take their captive.

At that time, the opponent, if he was able, should break free from his bonds, for doing so would win him a shekel from each challenger, and the next round would begin. Should the opponent fail to break free, the roles of challenger and opponent would be reversed, and it would be another player's turn to show his own strength.

Whoever had accumulated the most money when everyone had been tried would take every other player's pot.

There was one way to win more, however: any man who could pass four rounds without being held could name his own reward.

As Delilah had said, the stakes could be high, and the game pieces were the men themselves.

But, for Samson, the contest was predictable and boring so that his focus continually drifted to Delilah.

For the first round, Delilah posed the prescribed question. "Please tell me, Samson, what is the secret of your strength? If you were tied with seven fresh bowstrings, would you be held?"

How endearing she can be! Samson thought. Glancing at the seranim, who gathered at her back, he chuckled.

"If I were tied with seven fresh bowstrings that have not been dried," he said, rolling his eyes, "I would become as weak as any other man."

"Very well," Baldod replied, "so it shall be."

Leaving the room, the seranim sent a servant to bring the seven bowstrings, and in no time, Delilah had Samson bound in a chair. Laughing and giggling, she danced around him, twining the strings in and out of the chair's rails and creating intricate knots behind his back.

"Isn't this fun!" she said, a radiant smile on her face. "But I don't believe it will hold you, dear Samson!"

When she was done, she cried out for the men who waited in the parlor, "Samson, the Philistines are upon you! The Philistines are upon you!"

Taking the cue, which was all part of the game, the seranim came forth, but before they so much as threw open the door, Samson snapped his bonds like so many threads. And he stood before them, free of the worthless trap.

Laughing and clapping him on the back, the challengers congratulated him. Samson could scarcely believe they found this entertaining.

Following a round of drinks, the next episode of the game began, and Samson was again seated in the chair, enduring his challengers' second vain attempt.

"Hold still, love!" Delilah whimpered. "Must you be so headstrong?"

"Woman, it is a silly game! What is the point?" Samson growled. "Unless the seranim find a way to bind me so that I cannot break free, they will not win a thing!"

"I know!" Delilah cried, as she wrapped seven new ropes about his wrists. "But if they fail three more times to find a way to hold you, you may ask what you want, and they will be obliged to give it to you!"

Clenching his jaw, Samson wriggled in the chair. Though he knew very well that the ropes would be like so much twine against his invincible arms, she tightened them so that they cut into his skin, and he groaned aloud.

"Easy, Delilah!" he fumed. "I am flesh and blood, you know! I still say it is a foolish game! There has never been a fetter that could hold me!"

"Very well," she snapped, giving the ropes another tug and planting herself squarely before him, "then what are you complaining about? The game will end soon, and you can name your reward!"

Seeing his exasperated look, she said no more. In his eyes she read that there was no reward he wished, except to be free to go his way. At this realization, she bit her tongue, seething with jealousy at the thought of Samson with his Jewess bride.

"Dear, dear Samson," she lisped, donning a kittenish aspect, "it is almost suppertime. Let's not fight. Play along, just for me."

Then, turning to the door, she repeated the cry loudly enough for the men in the parlor to hear: "The Philistines are upon you, Samson! The Philistines are upon you!"

Again, the seranim entered the bedchamber, scrutinizing Delilah's handiwork, trying the knots and taunting Samson.

"Up, up, Israeli!" they laughed. "Let us see what you are made of!"

Of course, they were no fools. They knew the ropes were as useless against Samson as the thongs had been.

But, as though he needed instruction, Delilah spurred him, saying, "Rise up and break free!"

Sighing, Samson did as he was told, and in a moment the chair, ropes and all, clattered to the floor and his great arms were loosed. As he rubbed his wrists, the seranim departed, pretending amazement and shaking their heads.

"What will they invent now?" Samson asked, kicking at the tangle of knots at his feet. "I have no time for this!"

"No time?" Delilah purred. "No time to win whatever you wish from your enemies? This is your chance to win Gaza, if you desire! You let Baldod keep Gaza in the negotiations! This is your time to claim it for Israel!"

Wide-eyed, Samson looked at her. "Truly? I could claim so great a prize?"

"Of course!" the woman insisted. "What have I been telling you? This is not child's play!"

"I didn't realize . . . ," Samson said slowly. Looking at the door where the seranim had departed, he knew they plotted the next stage in the game, and he wondered if they over-heard.

"But they have not played to win," he noted. "If they could lose so much, why have they not tried harder?"

With a smirk, Delilah sighed, "Oh, Samson, did you live so long among the Philistines and not learn that we love playing our games nearly as much as we love winning them? Bariath and the others will not take this seriously until they are at the finish line."

Recalling the week of his wedding to Jezel, Samson realized Delilah's words were true. The wedding guests enjoyed the challenge of deciphering his riddle until the week was nearly past. Only then had they played with a vengeance, even threatening Samson's bride and her family in an effort to acquire the answer.

"So," he said, "the seranim have only two more chances to learn the secret of my strength. I suppose they are in earnest, now, to do so."

"Of that you can be certain!" Delilah smiled. "But, dear Samson, not to worry. Come," she offered, "supper is ready in the dining hall."

EIGHT

Samson scarcely noticed the food set before him that evening. The laughter and conversation of his Philistine hosts was all but lost on him, and he fingered the meat and fruit upon his plate without tasting it.

Despite Delilah's tempting suggestion that he might win Gaza if he continued to play her parlor game, he felt like a fool for having submitted thus far to the contest. He was winning, it was true. But he could not shake the sense that he was being used—that, at best, he was a clown at a Philistine sideshow.

Feeling strangely humiliated, he gazed with sad eyes into the fire at the end of the dining hall. Even now he should be arriving in Zorah, and by the end of the week he should be taking Marissa with him to Hebron. As the realization of his folly set afresh upon him, he gripped the pillow of his chaise lounge in an iron fist.

Darting a glance toward Delilah, where she reclined upon a nearby couch, he gritted his teeth. How was it possible, he wondered, that he was able to extricate himself from thongs and ropes, that he had been able to lift the gates of Gaza upon his shoulders, yet he had no strength to fight against designing women?

But as much as he wished to blame the temptress for his predicament, he knew she would have no power over him if he were a real man—and not a weakling.

As he considered this, he determined to escape her snare. Rising from the table, he left his couch and bowed to his companions.

"Gentlemen," he said, making his decision public, "you have been grand hosts. But I must be going. Your generosity has been flattering, and the games have been a challenge. But our business is done. I shall be going home."

Stunned by this unexpected announcement, the seranim stopped their feasting and pleaded with him, reminding him, in diplomatic terms, that he would be risking their goodwill to act so rashly.

Even so, Samson was not about to be detained again. "If our peace can be so easily strained," he warned them, "it was a tentative thing at best. Remember," he said, looking them each in the eye, "Israel is not to be mocked."

At this, he turned away, exiting the dining hall and heading for the gallery. Flashing a hand at his valet, he called him to pack and ordered his driver to ready his chariot.

Not even the sound of Delilah's footsteps hastening behind him could slow him as he grabbed his cloak from her room and looked about for any personal items he might have left there.

"Samson!" she cried, following him into the chamber. "How can you do this? You say you love me, yet you shame me before my own governors!"

Turning on her with hot eyes he growled, "Love you? When did I ever say I loved you?"

Delilah's awkward silence was short-lived. In truth, the man had never spoken these words. But she had seen the way he watched her . . . she had felt his touch. Besides, how could he be so certain what he had or hadn't said in the midst of their passion?

Sidling up to him, she stroked the lacing on his vest and purred, "Why, how quickly we forget! Can you deny the words spoken upon this very bed?"

His heart pounding in desperate denial, he jerked her hands from his chest and refused to look at the couch of sin. "I do deny it!" he shouted, pushing her aside and storming out of the room.

Astonished at his willpower, Delilah chased him as far as the hallway, then slumped against the doorpost of her parlor.

"What about Gaza?" she called after him. "You could win Gaza if you stay!"

"Ha!" Samson laughed. And without so much as a look back, he declared, "If Samson wants Gaza, Samson shall take it! And he shall carry its palace all the way to Hebron!"

DELILAH PACED her bedroom, back and forth, up and down, rubbing her hands in front of her and wringing them behind her. Her teeth bit into her lower lip so that they almost drew blood.

Samson was leaving; she had failed in her task of subduing him.

This woman, hardened as she was to normal emotion, was on the verge of real tears. Hot and stinging, they threatened to spill from her eyes and down her rouged cheeks. But she checked them, determined not to waste her energy.

Time was of the essence. She must think, and think quickly!

In one respect, she had accomplished a goal. She had bettered her rival, Mariah, by persuading Samson to stay more than a day. Of this she was quite proud. And she had delighted in the intimate favors of the man most coveted in Palestine for his amorous talents.

But such victories now seemed hollow. Not only was she about to lose him to a pauper Jewess, but she was about to forfeit the fortune, the lifetime of wages promised by the seranim.

Rarely since Samson arrived had she thought of the money. Delilah was as materialistic as any Philistine, but the money had been of much less interest to her than the winning of Samson's affections. So long as she thought she held his heart, the monetary reward was of little import.

Now, as she paced her chamber, rejected and humiliated, she thought otherwise. Anger and bitterness welled within her, as well as the desire for revenge. She must, she *would* gain something for her troubles!

Turning to her dressing table, she poured a glass of wine from the carafe that sat there and rebuked herself for lack of a plan. To the sound of a knock on her door, she jolted.

"Go away!" she shouted, not knowing or caring who stood outside.

"Delilah," came Bariath's voice. "Let me in!"

For a moment, she thought to refuse. But at last, composing herself, she went to the door and opened it. Without a word, she turned again for her wine.

"Tsk, tsk," taunted Bariath. "Is this the look of a scorned woman?"

"What do you want?" she snarled. "I don't want you here!"

"Ah, no," Bariath laughed, taking her by the sleeve and forcing her to face him, "I am certain there are other arms you prefer these days to mine. But we won't talk about that now."

Delilah wrenched in his grip. Tears no longer hid behind her lashes but came spilling freely down her cheeks.

"Quite so," she sighed. "You are the master. Always the master. Have you come to see your little slave squirm in her chains?"

"Oh, Delilah," Bariath chuckled, "you are quite the dramatic wench! Let's forget your infatuation for the moment and speak of our nation. Or have you forgotten your duty and why we hired you in the first place?"

Hating him intensely, Delilah speared him with a look. "I have not forgotten," she replied through gritted teeth.

"Then, dear lady, let us see what you are made of," he challenged. "Are you going to let our enemy slip through your fingers? Or . . . ," and here he paused, peering at her through gimlet eyes, "should we have hired Mariah?"

Lifting her chin, Delilah jerked free of his hold and stood arrow straight before him. A kaleidoscope of feelings spun through her—shame, jealousy, and hate.

"If I cannot undo Samson," she spat, "there is no woman alive who can!"

Bariath crossed his arms over his chest and rocked back and forth upon his soles. "Now," he exclaimed, "that's my girl! That's the Delilah I know!"

Delilah seethed. How she wished she could slap the pompous Philistine! But images of the money and the fame she would earn if only she could succeed in her mission stayed her itching hand.

Turning for her table again, she fondled the love oils and potions arrayed there in tiny flasks. Until now, she had not needed any of these devices to win Samson's passion. But sometimes a woman, even a woman like Delilah, could benefit from their use.

As she studied them one by one, Bariath slipped up behind her.

Leaning over her shoulder, he breathed into her hair.

"What was he like?" he hissed. "What was it like, my lady, to be with the strongman of Israel?"

Incensed, Delilah wheeled about, lightning flashing from her scandalized eyes.

She did not hesitate, this time, to retaliate. With a sweaty hand, she slapped the Philistine, leaving a welt upon his face.

Clutching his cheek, Bariath was about to cuff her. But he halted, and then did much worse.

Bowing low, he backed out of the room, leaving her with only the sound of his mocking laughter echoing down the hall.

NINE

*D*elilah hastened down the gallery to Samson's room. Actually Samson had been provided a suite of rooms for himself and his attendants, his apartment a sumptuous parlor filled with tapestries on the walls and floor, and with artwork of the loom and shuttle gracing each nook. Had he not been sidetracked by the temptress, spending all his time in her bedchamber, he would have enjoyed his surroundings for their warmth and style.

As she hurried, Delilah was careful not to drop the carafe she carried—the very carafe that had graced her dressing table—and two goblets. If she could get Samson to admit her to his room for a parting toast, she might yet have a chance to derail him.

To her disappointment, it was Samson's valet, and not the judge himself, who opened the door. "Tell your master I wish to part as friends," she said, holding forth the wine bottle.

Knitting his brow, the servant called over his shoulder, "Sir, it is the Philistine woman. She wishes to bid you good-bye."

"The same to her," came Samson's voice. "Give her my regards."

Exasperated, Delilah pushed past the valet. "By the gods!" she growled. "Get out of my way!"

Unnerved by her sudden appearance, Samson wheeled about. "What is it?" he cried. "Can't you see I'm busy?"

Upon his couch were his satchels, which he and his servant had been packing for the trip home.

"How can you leave, when all is not well with us?" she snapped. "If we must part, let it be as friends!"

Once again, she held forth the carafe as though it were a peace offering.

Bemused, Samson studied her outstretched hand. Surely she had nothing to gain by this overture, except his goodwill. Temptress she might be, but perhaps she was not totally evil.

With a sigh, he approached her, taking the goblet she held forth. "It is all right," he told the valet. "Return in a moment."

Dubious, the valet bowed and backed out of the room, shutting the door.

"Dear, dear Samson," Delilah whispered, "I knew you could not utterly hate me." Clinking the rims of their glasses together, she twined her wrist around his and pretended to drink. As Samson complied, sipping from his goblet, she restrained the wicked smile that tugged at her lips.

If the wine seemed unusually potent, Samson could do nothing to stop its effects. In only moments, it worked a strange sorcery upon him, dulling his senses and making his tongue heavy in his mouth.

"What sort of witchery have you worked this time?" he stammered, holding his head to stop the reeling of the room.

"Why, Samson," Delilah laughed, "you flatter me. Are you drunk with love?"

Taking him by the hand, she led him to the couch. "Here," she said, sitting down. "Put your head in my lap."

With no strength to resist her, Samson obeyed. And as he rested there, he was tickled with a light-headed giddiness.

"You are a strange woman," he laughed, gazing at her through a besotted haze. "How is it that you still think I love you?"

Delilah hid her delight behind a sullen pout. "Oh, I am a fool when it comes to you," she sighed. "Of course it is only wishful thinking that makes me speak of love when I am with you. After all, if you really loved me you would not mock me as you have."

With a snort, Samson reached up and stroked her hot cheek. "Mock you?" he slurred. "When have I ever mocked you?"

Pushing his hand away, Delilah pretended outrage. "Oh, you are cruel!" she whimpered. "You have mocked me again and again and have told me lie after lie! How can you say you have not?"

Samson's drugged emotions leaped from the giddy to the morose. "Dear woman!" he gasped. "When did I mock you?"

"You have lied to me twice about your strength!" she reminded him. "First about the bowstrings and then about the ropes! Don't pretend that you didn't!"

In his altered state, Samson almost believed her. "That was just a game!" he objected, trying to sit up.

But Delilah pinned him to her lap. "Not to me it wasn't!" she wept. "Had you spoken the truth to me, I never would have revealed it to a soul!"

"You can't be serious!" he laughed, clutching at his swollen head. Now it seemed the room was changing colors, the shadows swelling from gray to yellow and taking on monstrous shapes.

With surprising agility, Samson rolled off her lap and stood on wobbly legs, wondering if she was a mirage. "You, my lady, are enough to drive a sane man lunatic!" he howled.

"Tell me, then," Delilah challenged, "how *can* you be captured? What *is* the secret of your strength?"

Laughing hilariously, Samson staggered about the room, until he stubbed his foot against a small loom erected in the corner, the loom upon which the tapestries and rugs of the luxurious chamber had been fashioned.

"Here!" he cried, his face clownish. "Here is the answer!"

Picking up the loom, he moved it across the floor and rocked it back and forth in front of his tormentor. "I am afraid of looms!" he laughed. "Looms are my greatest enemy! Why, if you but take the locks of my hair and weave them into this loom, I shall be as weak as any other man!"

Aghast, Delilah watched his raving, fearing that she had underestimated the potion with which she had laced the wine.

"Samson, you frighten me!" she cried. Pulling her feet onto the couch, she tucked them beneath her, avoiding the gyrating loom.

"Samson, you mock me!" he hooted. "Samson, you frighten me!"

Raising the loom over his head, he would have heaved it against a wall, had the room not begun to spin like a top.

Suddenly, he could feel nothing, see nothing, hear nothing. He did not know that the loom toppled from his hands, crashing to the floor. He did not know that he, too, fell on his face, leaving Delilah to shake and quake upon the couch.

But, how quickly the woman composed herself! When the valet banged upon the door, inquiring about the ruckus, she calmly called out, "The master is asleep! Do not come back until he calls you!"

TEN

*D*elilah worked quickly. Kneeling beside the unconscious Samson, she took the seven braids of his hair and slid the loom close to his head. Then she began to weave the locks upon it, as though they were so much combed wool.

Back and forth the shuttle moved, the woman's shallow breathing keeping rhythm with its sound. She must hurry before the valet or some other suspicious servant came to check on the Nazarite.

She felt quite foolish following Samson's suggestion. But she was desperate enough to try anything.

Besides, it was just possible he had hinted at the truth.

Israelis and Philistines, like every culture of the region, held superstitious reverence for the hair. They believed it to be the favorite abode of spirits and all sorts of magical influences. Perhaps, indeed, this *was* the source of Samson's strength! After all, it was not for nothing that the vow he had taken, the one imposed upon him before birth, required him to grow his hair long.

Oh, she thought as she deftly hooked his hair between the cords of the loom, *can his secret be so simple? Has the source of his strength been so obvious, yet no Philistine ever suspected it?*

Still, he had tricked her heretofore. She would not call for the seranim until she knew good and well he had not tricked her again. When he awoke, she would test him and, if he broke free, she would at least save herself embarrassment. If he was incapacitated, she would hold him here and summon Bariath and the others.

Already she could feel the cool coins of her reward smooth upon her palm.

After a half hour of weaving, she had completed her task. How heavy was the fabric she had created—and how lustrous! Samson's hair formed a glistening tapestry a cubit long! Though she had not been concerned for any design, the outcome was worthy of a royal palace.

She scarcely surveyed her handiwork, however. She was interested only in its effect upon the man.

In haste, she poked the pin of the loom through the dark web, anchoring it to the cords. Then she leaned back upon her ankles, nervously twiddling her fingers.

When would Samson awaken? If she shook him, would he come to?

When a few minutes had elapsed, she grew more anxious. She would speak to him the words from the game, but this time she would not shout them.

Bending over him, she softly called, "The Philistines, Samson! The Philistines are upon you!"

When he slept on, she shook his lethargic body until his drugged eyes opened with a flutter.

"The Philistines are upon you!" she cried.

Like a fallen tree, Samson lay helpless on the floor, vainly wrenching his head from side to side, each twist sending spikes of pain through his skull.

"Delilah, what have you done?" he groaned, reaching for his aching head.

By the gods, she had him! Leaping up, she began to dance around, tormenting him with a mocking song. "Poor Samson!" she hooted. "Have you at last told the truth?"

But just as she was about to summon Bariath, adrenaline coursed through Samson's body, chasing the drug from his head. Like a mighty behemoth, he rolled over and hoisted himself from the floor, grabbing the loom in his great hands and yanking the pin from the cords.

Shaking himself, he freed his hair, unraveling the woman's handiwork and staggering out of her grasp.

Vaguely he remembered that he had spoken to her about his hair, his most cherished and sacred adornment. Struck with the realization that she had profaned it, that the hands of a pagan woman had touched his Nazarite locks, he was overcome with shame.

Stumbling across the room, he shoved her aside and headed for his dressing room. Upon the wall was a copper mirror and, with a groan, he surveyed his straggly hair . . . the symbol of his holy calling, now loose, unkempt, defiled.

Never in all his life had his hair looked so! Ever since the day Peniel had woven it, with loving hands, into the seven distinctive braids, Samson had kept that style. Except for times he had loosed it to wash and comb it, it had borne the mark of the Nazarite.

Filled with remorse, Samson wept aloud, "Oh, God! What have I done? What have I done?"

Delilah was unmoved by his shame. She was only outraged that she had lost again.

Running after him, she assailed him. "How can you say you love me?" she wailed, pummeling his broad back with her fists.

When Samson covered his ears, she howled the louder. "How can you say you love me when your heart is not with me? You have mocked me three times! Three times you have lied to me!"

Stupefied by remorse, the lingering effects of the drug, and days of Delilah's nagging, Samson finally turned on her. Forgetting his own strength, he grabbed her by the shoulders and would have shaken her head from her neck. But he stopped himself and, flinging her aside, staggered back to his chamber.

Then his valet at last intervened. As he threw open the door, he came upon the raging Delilah, the toppled loom, and the disheveled Samson. He was once again ordered away. The Nazarite, shamed to the quick, thrust him bodily from the room, commanding him not to return. Then, focusing his rage and humiliation upon Delilah, he raved crazily, revealing the terror of his heart.

"I am a Nazarite from birth!" he cried, hunching over the terrified woman. "A Nazarite! Do you hear me?"

Reeling about the room, clutching at his tumbled locks, he wept. "What will you do now, utterly shave me? There has never come a razor upon my head, for I have been a Nazarite unto God from my mother's womb!"

Stunned, Delilah watched as he tripped over the furniture and careened about the chamber like a wild boar.

"Don't touch me!" he cried, though she stayed well away from him. As if she were a legion of demons, he cried aloud each time he looked at her. "Don't touch me! If I be shaven, then my strength will flee! I shall be weak," he sobbed, "weak as any other man!"

There, it had been said. Delilah wanted the truth, and to Samson's desperate, outraged thinking, truer words were never spoken.

Slumping to the floor, he sat on his haunches, rocking back and forth like a lunatic. "Don't touch me!" he repeated, lifting his arms like a shield and weeping like a baby.

Though Delilah did not come near him, she breathed easier as she saw his wretched condition. Observing the fallen hero, his great body huddled like a beggar's, she raised her chin in scorn.

In a moment, he would swoon again. He would sleep deeply from shame and despair. This she knew . . . as well as she knew that this time, he had spoken from the heart.

Tiptoeing to the door, she leaned into the hall and summoned the terrified valet.

"Get Bariath," she commanded. "Samson is in trouble."

The Boy
and
the Blindman

ONE

*T*he streets of Gaza rang with music and celebration as the citizens awaited the arrival of their vanquished enemy. Samson the Nazarite, hero of Israel, oppressor of Philistia, was fallen! Any moment he would be entering the gates of the city, the new gates erected since he had uprooted the originals.

This time, he would not come in a show of power, he would shed no blood, level no walls. He would come in chains, prodded by the swords of his captors, the seranim of Philistia.

Above the ruckus of the streets, above the chanting, singing, and laughter of the vicarious victors, a young boy stood watch. He was barely big enough to see over the parapet of Dagon's temple, behind which he hid. But he stretched as tall as possible, gripping the rampart and pulling himself up so that his chest rested on the railing. Wide-eyed, he surveyed the milling masses and waited, as they did, for Samson's appearance.

But his heart was not with theirs. He took no joy in the knowledge that the hero was fallen. For him this was a sad, sad day. And not only because he was a Jew.

Dan's young life had been radically altered from the moment he had set foot in Gaza. Forever emblazoned upon his brain were the events that had brought him to serve, against his will, in this heathen house of worship. Eternal were the scars wrought by his erstwhile father, Josef. Everlasting was the memory of his night at Gaza Inn and the fragmented conversation he had overheard from the adjoining room.

Though he little understood it, he knew that the man the Philistines hated, the one they awaited with leering smiles and bared teeth, was his real father.

Today, when news had spilled through town and through the temple courts that Samson was vanquished, Dan had kept to himself. He had done his duties, performing the menial tasks required of him as a slave of the priests, but he had kept his eyes down and his voice low. When the crowds began to gather along the streets and upon the highways leading into town, he had showed no feeling.

Inwardly, though, he quivered with emotions too great for his young heart to name.

Outside the city, the roadways were becoming as congested as the boulevards and avenues within. People were arriving from up and down the coast, from Ashkelon and Ashdod, the maritime cities of the Pentapolis, and from the inland cities of Gath and Ekron. Now masses of humanity were pressing toward the Gaza walls, lining the seaward moat and packing the bridge. Only a narrow corridor was left for the arrival of the seranim, their entourage, and their captive.

Word of Samson's defeat had reached the temple early this morning. It was now well past noon. If the noblemen had left Sorek last evening, they would surely arrive soon.

The sound of a hundred drums heralded their coming. Somewhere up the northerly highway, where it merged with the road from the shephelah, the awaited procession had been seen. The news, carried on the wind by ten thousand voices, was now echoed by the beating drums.

Dan clung to the balustrade, scarcely breathing, until a tremendous swell of cheers and chanting pressed toward the city, moving through the gate and into the marketplace.

Yes, there they were! Dan could see them, the gaudy carriages and high-stepping horses of the seranim! Following after them were dozens of slaves and servants garbed like Dan himself, in immaculate white tunics. And marching before them were armed men with plumed hats and shining leather vests, prodding a hapless creature down the boulevard.

Taking a sharp breath, Dan gawked at the captive. Was it possible that this was the mighty Samson, the legend of Israeli song and the hero of every Israeli boy?

Where was his fabled hair, the mark of the covenant he had made with the Nazarites? And why did he stumble as he did, holding his gaze to the ground?

Surely this was not Samson! In truth, the prisoner was a big fellow, his physique in keeping with the tales rehearsed about Israeli fires. But this man appeared to have no strength and even now was being pushed like an aged bull down the thoroughfare. And his head was shorn, shaved from nape to crown, from ear to ear!

Yet, the crowd called out the name of Samson over and over, hissing and spitting upon the unfortunate one, laughing hilariously each time he tripped.

It was not until a guard, for no reason whatsoever, jerked the prisoner's chains and slapped him, that he raised his face to the people. Or perhaps there was a reason, for when the captive showed his face, the crowd cheered and laughed the more.

Lord God! Dan thought. *What have they done to him?*

Caked upon the prisoner's face, hardened upon his cheeks, was a layer of dried blood. The helpless victim staggered and stumbled because he could not see. His lids were sealed shut with the grisly substance, and a shock surged through the watching boy when he understood that the hero's eyes had been gouged out!

At this realization, Dan grew faint. Releasing his grip on the railing, he slid to the rooftop and curled against the low wall, holding his knees close to his little body and hiding his face against them.

Lord God, was it possible that this was his father? Was it possible the mighty one, whose escapades had fueled his boyish dreams, could fall so low?

Ever since Josef had abandoned him, one hope had kept Dan alive—the hope that one day he would find Samson, or that Samson would come for him, and they would live happily ever after.

Moaning softly, he held himself with his own feeble arms. The child whose mother had died before he was born, the child who only dreamed of love, tried vainly to comfort himself.

But as he huddled in his rooftop corner, the sounds of the street hammered harder, filling the temple with pagan rhythm.

They were bringing the captive to the priests!

Dan lifted his head and listened. Yes, Samson was about to be delivered into this very place!

Jumping to his feet, the boy ran for the ladder that led down from the roof. With all this activity, there would surely be work for him to do. He must not be caught spying when his keepers came looking for him.

Downstairs, the sounds of the central court grew louder in his ears. As he came to the court pavement, he skidded to a halt and hid behind a pillar. Holding his hands over his eyes, he clamped them tight.

Samson was just entering the compound, and Dan could not look upon him.

TWO

*A*ll that day and into the night, the Philistines celebrated in Gaza's streets. In the temple court, Samson, their prize, was set on display beside the statue of Dagon. Even the fishlike god and his consorts erected upon a splashing fountain seemed to be mocking the fallen Israeli.

Though little Dan wanted to avoid looking upon his hero, he was obliged to do so as he was sent on errands about the court, fetching wine, food, and dancing girls for the revelers' fathomless appetites.

His feet and head aching, the boy was at last released to go to his room, where he tossed and turned with nightmares through the dark hours.

Only with morning did the noise of the temple taper, and only with dawn did the street music grow quiet in a temporary lull. By afternoon, the besotted Philistines would be ready for another round of excess. But before they awoke, Samson was removed, consigned to the bowels of the pagan sanctuary.

Rousted from a tormented sleep, Dan rose to face the new day—and a mission more challenging than serving at the party.

Through the underground of the temple compound, he now crept like a wary mouse. He had worked in the house of Dagon for a full month, but never had he been obliged to wend his way through the maze of corridors that linked storerooms and closets with dungeons and sewers.

Though daylight did not reach these hallways, there were shadows cast against the damp walls by fiery torches. Who manned the torches, he did not know, though he knew the prison keepers who oversaw the criminals housed here. With a shudder, he wondered if other boys like himself must come here every day to light the flames.

Though he feared the eerie shadows, Dan moved through the tunnels on quick feet, trying not to slop the bowl of warm water which he carried. He did not want it to cool before he reached his destination, the room of the grinding wheel, where Samson was quartered.

As for the duty that lay ahead, he faced it with mixed feelings. It seemed unusually good luck that he, of all the youngsters working here, should have been selected to look in on Samson. On the other hand, he of all the lads had the most personal reason to fear the encounter.

He must be nearing the granary. The tunnel was becoming damper, and he had been told that the grinding wheel was housed along the compound's seaward wall. A narrow shaft opened from the grinding room to the marketplace above, he had been told, where sheaves of wheat and other grain were deposited. Across the top of the shaft, there was a grate, so no commoners could enter. But the presence of a little daylight would be his cue that he had found the place.

He wondered why the priests quartered Samson in the granary rather than in a prison room. But he had been too timid to ask. As he glimpsed daylight straight ahead, the hair on his neck bristled.

Was that the sound of the grinding wheel vibrating through the humid hall?

Tiptoeing toward an entrance, he set his bowl upon the floor and peeked through the door's barred window. Yes, this was the granary. Gray light filtered down a long shaft into the room, settling upon a huge stone wheel. Chained to the wheel was a giant of a man, his naked back striped with blood.

Riveted by the sight, Dan clung to the window bars, unable to look away, even when another huge fellow emerged from a corner of the room, lifted a whip, and lay it across the prisoner's spine.

A clot of fear rose in Dan's throat. "Samson!" he would have cried out. But it was best he could not.

Instead he knelt to the floor and took up the bowl in shaking hands. Catching his breath, he stood and knocked on the door.

"Enter!" cried the beastly guard. When Dan hesitated, the rude man stomped to the door and threw it open, revealing the wheel, the rancid room, and the pathetic prisoner in all their horror.

Dan would have explained his errand, but, confronted by the muscle-bound Philistine, he was speechless. Bare-chested, garbed only in an open leather vest and short leather skirt, the man had obviously been chosen for this duty because of his proximity to Samson's size.

"At last!" the ogre snarled, pounding the handle of his whip against the floor and shaking his bearded head. "What took you so long?"

Saying nothing, Dan entered, the guard prodding him with the tip of his wicked flail.

As if the boy were as blind as the prisoner, the guard growled, "There he is! Take care of him!" And slamming the door behind him, he trudged down the hall, leaving Dan alone with the Israeli legend.

Though the guard was gone, the prisoner continued to press his weight against the wheel's handle, turning the horizontal stone round and round and sending a shuddering song through the underground, of slab against slab, wheel against rock.

Now and then, the grinder let out a mournful cry, a wail of sorrow mingling with the rumble of the wheel.

Biting his lip, Dan suppressed his own despair and pulled a linen rag from his belt. On soft feet, he approached the hunched hero.

"Sir," he called. "I am here to help you."

All about the base of the stone there was a circular path, worn over the years by oxen feet. Today, however, the beasts were on holiday, replaced by the Israeli's brute strength. Stopping in the path, Samson cocked his head.

"Sir," Dan repeated, "sit awhile. I will wash your face."

Like a great bear, Samson straightened himself and weaved his head from side to side. It seemed he looked toward the sound of the boyish voice, but of course he had no eyes with which to see. The more he waved his head, as though much movement would clear his wanting vision, the more Dan fought to keep from crying.

"Here, good sir," he peeped. "Sit here."

Dan, too, made the mistake of gesturing as though Samson could see. Walking to the wheel, he patted it and, when the mighty grinder did not sit, he reached out a tentative hand, taking him by the arm and tugging him down.

"Is it a boy?" Samson croaked, straining his head in Dan's direction.

"Yes," the lad replied. "I am a boy. I am here to help you."

With trembling fingers, Dan placed the bowl upon the stone and dipped the rag into it. Then, wringing it out, he held it up to Samson's face and dabbed at the blood encrusted there.

Swallowing tears, the lad proceeded to wash the giant's cheeks, holding Samson's chin with one hand. *Oh Lord,* he thought, *I dare not touch his eyes! His eyes! There is nothing there, behind those swollen lids!*

How he managed to contain himself in the face of this grisly image, he would later wonder.

As he ran the rag over the marred visage, he reached up to stroke the giant's stubbled head.

At this unexpected gesture, the prisoner lurched backward and grasped the brave hand in a mangling grip.

"Do not touch my hair!" he commanded.

When the boy cried out, he released him, turning away as if to avoid a blow.

"I am sorry," Dan apologized. "No one will hurt you. We are alone."

Slumping forward, Samson buried his bloody face in his hands and let out a groan. But, when he inadvertently touched his vacant sockets, he threw back his head, sobbing again.

"God of Abraham!" he wept. "My hair! My eyes!"

Terrified, Dan moved aside. And none too soon, for suddenly Samson was on his feet, swinging his chained arms in the air and bellowing like a caged bull.

"My hair!" he cried. "My eyes! Oh, what have I done? What have I done?"

Pacing like a trapped lion, he threw himself from side to side of the wheel.

"Delilah! Bariath!" he roared. "Where are you?"

For many moments the tirade continued, as Dan watched from a corner of the room. Tears streamed down the lad's cheeks, and for the first time since hearing of Samson's defeat, he was free himself to weep.

Such a pair they were, blind giant and slave boy! Cameos of anguish, profiles in pain.

But more than mutual horror coupled them. Had either of them been able to observe, they would have marveled at their similarities, their matched complexions, their coal black hair. And Samson's eyes . . . they had been dark and deep like the boy's.

At last, spent of voice and strength, the giant collapsed against the stone wheel. Releasing the handle, he slid to the floor and lay in a huddle.

When Dan peeked up from his own curl of fear, he took a shuddering sigh. How long he sat watching the giant, no one would know. But at last, he remembered the bowl of water and the bloody rag that rested in it.

Crawling toward the prisoner, he scooted beside him and lifted the huge head, making a pillow of his own lap.

From the scarlet water he withdrew the rag, and as he swabbed the scales of blood from Samson's tortured face, he continued to weep.

Escaped into a fog of slumber, the giant did not know that Dan's tears mingled with the bath, or that his ministrations were more from love than duty.

THREE

*I*t was the seventh day of Samson's incarceration in the Philistine grinding room. This morning when Dan followed the hallway toward the foul chamber, it was with a lively tread.

Not only had the young boy learned not to fear the underground shadows, but each day since his first meeting with the Israeli, he had become more comfortable with him.

He kept to himself the fact that he enjoyed the hero's company. Were the priests to learn that he did much more than was required of him in caring for the prisoner, they would have jerked the privilege from him.

Certainly his kindnesses did not go unnoticed by the prisoner. If Dan was sent to fetch water for Samson to drink, he brought a cold, brimming cup. When he brought him meals, they were heaped in generous portions. Without being asked, the boy removed Samson's sandals, washing his feet when they bled from his passage about the stone.

Fortunately, the guard used Dan's arrivals as opportunities to break from his duty. So the two were always left alone.

The first few days, Samson hardly spoke. But the boy reached out to him with kind words and sensitive silences. Yesterday, he had noticed a change in the Israeli. His countenance seemed lighter. He still said little, but he brightened at the sound of Dan's entrance, as though he looked forward to it.

Today, before Dan reached the room, he noticed that the turning wheel was louder, as though the stone moved faster. When he arrived, he was amazed at Samson's energy.

Surely, the hero had no love for his dreary task. But he was becoming stronger by the day and now threw himself against the handle with a vengeance.

When the guard greeted the boy with his harsh growl and then departed, slamming the door behind him, Samson stopped his work and almost smiled. "Good day," he called.

Astonished, Dan received the salutation with a stammer. "Good day," he replied.

Without being told to, Samson sat down on the rock, ready for whatever the lad had to offer.

"You are looking well," Dan observed, as he ran a cool rag over the giant's brow. "And your hair . . . I will not touch it," he assured him. "It is growing!"

When Samson suddenly reached for the boy's hand, he pulled away in fear. But Samson tugged at it, placing it upon his head.

"Yes!" the prisoner exclaimed. "It *is* longer, isn't it!"

Fearfully, Dan stroked the locks as one would stroke a lion's mane.

"And I am stronger!" Samson declared. "Longer . . . stronger!"

At this, the mighty captive actually laughed a little, and Dan, wiping his face again, laughed with him.

At the sound of Dan's giggle, however, Samson was suddenly silent, cocking his head as at the song of a bird.

"Your voice—" he gasped. "it is the voice of an angel!"

Not knowing how to take this, Dan kept quiet. But Samson grew anxious. "Oh," he cried, "do not stop! You are my angel!" he pleaded. "My ministering angel!"

Taking the rag from Dan's hand, Samson held the small fingers flat upon his broad ones.

"The hands of an angel," the hero insisted. "And the voice. But tell me, my boy, how is it that you speak Hebrew? Are you a Hebrew angel?"

"I am," Dan answered. "Not an angel," he laughed, "but a Hebrew!"

Leaning back against the stone, Samson chuckled. But then he grew somber. "How, dear boy, did you come to this wretched place? Were you captured, like me? Were you sold here?"

Such dreadful incidents were not uncommon in this pagan nation, especially with the rivalry between Israel and Philistia. There was little conscience in regard to making slaves of Hebrew children when they could be had.

But Dan's story was not quite so simple. And he choked on its memory.

"I was not captured," he said.

As soon as he had confessed this, however, he regretted it. He dare not speak freely of his past, lest he reveal his relationship to the prisoner. And that must not happen.

Not only might there be dire consequences to himself should word of his kinship be leaked, but the reality was so awesome to his young heart that he dared not frame it in words.

"Then how did you come here?" Samson persisted. "Surely if you had a Hebrew family, they would never sell you!"

At the truth so plainly spoken, at the remembrance of Josef's abandonment, Dan was dumbstruck. Trembling, he pulled away from Samson's kind touch.

"I . . . I cannot remember," he lied.

Without a further word, he backed toward the door, stumbling over his water bowl.

Hearing him leave, Samson beckoned to him. But Dan was already in the hall.

Only the sounds of his running feet, as he escaped exposure, proclaimed his private torment.

SAMSON was still sitting beside the wheel when the guard returned. He had not risen to continue with his labors, but sat in silence, wondering at the lad's reaction.

"Up!" the guard shouted, kicking the discarded water bowl. "Where is the boy? Why are you sitting?"

When Samson felt the whip whiz past his head, ready to come crashing down upon his back, he reached forth, not this time to shield himself, but to rip it from the ogre's grip.

With one stunning flash, he tore the cruel instrument from his oppressor's hand and brought it up against the Philistine's gullet, pulling it tight with both hands.

When the guard reeled backward, crashing into Samson's chest, the mighty Israeli thrust a shackled ankle between his legs and threw him to the floor.

Looming over him, Samson held the whip aloft. "I cannot see, but I can hear perfectly well!" he warned. "One move from you and you shall know pain as I have known it!"

Disoriented, the guard could only mutter, but Samson knew he would comply. Placing a foot upon the man's neck, he bellowed, "I shall work your stone!" he cried. "Oh, how I shall work it! Your head shall be the grain, ground to powder, unless you tell me what I want to know!"

"Speak, speak," the ogre pleaded. "What do you want?"

"Tell me about the boy!" Samson spat. "How came he to be in this unholy place?"

When the guard only rocked his head upon the pavement, Samson pressed harder with his foot, until the fellow's face turned blue.

Struggling for air, the Philistine grabbed Samson's ankle and tried to push him off. But the Israeli relieved the pressure only enough to let him speak.

"I know nothing!" he asserted.

"Nothing?" Samson snarled, resting his weight upon the neck.

"He is a Hebrew," the guard choked. "This, and nothing more."

"Who sold him here?" Samson prodded, digging the nose of his sandal into the guard's chin.

"An Israeli," he croaked.

"You lie!" Samson growled. "Israelis do not sell their own!"

"I know nothing!" the Philistine insisted. "He had the right!"

"What right?" Samson grilled him, pressing down again.

"He was his father!" the Philistine gargled. "Hasn't a father the right . . . "

"Not in Israel!" Samson bellowed.

"I cannot say . . . ," the Philistine sighed, nearly fainting for lack of air.

"I can!" Samson declared. "I was judge in Israel!"

By now, the ogre was no longer struggling. Woozy, he lay still upon the floor, barely hearing as Samson lifted his foot and bent over him.

"Who was he?" he breathed into his bearded face. "Who was the wretched Jew?"

Through a haze, the Philistine sensed that Samson would surely kill him. "No name," he sighed, "he had no name . . . Zorah . . . he was from Zorah. . . ."

Astonished, Samson went white. And with leaden ears, he heard the Philistine's fading defense. "The boy is not all Jew . . . the man did not want him. . . ."

══ FOUR ══

*N*ighttime was the worst time for Samson.

Through his unsighted eyes he received no light, even at high noon. But during the day, he could sometimes feel the rays of the sun upon his back as they spilled through the high shaft. And he could hear the sounds of life, however bleak, within the underground, and the echoes of traffic in the street above.

At night, though, his darkness was shrouded in gloomy quiet.

This was the eighth night of his imprisonment. This time, however, his personal circumstances did not press in upon him with quite such heavy weight, for his concerns ran to the boy and what his story might be.

Apparently the child had been abandoned, sold here, of all things, by a Jew! This fact alone was not all that haunted Samson. Undoubtedly he knew the Jew, if he was from Zorah. The question of who the monster might be was enough to keep Samson's head churning through the wee hours.

It must have been nearing cockcrow when a grisly picture formed itself in his mind, pieced together from the bits of information he possessed.

As the picture grew more distinct, Samson fought against it. But the facts were frighteningly suggestive.

The man he contemplated was a Zorahite, likely a merchant or businessman, for only such a Jew would have come into Gaza. He had been married to or had consorted with a pagan woman, if the child was "not all Jew."

If the child's mother was, as Samson suspected, a Philistine, she must have abandoned the boy early on, or possibly she had died, leaving him to the Jew. Judging by the boy's age, that had been about seven years ago.

Furthermore, the Jew must be of shallow conviction, or of none at all, for no Jew of conscience could sell a child! Not even a shallow Jew could do so. Unless . . .

Here Samson trembled, wondering at the direction of his logic.

Unless . . . the child was not his own, after all.

Pulling his feet beneath him, Samson stared with vacant eyes through the tunnel of his solitude.

Perhaps the miseries of recent days had affected his brain. Surely the possibility that the facts proposed was a product of dementia.

But the more he pondered it, the more plausible it seemed.

Cold sweat dotted Samson's forehead. He had not worked for hours, yet his heart drummed as though it would break through his chest.

If he followed this trail of logic to its conclusion, he could not stop with the Jew, the woman, or the boy. The path led unrepentantly toward himself.

Suddenly, in his mind's eye, he stood before the fallen house of Mardok, before the smoldering ashes in which Jezel had died, in which the child she carried had died with her. And, in this imaginary episode, his logic made an unavoidable leap.

Was it possible that the child had *not* died? That the child had *not* been Josef's, but that Josef had found him and kept the secret of his birth to himself?

It was, indeed, as likely that the child was Samson's as Josef's! For Samson was certain Josef would never have sold his own child!

Lord God! Samson sighed. *Tell me it is not true!*

But the instant he thought this, something more primal than fear rose to squelch the plea. If the boy *was* Samson's, he was a gift from heaven, a gift beyond all dreaming and all asking, come to him in his deepest, most hopeless hour!

Back and forth Samson's heart wrestled, first resisting, then longing for the possibility.

Was there a way to know the truth? Surely Josef would never have told the boy the reality of his origins! If Samson were to suggest the idea to the lad, it could scar him beyond all the cruelties life had dealt him.

Dawn was creeping down the shaft from the street wall. Samson saw no light, but he could hear the sounds of life stirring above, and soon the dungeon was growing warmer. Any moment, the guard, who had survived the Israeli's inquisition, would be returning. And his whip would be more vicious than ever.

But Samson would not be undone. He had a mystery to solve, a puzzle to unravel. The mystery was not a simple mind game. It involved himself, his blood, and his deepest longings.

He must discover if the boy was his own! For if he was, Samson's heart would soar above the prison walls. If the boy was his, no dungeon could confine him.

Though he were to live here the rest of his life, though he were to die here, he would be no man's true captive. For he would have a stake in the future, and his heart would be free to dream.

═══════ FIVE ═══════

About the same time that Samson deduced the truth, his granary guard lay face up on Mariah's bed, cringing as she applied ointment to his bruises and scrapes.

Her red hair fell across his chest as she spread the salve, and he fingered it fondly.

"You are a fine woman," he said, trying not to wince. "You know more than one way to make a man feel good."

"That Samson is a wild man!" she exclaimed, as she inspected the damages. "What happened to make him turn on you?"

"It was the oddest thing," the Philistine recounted. "For some reason, he has taken a great interest in the boy who looks after him. You know, the one you and Josef sold?"

Mariah glanced up, her hand in midair. "Dan?" she gulped. "Little Dan is his keeper?"

"Yes," the guard replied. "They have become fast friends." This seemed to tickle him and he snickered.

But Mariah was not amused. Running a streak of salve across a cut, she asked, "So, what did he want to know?"

"He asked how the boy came to be at Dagon's house," the guard reported. "He went mad when I told him a Jew had sold him there."

Pulling back, Mariah scowled. "You told him *that?*" she gasped.

"I did," the guard affirmed. "Is that a problem?"

Clenching her jaw, Mariah continued her work. "What else did you tell him?" she inquired.

"He wanted to know the Jew's name," he hedged. "I didn't tell him."

Relaxing a little, Mariah proceeded to dab ointment here and there. "Is that all?" she probed. "Did you say anything else?"

The guard reflected. "So what? So what if I did? He would make nothing of it."

Mariah bore down harder than she needed to, her nails digging into one of the abrasions.

"You *did* say more!" she snarled. "What did you tell him?"

"Only that the Jew was from Zorah!" he replied, shielding his chest. "That is nothing."

"By the gods!" the woman spat. "Do you forget that *Samson* is from Zorah? Don't you think he knows everyone in that puny place?"

Jumping up, she huffed, "Just how many Zorahite men are there who would stoop to selling a child?"

The guard watched her rave, wrinkling his forehead.

"How should I know?" He shrugged. "What difference does it make?"

Mariah wheeled on him with hot eyes.

"To you, none," she asserted. "To me and Josef, a good deal!"

Now the giant was quite uneasy. "I don't understand," he said. "Even if Samson did put Josef's name to the deed, how would he trace anything to you? And if he did, why should he care? The boy is not his."

At this comment, Mariah's cheeks burned. She had better watch herself or she would give everything away.

Her reaction, however, did not escape the guard.

"What is it?" he asked, surveying her suspiciously. "Is there more to this than I already know?"

With a forced smile, Mariah returned to the bed and proceeded with the nursing.

"It is only . . . ," she lied, "only that Samson is a very dangerous fellow. Look what he did to *you!* If he has developed a fondness for the lad, we are all at risk."

"Well," the guard teased, showing his yellow teeth, "perhaps you will think twice before you sell a child again."

Mariah gave him a threatening look and he flinched. Thinking it best to leave, he sat up and pulled on his shirt.

"Not to worry, my lady," he assured her. Slipping two coins into her hand in payment for her services, he laughed. "Samson is no real danger to anyone. You ought to see the poor creature . . . blind and all. A sorry sight it is!"

He was about to depart, when, turning from the door he called, "By the way, you *shall* see the poor beast, at Dagon's festival! Samson will be on display, for all the world to see!"

Ducking out, he disappeared, leaving Mariah to grapple with her fears.

But as she straightened the now-vacant bed and replaced the ointment jars upon her table, she remembered what had led her to suggest selling the boy in the first place.

"What would wound Samson more," she had asked Josef, "than for his own son to serve in the house of his enemies' god?"

Perhaps Samson would trace the deed to Josef, and perhaps, knowing not even Josef would sell his own offspring, he would deduce that the boy was his.

But wouldn't that be a dream come true? Secret vengeance was unfulfilled vengeance, she had told Josef.

Samson was big and strong, but he was not dumb. He had probably already deduced the facts. Licking her lips, Mariah

311

turned to the chamber window and looked out on the acropolis, the rise on which Dagon's compound sat.

Somewhere in that labyrinth of buildings and dungeons, Israel's blind hero sat, his torment intensified by his son's enslavement.

"Aha!" she cackled. "Revenge is sweet, indeed!"

Down below, on the street, the guard returned to his appointed station. Suddenly, a wicked hope flashed through Mariah's heart.

"Hello!" she hailed him, waving from the window. "Don't go away mad."

The guard stopped and bowed to her.

"Tell me," she called, "will the boy be with Samson at the festival?"

"I suppose," he chuckled. "The poor blind man will need someone to lead him!"

"Good!" she replied. "I will get word to Josef. We will both want to see that!"

═══ SIX ═══

*R*egarding the attitude of the guard upon his return to the grinding room, Samson was not mistaken. Having revived under Mariah's ministering touch, the oaf came back with a vengeance and, standing out of reach of the prisoner, whipped him mercilessly.

Then he shouted up the shaft to a waiting wagon, "Send down the sheaves! Samson will have them ground by evening!"

With a thud, several heaps of wheat and rye came tumbling down the hole, and the guard gave Samson a kick. "See that you do not make me a liar!" he growled.

Storming from the room, he left Samson to lie in silent pain.

For a long moment, Samson sat huddled upon the wheel. Any attempt to move brought searing pain across his slashed and bloody back. But at last, with a mighty cry, he managed to stand, and throwing himself against the wheel's handle, he began again to work.

No one heard the prisoner's cry, save little Dan, who stood even now shaking and trembling outside the granary door. From the moment he had run away, leaving Samson to the cruelty of the guard, he had been ashamed of himself. And he was determined to make amends.

Steeling himself, he crept to the entry's barred window and peeked inside.

"Lord Adonai!" he whispered. "Poor, poor Samson!"

The sight was more gruesome than he had feared. Hunched in torment, the hero of Israel trudged around the stone, his torn back oozing scarlet streams from countless furrowed welts.

Impulsively, the boy threw open the door and ran to the giant. Taking a clean rag from his belt, he doused it with water from a skin bottle and called the prisoner to him.

"Samson!" he cried. "What have they done to you?"

Stopping in his tracks, Samson shook his head. "Go away, boy," he commanded. "It is not safe for you to be here!"

"But the guard sent me," the boy replied. Tugging on Samson's hand, he bade him sit.

"You are kind," Samson said. "But I know better. The guard prefers to let me suffer."

Ignoring this, Dan dabbed at the giant's wounds. But he kept a wary ear cocked toward the door, for indeed, he had no business being here.

Slumping beneath the lad's tender hand, Samson found a little relief from his pain. And once again, the mystery of Dan's identity played through his heart.

Should he or should he not inquire further?

"Boy," he said at last, "do you know why the guard beat me?"

Swallowing hard, Dan replied, "They say you wrestled him to the floor and held him fast! Is that true?"

The hero worship in his young voice was evident. And Samson managed a smile.

"I did," he answered. "Longer . . . stronger!"

Together they laughed, and Dan sat down beside the prisoner as he continued to wash his back.

"Can you imagine why I would do such a thing?" Samson went on.

When the boy was silent, he said, "The man lied to me, boy. He told me that your father sold you here."

Fumbling with the rag, Dan ceased his ministrations, and Samson sensed his unease.

"The man who sold you was *not* your father, was he?" Samson prodded.

When a long, tense moment was broken by the boy's soft weeping, the prisoner straightened. Had he gone too far? Was he being cruel?

"There, there," Samson whispered. Placing an arm about Dan's narrow shoulders, he drew him close. "Shall I tell you a story?"

With a shuddering sigh, Dan nodded his head.

"There once was a wee lad whose mama died, just as he was born. And that wee lad was stolen by a wicked fellow named Josef."

At this, Dan lurched in Samson's embrace. But the mighty judge held him more tightly.

"Evil creature that he was, Josef sold the precious boy," Samson continued. "But Adonai was with him. And bringing him to the granary of his enemies, he gave him to his real papa. His lonely, helpless papa."

How Samson had deciphered the truth from all the shrouded past, Dan could not imagine. But hearing it so plainly put cut through his young soul like lightning.

Weeping sorely, he huddled against Samson's chest and emptied his heart with tears.

"How did you know?" the boy cried.

Samson lifted the lad's chin with his fingers.

"I am right, then?" he asked. "You learned this yourself?"

"I did," Dan confessed.

"Wicked Josef!" Samson groaned. "Did he delight in heaping this cruel truth upon you?"

"He never knew I knew," Dan admitted. "I overheard him tell a red-haired woman."

Samson pondered the description. "Red-haired?" he stammered. "Where, child? Where did this happen?"

As Dan told him how Josef had taken him to Gaza Inn, and how the scarlet woman had colluded with him, Samson's stomach tightened.

"Lord God!" he groaned, leaning his head against the wheel. "Is there no end to the fruits of my sin?" His lips quivering, he searched for words to express his shame, but none came.

Dan, who could only behold his father's agony, did not understand how entangled Samson was with the sorry tale. And when the huge man hunched over him, embracing him and sobbing, he could only tremble.

"Forgive me!" Samson wept. "Forgive me, my son!"

Resting his tousled head upon his father's chest, Dan wondered what there was to forgive. "I am with you," he pleaded. "Please be happy."

At this, Samson stopped his weeping and held the boy closer. The lad's childlike trust had pierced him to the quick, and stroking the boy's dark head tenderly, he said, "You are the gift of God! Perhaps it matters not how you came to me."

Then, with utmost tenderness, he held the boy's face between his hands, tracing it gently with a forefinger. "You are my son," he sighed, "and yet I do not know your name."

Looking at him wistfully, the boy replied, "Dan, sir. My name is Dan."

Samson brightened. "Old Josef did one thing right!" he proclaimed. "He named you after my tribe!" Then with a broad smile, he added, "But you are so dear. May I call you Dani?"

The boy tucked his head into the hollow of Samson's shoulder. The big man had no idea how this special name touched the lad's heart. "You may," he enthused, "if I may call you Papa!"

Almost as one, the two sat entwined, prisoner and ministering angel, father and son, taking strength from their mutual embrace.

When morning filtered down the grain tunnel, a shaft of sunlight illumined them, as though the eye of heaven knew their whereabouts and overwatched them with love.

PART NINE

The Temple
and
the Triumph

ONE

Marissa sat up from a half sleep and drew her blanket to her chin. The night was very dark over Zorah. There was no moon, and no shadows played against her bedroom window.

Had she not been half-awake, she would have thought the sound at the door was a dream. But she was certain she had heard a knock, and she feared to answer it.

Fear had become quite familiar to her. Ever since the day when Samson was supposed to come for her, she had lived in a limbo of dead hopes and shattered promises.

It had been a shame to approach her wedding day without a groom, and humiliating to hear of his liaison with Delilah. But such feelings had been overwhelmed by a greater horror, by news of Samson's defeat at Sorek and of his subsequent incarceration.

Helpless, Marissa had retreated into a gloom of despair, keeping close within her house, receiving no visitors and doing no business.

For someone to come calling in the middle of the night sent new terror through her already-terrorized heart. Lying still upon her bed, she hoped the knock she heard was only the rustling of branches at her front porch.

But here it came again. *Knock, knock, knock.* When this was followed by a woman's desperate voice, Marissa leapt from bed and rushed to the door.

"Rena?" she called. "Is that you?"

"Marissa, let me in!" the old woman replied. "There is trouble!"

The last time Samson's mother had stood in Marissa's parlor had been the day the women of the village came for the fitting of the bridal dress. Such a happy time that had been as Samson's betrothed had twirled before them, showing off the handmade gown.

But there was no joy in Rena's eyes this night as she shared the latest crisis.

"Manoah is very ill!" the old woman exclaimed. "I don't know how much longer he will hold on!"

Samson's father had been in poor health for many months. His spirit had revived somewhat with the anticipation of the wedding, only to fall to a deeper low when Samson did not appear. News of his son's imprisonment was killing him.

"I am coming," Marissa announced, grabbing her shawl and ready to accompany Rena home.

But the old woman stopped her. "No, my dear," she said. "It will do no good for you to see Manoah. The doctors are with him. But he calls over and over for Samson. Even if he lives through this night, only the sight of his son will give any hope at all."

Marissa's face paled. "What do you want me to do?" she asked.

When Rena gave the dreaded answer, the younger woman was stunned.

"You must go to Samson!" the old mother commanded. "No one else will do!"

Aghast, Marissa shook her head. She had gone in search of Samson once before, stripping herself of all feminine pride by making a journey to Hebron. She would not, she could not, lower herself to such a thing again!

"What makes you think I would be permitted to see him?" she cried. "And even if I could, he is a prisoner! I can do nothing!"

Tears swam in the elder's eyes. Weeping, she pleaded, "You can tell him his father's long-kept secret. It is time, Marissa, that Samson knew the truth of his calling!"

Holding her shawl tight to her chest, Marissa marveled. "What secret, Rena?"

Hesitating not a second, the old woman revealed the story of the angel's pronouncement, how Samson would be destined from birth to save his people from their enemies.

"He was born to *overcome* the Philistines," Rena insisted, "not to be their captive!"

Quaking with awe, Marissa closed her eyes.

"But it seems Samson has given up," Rena persisted. "What hope is there if someone does not go to him, if someone does not tell him the end is not yet?"

When the old woman saw tears along Marissa's lashes, she stroked her arm. "The Lord is your protection," she exhorted her. "You must implore our son to rise up against his enemies! This is the desire of his dying father!"

Speechless, Marissa absorbed the insane petition. As though no time had passed, she recalled the horrid dream that had sent her to the camp of the Nazarites. She remembered God's persistent command that she find Samson and warn him of the evils plotted against him.

But she had done that, and what good had it done? Samson had walked headfirst into the Philistine trap. He had succumbed to his greatest weakness and had fallen prey to the wiles of a seductress.

"Rena," she objected, striking a dauntless pose. "You are overwrought. You do not know what you ask!"

For an uncomfortable minute, the two women locked eyes, Rena's plaintive, and Marissa's defiant.

At last, seeing that Marissa would not budge, Rena turned for the door. "Very well. You are right," she conceded. "Such a journey is no undertaking for a woman."

Then, just as she was about to enter the street, she seemed to brighten. "Josef!" she exclaimed. "Josef is going to Gaza! I will ask him. He will surely help us!"

Like a knife, the name of Samson's enemy shot through Marissa's heart. Bolting after the old woman, she stopped her short.

"Wait!" she cried. "Do not trouble Josef!"

Glancing sideways, Rena shrugged. "Why not?" she asked.

Pulling back, Marissa choked on the epithets she wished to heap on Josef's name.

"Do not trouble him," she sighed. "I will go to Gaza. A woman might have more luck on such a mission than a man."

Having gotten what she was after, Rena hid a victorious smile. For once in his life, Josef had served a good purpose.

INTERLUDE

Marissa leaned against the wall outside the granary, her heart drumming like a hammer. She had come many miles through wintry terrain, had entered the compound of Dagon's pagan temple, and had been escorted to the prison cell of the great Israeli judge by a mysterious young boy. All this, only to find the Shining Sun of her fondest dreams hunched in helpless dejection, blinded and bound by the Philistines' cruelest tormentors.

"Lord God! Help me! Help me remember why I am here!" she prayed.

As she had done when she had gone to seek Samson at Hebron, she tried to focus on a purpose higher than personal desires.

Still, the thought of her beloved having fallen to such a dreadful depth made her stomach churn. She might not have summoned the courage to reenter the grinding room had not the little servant boy come looking for her in the hall.

"Miss," Dan called, stepping out of the dark hold, "the prisoner wants to know who you are."

This was asked in such a stalwart tone, Marissa could not help but be impressed by the boy's commanding spirit. Indeed, he seemed quite protective of his blind charge, and this she found appealing.

Bending down and looking him in the eye, Marissa replied, "As I told you, I am a friend. Perhaps the best friend Samson has ever had."

Marissa did not realize that Samson could hear her. In his sightless state, he relied far more on his hearing than he had before, and it had grown quite acute. He easily picked up Marissa's declaration.

Suddenly, from the solitude of his dungeon, he cried aloud, "Lord God, you have blessed me twice over!"

At the sound of his voice, Marissa straightened, gazing fearfully toward the prison door.

"He knows you!" the boy exclaimed, taking her by the hand. "Come. Don't be afraid."

Following his lead, Marissa reentered the chamber and found, to her amazement, that Samson was standing, his face uplifted as if to an invisible light.

Quoting a Hebrew proverb, he proclaimed, "You give fathers to the orphans, and the lonely you put in families!"

Trembling, Marissa surveyed her hero, the man she had never ceased to love, though she had ceased to believe in his love for her.

As he strained through vacant eyes to see her, turning his face toward her with a smile of utmost joy, Marissa held tight to the boy's hand.

"Who did this to Samson?" she whispered, hoping that this time he would not hear.

"The Philistines," was the simple reply.

But Samson *had* heard. Shaking his head, he cried, "Not only the Philistines, Marissa! It was myself, my own weakness, that brought me to this! Come, my lady, let me touch you and I shall be redeemed!"

When the woman hesitated, Samson lowered his head, like a lonely lion.

"Am I so dreadful?" he moaned. "Am I a monster, and not the man you love?"

With a heaving chest, Marissa ran forward, stopping just short of his outstretched hands.

"Oh, dear Samson!" she cried. Grasping his fingers in hers, she brushed them with a kiss.

At last, falling into his arms, she wept, disconsolate, upon his shoulder.

Pressing her head to him, Samson held her tenderly, weeping with her.

"Can it be that you forgive me?" he cried. "Tell me it is so, Marissa. For I have died a thousand deaths since last I saw you!"

By impulse, Marissa would have replied that she *had* forgiven him. But, suddenly, the thought of her beloved in the arms of notorious Delilah raged through her, and she would not be so easily won.

Pulling back, she stared at the pathetic beggar.

"You ask forgiveness?" she groaned. "Am I a puppet, that you think to pull my strings?"

Turning his face to the floor, Samson took her castigation like another whip upon his back.

"You have betrayed me again, Samson!" she cried. "Again and again!"

Shamed to the core, Samson put his hands over his face.

"My eyes! My eyes!" he wailed.

His plaintive cry sent a chill down Marissa's spine.

But he was not seeking pity.

"It was my eyes that undid me!" he confessed. "Eyes of lust and sin! How often did I pray that God would strike me blind, so that I could sin no more!"

Stumbling backward, Samson collapsed upon the wheel and wept more loudly.

"My prayer has been answered!" he moaned. "The ways of God are surely above ours! And all his ways are right!"

Red-faced, Marissa raised a hand to her throat and stood before her betrothed in silent horror. She dare not rebuke him a second time. She knew now that he had suffered far more than anyone could have dreamed, and she loved him as never before.

Tiptoeing to him, she gently reached for his broad hand and, pulling it into her lap, sat beside him on the wheel.

Little Dan, round-eyed, observed the strange couple in silent wonder.

"Samson," the woman sighed, "I have come not only because I care, but because your mother sent me. Your father is very ill and sends word to you."

"Father?" Samson gasped.

"They—they say he is dying," Marissa stammered. "He begs that you avenge yourself, Samson! Oh, my dear, you must rejoice his heart in his last hours!"

Rising up from the wheel, Samson stood dumbfounded in the rut his feet were accustomed to treading. "Papa!" he wept, not seeing little Dan shudder at the sound of that word.

"God has not left you!" Marissa said, going to his side. "Your mother has told me a secret, Samson. One she and your father have kept until now!"

With this, she relayed the story that Rena had told her. "You are blessed of God," she concluded, "destined from birth to save us all from the Philistines!"

Shaking, Samson reached for the wheel and leaned against it. In a flash of seconds, it seemed the riddle of his life might have a solution, and the possibility was too much to grasp.

"You are still the strongman of Israel!" Marissa repeated. "You are still our hero! Avenge yourself! For the sake of your family and your nation!"

But just as hope sprang forth, Samson shook his head, clutching his growing curls. "Delilah thought my hair was my strength!" he sneered. "But it was not the loss of my hair that defeated me! The Lord withdrew himself from me because of my sins!"

With gentle fingers, Marissa stroked his dark locks. "Will the Lord punish forever?" she asked. "Will he never forgive?"

When he turned his pathetic face toward her, seeking through sightless eyes for a ray of hope, she proclaimed, "You are the Star of Israel, my beloved! Rise up and take back your good name!"

For a long while, Samson was silent, turning her words over in his beleaguered mind. Then, resting on the wheel, he gestured to her and little Dan to sit beside him.

Throwing back his shoulders, he lifted his face to the damp ceiling, recalling another time long ago when the puzzle of life had seemed beyond solving.

"Once," he said, "the Lord gave me a riddle with which to stump my enemies. I thought I knew the meaning then. But I saw only the shallowest level."

"A riddle?" Dan brightened. "What was it, Samson?"

"Out of the eater came something to eat," he replied, his lips stretching in a smile. "And out of the strong came something sweet!"

Marissa pondered this, wondering what chapter of her beloved's life had produced such a paradox.

"What did it mean?" Dan prodded.

"What it meant then is not important," Samson reckoned aloud. "What it means now is that in my deepest trial, God has given me my heart's desire!"

Drawing Marissa to him, he breathed into her hair. "Love, you are my love!" And then, placing Dan's little hand in hers, he said, "This is my son, Marissa! Bone of my bone, flesh of my flesh. And he would have been yours, for his spirit is akin to yours, my wife!"

Scarcely comprehending what Samson was saying, Marissa gasped, "Your son?"

"Spared from the ashes of Mardok's house! Josef stole him from me, before I even knew I had him, and raised him as his own!" Then, with a sigh, he added, "But in this house of death, he was returned to me! And now, dear lady, take him! Save him for me, until I can be with you both!"

Incredulous, Marissa looked at the slight child. In his dark winsomeness, she could not help but recognize a shadow of her beloved.

But the boy snatched his hand from hers and cuddled close to Samson. "Papa, do not send me away!" he cried.

"Hush, hush," the giant soothed, placing the little hand again in Marissa's and holding his newfound family close to his heart. "Of course, I will join you. And you will not leave just yet. Stay with me for now, until the sun peeks through the window."

With bewildered sighs, Marissa and her new charge huddled in their hero's arms. Moonlight spilled through the shaft above, and in time they fell into a dreamless sleep, the wheel of torment transforming to a cradle, and the breath of contentment covering them like a mantle.

TWO

Sunlight did not reach the threesome in the dungeon before the sound of many voices and rumbling wheels roared down the shaft from the temple boulevard. Lurching awake, Dan jumped to his feet and ran for the granary door.

"I must go!" he cried, waking the dozing couple. "Today is the sacrifice to Dagon, and the keepers will be looking for me to help!"

Sitting up in rigid fear, Marissa clung to Samson's embrace. But the prisoner gently pushed her from him.

"You must show our lady the way out!" he commanded. "She must not be seen!"

Flustered, Marissa gathered her cloak, but hesitated to leave. "What sacrifice?" she inquired. "Why are there so many people in the court?"

Preferring to be vague, Dan replied, "It is a celebration. There will be a big party. . . ."

But Marissa detected his reticence. "What do they celebrate?" she asked.

"It is a holy day to their god," the boy replied, "and they celebrate the defeat of their enemy!"

When Samson slumped a little, turning his face downward, Dan began to cry. "They are bad people, my lady. Very bad!"

"Go, Dani!" Samson ordered. "Take Marissa to a safe place!"

But the woman clung to the prisoner more tenaciously. "I will not go!" she insisted. "How can I leave you now?"

Pressing her head to his chest, the mighty judge listened to the predawn crowd gathering in the mammoth court and along the street outside. "It is a good day," he declared. "A good day to trust the God of Israel! Go, Marissa. Meet me in Zorah!"

With this, he shoved her to her feet and sent her to Dan.

"Come!" the boy whispered. "The guard will be here soon!"

Tears coursing down her cheeks, Marissa turned for a last look at her betrothed. "I love you!" she called, holding fast to the doorpost.

As Dan pulled her away, Samson bit his lower lip. He could only nod his head, feeling too much for words.

His THOUGHTS leaping back and forth from Marissa's safety to the meaning of the sounds overhead, Samson paced the path that circled the stone.

It was almost dawn, and the brutal guard still had not looked in on him.

When he felt the first rays of sun spill through the shaft, a great cheer rose from the court, and rollicking music and ribald singing filled the streets.

Familiar with pagan ways, Samson knew that this was only the beginning, and that the party would last into the night. What he did not know was what the Philistines had in store for him. If this celebration revolved around his captivity, he was certain that he would be put on display. But he feared to imagine more than that.

Never, in fact, had he been so afraid. In all his testings, when he had come against his enemies and they against him, he had known anger and revenge—but rarely fear.

At Etam, the "hawk ground," where he had almost died of dehydration, he had known the fear of death. But today's torment was fear of the unknown. This time, if the Philistines came for him, he would be blind and stumbling. And he still reeled from guilt. His parents' late-coming story was his only cause for hope.

Soon after the music and dancing started, the burly guard appeared inside the prison. Throwing open the door, he found Samson slumped upon the wheel and whipped him severely, forcing him to stand and push against the bar.

Then, gritting his teeth in delight, he spat something to the effect that the wheel was nothing compared with what was to come.

When noon arrived, there was no small boy to give Samson water. Sweat pouring from his body, he listened tensely as the celebration tapered and a solitary voice, bellowing across the courtyard, announced the purpose of the party.

Thrilling up the pillars and ricocheting across the terraced rooftops of the temple's colonnaded halls, the voice sent a chill to Samson's heart.

"Bariath!" he groaned.

Yes, it was the blond fiend of his worst nightmares, the very man at whose command his eyes had been gouged out, the one whose plot to vanquish him had been realized, and whose mistress had been his downfall.

Even now, in his permanent darkness, with no eyes to close against it, Samson relived the memory of the white-hot rod used to blind him. He could see, in his mind's eye, the way it had flashed before his horrified gaze and then had been plunged directly toward each iris, causing him to cry aloud.

Excruciating pain, as hellish as any man had ever endured, had been his that fateful day. He had learned what it was to die and yet live, to wish above all that he had entered the halls of death, only to be thrust screaming into the jaws of ongoing life.

But even as the memory of his cry died away, Bariath was still speaking: "Men and women of Philistia! Worshipers of our great Dagon! We are here today to celebrate the conquest of our most dreaded enemy, the ravager of Ashkelon and Gaza, the uprooter of our sacred gates, the monster of Israel, *Samson!*"

At the sound of that name, the crowd went wild, stomping and clapping and shouting until the prisoner thought the temple mount would surely crack asunder.

"We are here to make the sacrifice of thanksgiving!" the Philistine governor announced. "And we are here to enjoy the liberties won for us by our great god, Dagon!"

Music and pounding drums echoed up the temple mall as Samson cowered in his dank hold. In dark visions, he could imagine what transpired above, as the Philistines, besotted with wine and ritualistic frenzy, approached the platform of Dagon's altar, bringing sacrifices of food, drink, gold, and blood. And the parade of worshipers would not cease until nightfall, when the courtyard gutters flowed red and the city drains were choked with crimson.

Then what? Samson wondered. Would he be the ultimate blood-gift? He had heard that, from time to time, in moments of either national crisis or ecstasy, the Philistines had condoned human sacrifice!

Slipping from the wheel's handle, he collapsed numbly to the floor.

How long he sat there, weak and shaking, he knew not. But with the rising of the moon, his demon-sponsored fears were spurred to ever-higher peaks by the sound of a chanting chorus.

It began from somewhere across the court and grew in tempo and timbre until he almost went mad:

"Our god has given Samson our enemy into our hands!
Dagon has given Samson our enemy into our hands!
The destroyer of our country! The slayer of many!
Our god has given our enemy into our hands!"

Ten thousand voices raged with the chant, taunting the man
in chains. As they did so, he shriveled upon the wheel, pulling
his knees to his chin and choking himself with tearless sobs.

AT MIDNIGHT, Samson was roused from his nightmarish slumber.

A small, soft hand, incongruous with his hellish dreams,
shook him by the shoulder. When he sat up, grasping it in a
clammy grip, the owner whimpered.

"Papa!" Dan cried. "It is only me!"

With a loud groan, Samson pulled the boy close. "Thank
God!" he cried. "Is it over?"

As slumber fell away, his own ears answered the question.

The grating chant still echoed through the court, spurred
to ever greater frenzy by alcohol and lust. Dan trembled as his
father listened to the devilish song.

"It will end soon," he whispered. "They are calling for you.
And when they are done, you will be safe."

Aghast, Samson drew back. But Dan insisted, trying to
convince himself as well, that no real harm would come to the
prisoner.

"They say they want to see you," he croaked. "They want
you to . . . dance . . . for them."

This was almost as hard for Dan to report as if they called
for Samson's death. He knew how devastating such sport
would be to the strongman's pride. But when they were done
with him, surely he would return safely to the granary.

"They sent you to tell me this?" Samson bellowed. "I am to
dance for them, and they sent a little child to fetch me?"

Staggering to his feet, Samson roared, "Shameless cruelty! Lord God! Barbarians, all of them!"

Then, turning to Dan, he commanded, "Run, boy! Run for your life! Such madmen mean no good for you! Spare yourself!"

But Dan, clinging to the prisoner's mighty legs, wept louder. "No Papa! I will never leave you! I am glad they sent me, so I can be with you!"

Heaving a sigh, Samson slumped beside the lad and embraced him fervently. Then, holding his small face in his titanic hands, he anxiously asked, "Marissa. Where is she? Did she escape to Zorah?"

Dan swallowed hard. "No, sir," he replied. "My lady would not leave you, either. She waits above, hiding on the granary stairs."

THREE

*M*arissa clung to the handrail of the stone steps leading from the granary to a back corner of the court. She had stayed here all day since before dawn, when the boy had meant to help her escape.

"I cannot leave Samson!" she had pleaded. "Not now!"

So little Dan had left her here, telling her to keep low if she did not want to be seen, and checking on her throughout the intervening hours.

She might have gone out into the crowd. It was a cosmopolitan gathering. In her festive gown, the one she would have worn for her own wedding, she could fit in with the revelers. But there was always the chance she would be recognized as a Jew, and so she stayed low.

While Samson endured the sounds of the wild festival, Marissa was obliged to witness its sights and smells. By now the hilarity was unbounded, and crazed celebrators danced and gyrated and frolicked wantonly in the square. The aromas of warm wine, sacrificial blood, and perfumed bodies combined to make a stench that was especially nauseating to a sheltered Jewess from an Israeli hamlet.

Light-headed, Marissa looked on as thousands upon thousands of small animals—pigeons, goats, and sheep—were slain upon Dagon's altar, a high platform raised at the center of the court. She feared to imagine what the Philistines had in mind for Samson.

It was easy to guess that the blond giant who announced the festivities was the same man who had secured her beloved's downfall. When he was joined upon the stage by a ravishing, dark-eyed woman, Marissa's heart sank.

Surely this was Delilah, the ultimate Philistine weapon.

When, at the knell of midnight, this seductive creature took her stand at the head of the crowd, the manic cry of ten thousand voices shot to the skies.

If Marissa was not already certain of the woman's identity, the chant left her with no doubts.

"Delilah! Delilah!" it rang out. And soon it was coupled with the name of the Philistine goddess, whose great bronze image competed with that of Dagon himself. "Ashtaroth! Ashtaroth! Your blessings on Delilah!"

Growing pale, Marissa trembled at the sight of the vampish female, and slumping to the steps, she fought to keep hot tears in check.

How like the image of Ashtaroth the Philistine woman was! Tall, broad-shouldered, and amply endowed, she wore a clinging gown of gold that shimmered and gleamed in the light of a thousand torches. More glorious than the goddess was she! What statue of cold bronze could rival such flesh and blood as Delilah's?

While the crowd praised Delilah, she gave her worshipers a condescending smile. Then she whispered something in her paramour's ear.

Bariath, brightening, raised his hands to silence the adoring masses.

"Ladies and gentlemen!" he cried. "Our lady, who has done us such great service in subduing our enemy, has made a request. Should we not oblige her?"

Star-struck, the crowd whistled and applauded, ready to please her in any way possible.

"Our lady wishes to see her vanquished enemy!" Bariath announced. "She says that since she entertained him, she would like him to return the favor!"

Cheers and shouts followed as all eyes turned from Delilah to the court gate, expecting that Samson would at any moment step forth.

"Send for the prisoner," Bariath commanded, "that he may dance for us!"

Such amusement was too good to be dreamed of. The crowd went wild and began to chant Samson's name in place of Delilah's, demanding his appearance with lusty bravado.

"Samson! Samson! Samson!" they shouted. "Dance for us! Sing for us!"

Stomping and clapping, they set up a rhythmic vibration that echoed down the temple mount and filled the city with thunder.

Terrified, Marissa huddled upon the stairs, standing now and then to peek behind her, lest the prisoner should be brought forth from that direction.

But, as the revelers expected, Samson would be escorted through the underground and into the court through the central gate. When Marissa saw that the crowd's attention was riveted away from her, she slipped cautiously toward the head of the congregation, hiding her face with her mantle, shivering with terror.

It was not long before the drums grew louder, and, as the people fairly salivated with anticipation, Samson appeared between two pillars inside the temple gate.

To Marissa's horror, she saw that little Dan had been assigned to lead him. Squelching a cry of despair, she clapped her hand over her mouth and shrank back into the crowd.

No sooner had she done this, than she was greeted from behind by a distinct hissing sound, and as surely as though a serpent wound up her arm, she felt a slithering hand entwine her elbow.

Wheeling about, she was confronted by the beadiest set of eyes she had ever seen. Half a head beneath her chin, they drilled her through with the light of purest hate.

"Josef!" she gasped. But even as she did so, her intellect fought the impression. Was it possible that this hunched and wizened creature was the Josef of her youth, the shrewd businessman and calculating suitor? It had been years since she had seen him. Yet, in all the earth there were no other eyes like his.

"Marissa!" he hissed, baring his teeth like fangs. "What brings you here?"

Recoiling from his grasp, Marissa stood shivering before him. A thousand questions—and a thousand accusations—rushed to her lips, longing to be voiced. But she suppressed them, staring in wonder at the macabre specter who had starred in her worst nightmares.

Beside him, her arm twined about his scrawny neck like a leash, was a fire-haired woman, nearly equal to Delilah for glamour if not for sophistication. Though she surveyed the Jewess up and down, she seemed to look through her and not at her, her expression one of utmost disdain.

"Who is *this?*" she lisped in Josef's ear.

"Samson's lover," he replied, loudly enough that Marissa received the impact of his words. "But not like you were, my dear."

Lifting her chin, the siren shrugged and gave Marissa a sneer, as though to say that no man would have had the Jewess lest he was utterly starved for company.

Focused on Marissa, Josef hissed again, "What brings you here? Do you think to save Samson yet? Do you think to take him home, your faithful husband after all?"

Cringing, Marissa turned to run, but was hemmed in by the pressing crowd. Captive to Josef's taunts, she listened with burning ears as he rehearsed Samson's well-known betrayals.

"You think that he would have you now?" he spat. "A man who has had the likes of Delilah?"

When his scarlet-haired companion straightened, spearing him with a look of jealous spite, he quickly added, "—the likes of Delilah *and* my beauty Mariah!"

Pricked to the heart, Marissa could scarcely believe her demon had found her. In desperation, she forced her way through the crowd, managing again to reach the front, where she leaned against a court wall, trembling and panting as though her soul would burst.

"Samson!" she wept, caring not who heard her.

But no one heard. The drums were raging now, and Bariath shouted, "Let the prisoner stand at the head of the square! Let him dance for us between the pillars, that all may see!"

There were hundreds of pillars arrayed about the temple compound, some purely for adornment and some for function. But the pillars to which Bariath referred were the keystones of the central edifice, the supports of the main hall and of the terraces that graced its roof.

Beneath this roof, thousands of people stood in eager wonder. Upon that roof, thousands more milled about, straining for the best possible view of the court and its activities. Just as the people outside the gate peered through, jostling and pressing to see what transpired, and just as the folks on the court floor vied to be nearest the front, so did those upon the pillar-footed roof compete, leaning over the railing and even perching precariously upon the balustrade.

"Sing, Samson!" they commanded. Three thousand specta- tors leered down upon him, and thousands more clapped and stomped upon the pavement below. "Dance!"

Holding tight to the prisoner's hand, Dan began to weep. It was all Marissa could do to keep from running to the lad and sweeping him into her arms.

But she dare not. Any focus placed upon Dan and his connection to the prisoner would only endanger the lad. As much as Marissa wished to wheel on Josef, to tell him his plot against the child had produced the single happiness Samson and Dan had known in their bleak enslavement, she dared not indulge such passion.

So she restrained herself, observing mutely as the child led the hero of Israel to center stage.

Now the drums increased their tempo, and Dan looked desperately about him. Standing on tiptoe, he pulled Samson's great head downward and whispered in his ear.

Only Samson could hear the word "Papa," as the boy ad- dressed him. "Dance!" he pleaded. "Then they will let you go."

Standing upright, Samson pressed the lad's head to his thigh, and then heaved a great sigh. Momentarily, he did as he was bid, shuffling his feet like a swaying bear to the music.

As the crowd hooted and laughed, Dan held fast to the prisoner's broad hand, and Marissa's heart nearly broke.

But what was this? The prisoner seemed to grow weary, and calling out to the boy, loudly enough that the crowd could hear, he begged, "Let me feel the pillars, that I may lean against them!"

With a look of wonder, Dan did as he was told, straightening Samson's mighty arms so that they spanned the distance between the two supports and placing his broad hands upon them.

At this, the audience began to hiss and boo, shaking their heads and mocking: "Where is your strength, mighty Samson? Can't you even stand on your own feet?"

But as Marissa looked on, an expression crossed Samson's face that those who knew him less well should have noted. He was still dancing, if his reticent plod could be called dance, swaying back and forth between the pillars, as he pressed his hands against them. But his chin was now uplifted, and he seemed to hear something beyond the music and the mocking crowd, beyond, even, the whisper of the child.

As though it were yesterday rather than half a lifetime ago, Marissa knew where she had seen that look before. She remembered the first time she had ever noticed the farm boy from the Zorah hills—the day when, though she had met him a hundred times before, she had first observed his spirit.

On that day, little Josef had been trapped beneath a wagon and would have died had someone not been able to lift it. On that day, the boy Samson, strapping as a young lion, had raised his face to heaven, hearing, as he did now, the voice of God.

And on that day, he had cried out, words that shook Marissa's soul, placing her heart forever in his hands.

Bracing herself, Marissa now stood in the pagan court, awaiting those same words. Surely, any moment they would ring forth, Samson's echoing hallmark.

As she relived that distant hour, the past and present came together. Suddenly, all the intervening years, all the heartbreak took on meaning . . . and the ways of God with Samson became clear.

"O Lord God!" he cried, "Give me strength!" Throwing his huge head backward and bracing himself between the pillars, he wept, "Please remember me! Strengthen me just this once, O God, that I may be avenged of the Philistines for my two eyes!"

Then, throwing himself against the pillars, he pressed into them with all his might.

Watching him, the crowd laughed all the more, thinking him a clown. Such a spectacle he made! This was more than they had hoped for!

But while they roared with hilarity, Marissa slipped toward the gate, catching Dan's eye and beckoning to him.

When the lad hesitated, clinging to Samson's bulging thigh, she pointed to the roof, where already plaster was cracking and flaking.

Only a Jew would have looked for this, only a Jew or Jewess who still believed in the power of God Almighty. No one else, no Philistine, no lost soul upon the court below, would have thought to look above, to take Samson's actions seriously.

The instant Dan observed the buckling pillars, he was torn in two directions. Could he leave his beloved Samson, now, after all they had come to mean to one another?

"Papa!" he cried.

"Go, Dani!" Samson bellowed. "Go, my son! Care for your mother!"

And with a heave of his mighty leg, he thrust Dan from him.

Weeping, the little boy ran for Marissa's outstretched hand.

And just in time. For the crowd itself had suddenly grown fearful. Now all eyes traveled from the lion of Israel to the rocking pillars, from the pillars to the shaking roof . . . and from the roof to the people upon it.

Suddenly, the entertainment was not so amusing. Folks who had been clinging to the balustrade slipped from it and plunged to the pavement below. Those who enjoyed a rooftop view toppled upon one another, landing on the rocking terrace.

Instantly, the music and chants became shrieks and screams. Laughter was exchanged for terror, and the entire pillared mount became a tremor of tottering porches and swaying supports.

Incredulous, the people turned for the exits. But in their panic, they made matters worse, congesting the aisles and jamming the colonnades.

Taking their lives in their hands, many jumped from the rooftops, as building after building fell like game pieces. Crawling over broken bodies, those who had not jumped made ladders of one another, seeking a downward passage.

Meanwhile, thousands below scrambled to avoid catapulting bodies, screaming as they careened into one another and dodged splintered walls.

In the center of the square, the great Bariath and his lady hunched together upon the altar stage. But they would find no security in one another's arms. They were no more safe than Josef and his terrified Mariah, who vainly sought an exit.

In fact, at this moment, as the world toppled about them, those who had mocked Samson were all alike. Rich or poor, Jew or pagan, male or female—there was no distinction.

The man of God would have his day . . . and his day had come!

"Remember me!" Samson cried, his voice thundering over the din like the call of an avenging angel. "Remember me and strengthen me, that I may die with the Philistines!"

With one last heave, he leveled the keystones to the pavement, reducing the entire house of Dagon and all its courts to a mountain of rubble.

The man who had slain thousands in his lifetime now slew ten thousand in his death. And even as the walls of darkness encompassed him, his voice split the hearts of any left to hear:

"Remember me! God of my fathers! Be my strength!"

O Lord, please remember me . . .

JUDGES 16:28

EPILOGUE

A low moon hung over the little town of Zorah, speckled by soft clouds that flitted across its face. Below, a summer breeze played among the willow fronds that dangled in Zorah's shining brook.

Though most of the village women were finishing up their evening housework, Marissa was not obliged to stay in any kitchen. Single all her life, she had learned to relish her private moments. On such an evening she would sooner be caught dead than indoors.

Sitting upon the bank of the flowing stream, she let the clear waters sing between her toes while she ran a comb through her long, silver-streaked tresses.

Though she liked her solitude, however, she also enjoyed the sound of men's voices as a soft song of Israel spilled across the square from the town's humble gathering place.

It was not the Sabbath, but for many a year the men had gathered at odd times in the meeting hall, "just for fellowship." The women knew their men discussed the future of Israel and that they debated what course the country should take now that they were beginning to gain fuller stature as a political entity.

There were those who argued for a monarchy to replace the antiquated judgeship of the past. And, as could be expected, there were those who clung to the old ways, who believed God was King of Israel, and that any elevation of a man to such a position would be idolatry. On the other hand, it was true that Israel's growing strength, as well as her tendency to take up pagan ways, demanded more structure than the itinerant judges had afforded.

Marissa had lived long enough and seen enough in her lifetime to know that regardless of how the men debated, God would ordain the perfect plan. She cared little whether that plan involved a judge, a king, or some new, untried form of government. She also knew that as much as things might change on the surface, Israel was at its heart an eternal thing, bigger by far than rule and rulers.

Still, it gave her immense pleasure to remember how Adonai had used one fumbling man to move Israel along. As she thought of Samson, she wondered who would be next on the scene to direct her beloved people.

Only one thing could have torn Marissa away from the bubbling brook this evening. She was obliged to care for only one other human being, and when she heard his voice calling to her across the common, she jumped to her feet and hailed him.

"Over here, Dan!" she replied. "Is the meeting done?"

As the meeting hall emptied, the elders and the young family men bid good-night and departed for their homes. Dan left the steps and crossed the moonlit square.

"Where is your shawl, Mother?" he called, joining her beside the brook. "The breeze is growing cool."

"Fuss, fuss," she rebuked. "You worry over me too much." Sitting down again, she patted the ground and bade him join her. "You, my boy, are overheated by too much 'fellowship'," she quipped. "What do you men think, spending all night in that stuffy place?"

"Oh, Mother," Dan cried, "I wish you could have been there! We are making plans . . . you will see!"

Glancing sideways at her handsome companion, Marissa sighed. How he looked like Samson! Not in stature so much as through the eyes and face. He was, in fact, quite slender, but his build was deceiving. Marissa knew by his firm embraces and his endurance in the reapers' fields that he was a sturdy fellow.

Still, it was not so much his lustrous locks and olive complexion that reminded her of Israel's hero. He had these, to be sure, as well as dark, dancing eyes that could melt the strongest female heart. No, far beyond these things, it was Dan's spirit that revealed his kinship to Israel's great savior.

That spirit had never been roused to feats of physical prowess. It had always been turned, instead, to more intellectual interests. He was, in fact, much like his grandfather, the wise Manoah. Already, at his young age, he had become a leader among the people.

Yet how often when Marissa looked at him was she reminded of her Shining Sun!

"Dear Dan!" she laughed, her eyes tender. "You always tell me how the men are planning this and that! What is it tonight? A war against the Hittites, or a trade embargo on Egypt?"

"Neither," Dan said, snickering, looking at the woman fondly. "Take me seriously. We will have a king, you will see! Father was the last of the great judges!"

When Marissa listened thoughtfully, Dan went on. "Oh, Samuel is a great and good judge, and he has done well by the people. But there is much pressure on him, and word from Shiloh has it that he is looking for a suitable candidate for king!"

"Well," said Marissa, brightening, "tell him he need look no further. We have just such a fellow in Zorah!"

Shaking his head, Dan rolled his eyes. "Mother," he teased, "you have raised me well, but it is not my calling to sit upon a throne. Let me teach forever in the meeting hall and I shall be content."

With a conceding nod, Marissa praised him. "How like Manoah you are! If only your grandfather could have known you!"

Dan remembered how, when they escaped the fallen temple of Gaza, Marissa had taken him home to live with her and had loved him as though he were her own. There Dan had brought great joy to the heart of Rena, his grandmother. Sadly, Manoah had not survived the loss of Samson and had died in Zorah the day the temple fell.

"So tell me," Marissa queried, "what great things did you teach this evening? Is an old woman privy to such lofty matters?"

"Privy?" Dan chuckled. "You are the one who taught me these things to begin with! I spoke frankly of my father. I told the men they must learn from his example, from *all* that he went through in the years he was our people's judge."

Pondering this, Marissa closed her eyes. "You have spoken well," she agreed.

"I knew you would think so," Dan said with a smile. "For it was you who taught me how Samson was an image and a likeness of our nation."

Recalling the childhood lessons she had given the boy, and the many hours Dan had spent absorbing them, Marissa smiled back at him.

But he was lost in the same recollections and rehearsed them thoughtfully.

"We are all enticed to bitter fruits," he said, "but we are never beyond God's grace. Through our greatest failings, he can bring great triumph."

"Ah," the woman chuckled, "you are an able student!"

"It is this I spoke of tonight," Dan asserted, standing up and pulling his mother toward him. Taking off his cloak, he wrapped it about her shoulders and walked with her beside the brook.

"My father's cry is still in my ears," he proclaimed. "'Remember me!' If I have my way, Mother, they shall never forget!"

For a long while, the two stood together, enfolded in silver light. A lifetime ago, upon this very bank, Samson had promised Marissa his love. As though she were a girl again, she pressed her head to a young man's chest and listened to his heart.

"My son," she whispered, "as long as there are men like you in Israel, Samson will always be remembered."